KT-466-815

Sales and Service for the Wine Professional

Second Edition

BRIAN K. JULYAN

NORWICH CITY COLLEGE LIBRARY			
Stock No.	207911		
Class	642. 6 JUL		
Cat.		Proc.	IWL

THOMSON

Australia • Canada • Mexico • Singapore • Spain • United Kingdom • United States

THOMSON™

Sales and Service for the Wine Professional: Second Edition

Copyright © Brian Julyan 2003

The Thomson logo is a registered trademark used herein under licence.

For more information, contact Thomson Learning, High Holborn House, 50–51 Bedford Row, London WC1R 4LR or visit us on the World Wide Web at: http://www.thomsonlearning.co.uk

All rights reserved by Thomson Learning 2004. The text of this publication, or any part thereof, may not be reproduced or transmitted in any form or by any means, electronic or mechanical, including photocopying, recording, storage in an information retrieval system, or otherwise, without prior permission of the publisher.

While the publisher has taken all reasonable care in the preparation of this book the publisher makes no representation, express or implied, with regard to the accuracy of the information contained in this book and cannot accept any legal responsibility or liability for any errors or omissions from the book or the consequences thereof.

Products and services that are referred to in this book may be either trademarks and/or registered trademarks of their respective owners. The publisher and author/s make no claim to these trademarks.

British Library Cataloguing-in-Publication Data
A catalogue record for this book is available from the British Library

ISBN 1-84480-053-9

First published 1999 by Continuum
Reprinted 2001
This edition published in 2003 by Continuum
Reprinted 2003 and 2004 (twice) by Thomson Learning

Typeset by Kenneth Burnley, Wirral, Cheshire
Printed in the UK by Ashford Colour Press, Gosport, Hampshire

Contents

Preface

Today's sommelier (drinks server) requires a good knowledge of all beverage products, a comprehensive understanding of the drinks available in his or her establishment, and the technical ability and skill to provide a high-quality service. The aim of *Sales and Service for the Wine Professional* is to provide easily understandable information on the various products in general use and to explain the social and technical skills needed to meet the demands of the customer. It is intended as a base on which to build, for those entering the industry, and not as a definitive study. While every effort is made to ensure the information is up to date, changes are constantly taking place in the categories and classifications of wines and even in the definitive districts in some countries. It should, however, prove to be a useful source of reference for working sommeliers, and those involved in training staff.

It is ideally suited to those studying for the NVQs/SVQs On-Licensed Premises Supervision, Drink Service Advanced Craft, and On-Licensed Premises Management, WSET, AFWS courses and the Court of Master Sommeliers Certificate and Advanced Certificate programmes. It also provides customers with information on the wines and other drinks they will be offered in a restaurant and an insight into the service they are entitled to expect.

NOTES TO STUDENTS OF WINE

To the top professionals, wine is not only an important part of their day-to-day duties, it is a way of life and becomes an all-consuming subject of study. Wine should always remain an enjoyable subject and should be a source of great pleasure to top professionals as well as to those who take it less seriously.

The appearance, bouquet and taste are the basic foundations on which to build your knowledge. Take every opportunity to taste good-quality wines and wines from unfashionable areas. Take advantage during foreign holidays to taste the drinks of the country, they are usually more reasonably priced in their countries of origin than when imported into your own country.

Make short notes on the wines and other drinks tasted (e.g. brandies and malt whiskies) and these can then be studied at your leisure. Suggested headings for wine tasting include:

- date tasted;
- name of wine;
- vintage;
- shipper/producer;
- country and district of origin;
- grape variety/ies;
- colour;
- bouquet and taste characteristics;
- quality;
- readiness for drinking.

These notes will help you to build up your knowledge and will be helpful when selecting and purchasing these products at a later date.

Acknowledgements

Association of German Prädikat Wine Estates
  (VDP)
Australian Wine Export Council
Comité Interprofessionnel du Vin de Champagne
Devon Fire Service
German Wine Information Service
Investimentos, Comércio e Turismo de Portugal
Italian Wine Centre
New Zealand Wine
Percival Brown, Heyman Barwell Jones
Pierre Cheval, Champagne Gatinois
Christopher Piper Wines
Walter Hicks Wines, St Austell Brewery
Phillips of Bristol
South African Wine Farmers Association

Wine Institute of New Zealand
Wines of Chile
Wines of Portugal
Wines of Spain
Wines of South Africa

Illustrations
Original illustrations: Keith Bloor

Sources
Debretts Correct Form
Stephenson, T. (1966), *World Wine Encyclopedia*,
  Dorling Kindersley
Robinson, J. (1999), *The Oxford Companion to
  Wine*, Oxford University Press

CHAPTER ONE

The Hotel and Catering Industry

CAREERS IN BEVERAGE SERVICE

There is a multitude of opportunities for both full-time and part-time employment in beverage sales and service. Careers may culminate in management and ownership. The following is a list of possible jobs within the industry:

- Barperson
- Cocktail barperson
- Bars manager
- Publican: public house manager, tenant or proprietor
- Area/Regional manager
- Wine bar manager
- Commis du vin
- Sommelier
- Head sommelier
- Station waiter, Chef de rang, Captain; serving own customers with drinks
- Station head waiter
- Restaurant manager
- Food and beverage manager
- Restaurant proprietor
- Wine salesperson
- Wine/Liquor store manager
- Wine merchant/distributor
- Wine writer
- Educator

PROFESSIONAL ASSOCIATIONS

There are a great number of professional and technical associations related to beverage sales and service. The following is a shortened list of these associations, each with its abbreviated aims. A full and complete list is available from the Hotel, Catering and International Management Association (HCIMA).

Academy of Food and Wine Service
Aims: to improve the standard of education in food and wine service.

The British Hospitality Association (BHA)
Aims: to give help and advice to its members on legal aspects, purchasing, staff training and day-to-day problems. It represents its members' views to the government.

British Institute of Innkeeping (BII)
Aims: to promote and maintain nationally recognized levels of professional competence among licensees and those directly involved in the supervision of public houses, to help members develop business skills, to assist them with training and to set and maintain standards.

City and Guilds
This is a non-profit-making examining body which oversees the development and assessing of technical courses, including many for the hotel and catering industry, and the licensed trade. Its NVQ and GNVQ certificates enjoy worldwide recognition.

Cookery and Food Association (CFA)
Aims: to assist in the education and training of young people, chefs and others connected with the catering industry.

Court of Master Sommeliers Worldwide
This is the examining body for the Court's Certificate and Advanced Sommelier programmes and for the prestigious Master Sommelier Diploma. It is dedicated to education and training within the industry. Aims: to set, maintain and promote high standards of service of wines and other beverages, to improve the knowledge of sommeliers through its education programmes, to improve the status of the sommelier, and to promote a wide interest in wines, beers, spirits, liqueurs, non-alcoholic drinks and cigars. The Master Sommelier Diploma is the ultimate in worldwide professional qualifications in the service of wine, spirits and other alcoholic and non-alcoholic beverages.

Guild of Professional Toastmasters
Aims: to set and maintain standards and to promote and protect the professional standing of toastmasters.

Hospitality Training Foundations (HTF)
Aims: to encourage and develop training in the hotel and catering industry.

Hotel, Catering and International Management Association (HCIMA)
Aims: to promote standards of good practice in catering and accommodation management, to advance education, training and research, to establish and maintain standards of competence for managers in the industry.

Institute of Masters of Wine
Aims: to promote a high standard of knowledge of wines and all subjects relating to the wine trade, and to promote a high standard of professional practice among its members.

National Association of Licensed House Managers (NALHM)
Aims: to secure for its members the maximum benefit in their terms and conditions of employment.

Federation of Licensed Victuallers
Aims: to protect and improve the interests and welfare of its members, and to give advice on business queries.

The Restaurant Services Guild
This body is affiliated to the Cookery and Food Association. Aims: to improve the status of restaurant service workers, to improve national standards of restaurant service, to promote career development and to act as an advisory body for craft education.

The Restaurateurs Association of Great Britain (RAGB)
Aims: to protect and promote the interests and welfare of its members and to represent their views to the government.

The Scottish Licensed Trade Association
Aims: to protect and promote the rights and interests of the licensed trade in Scotland.

United Kingdom Bartenders Guild
Aims: to set and maintain standards of bartending and to assist with education and training.

Wine and Spirit Education Trust
Aims: to set standards of knowledge, education and training for those engaged in the wine and spirit trade.

CHAPTER TWO

Preparation and Maintenance of Bar and Cellar

TOOLS AND EQUIPMENT FOR RESTAURANT, BAR AND CELLAR

Bottle openers and corkscrews

Waiter's knife or waiter's friend
The points to look for in a good waiter's friend are an adequate number of coils on the screw, and as wide and long a screw as possible. The lever should hold its position when opened, not flop about. See Figure 2.1.

Wing screw
This is not convenient to carry in a sommelier's pocket. In addition, it has no knife. See Figure 2.2.

Double-action screw
This is good for removing corks from old bottles but has no knife and is not convenient to carry in a pocket. See Figure 2.3.

T-shaped wooden-handled screw, single pull
This corkscrew is not very useful. It has no knife or lever. The cork extraction is uncontrolled, resulting in a loud pop as the cork is pulled. It is of no use for extraction of corks from bottles which have a sediment, and should not be used to open wine in the restaurant. See Figure 2.4.

Screwpull corkscrew
An American invention, which is extremely efficient for removing corks from old bottles, but is less convenient to carry than a waiter's knife. See Figure 2.5.

Bench corkscrew
Ideal for a dispense bar or a wine bar. It is particularly useful in a dispense bar for function catering where set wines are being served. See Figure 2.6.

Figure 2.4   *T-shaped screw*

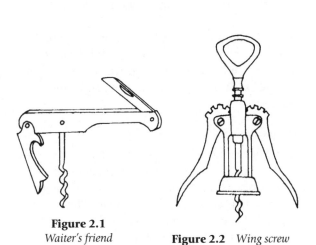 

Figure 2.1
Waiter's friend

Figure 2.2   *Wing screw*

Figure 2.3
Double-action screw

Figure 2.5 *Screwpull corkscrew*

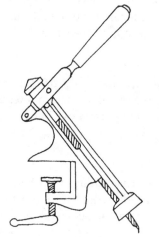

Figure 2.6 *Bench corkscrew*

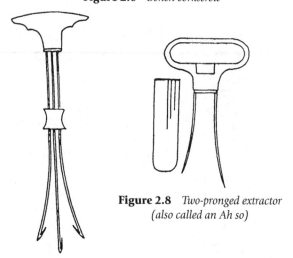

Figure 2.8 *Two-pronged extractor (also called an Ah so)*

Figure 2.7 *Broken cork extractor*

Broken cork extractor
Used to remove a broken cork which has been pushed into the bottle. The three wires of the extractor are inserted into the neck of the bottle until the claws are below the piece of broken cork. The wire or plastic ring is moved towards the handle so that the wires expand outwards. The extractor is then pulled out with the cork trapped between the wires and the claws. See Figure 2.7.

Extractor
The capsule of the bottle is cut in the normal way. The two-pronged extractor is removed from its sheath. The two prongs are inserted between the cork and the neck of the bottle and twisted to remove the cork. See Figure 2.8.

Fruit knife and board
A small stainless steel knife is required for the bar for cutting oranges, lemons and other fruit to be used in drinks. There should also be a bar-board on which to cut this fruit. See Figure 2.9.

Fruit squeezers
There are two types of fruit squeezer in general use:

1   The small glass, plastic or stainless steel type (Figure 2.10).
2   The bar press or bench type, usually made from cast aluminium or stainless steel.

These fruit squeezers are becoming increasingly popular in bars, wine bars and anywhere that fresh fruit juices are served. Ensure these are clean before use and thoroughly washed and wiped after use.

Coasters
Wine bottles are placed on coasters to protect the table. They are made from metal (usually silver or stainless steel) and wood. See Figure 2.11. Sometimes small card or paper mats, placed under glasses containing drinks, are called coasters. They often advertise the establishment or a product.

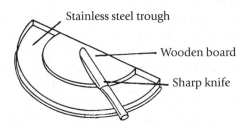

Figure 2.9 *Fruit knife and board*

Stainless steel trough

Wooden board

Sharp knife

Figure 2.10 *Squeezer*

Figure 2.11 *Coaster*

Figure 2.12 *A non-drip optic*

Optics

Optics include free-flow dispensers as used for some wines, non-stamped measures for vermouths, cordials, etc., and government-stamped measures for spirits (UK). Modern optics are non-drip. See Figure 2.12.

The UK government-stamped and sealed optical measures must not be tampered with (see Chapter Eleven). There are a number of computerized systems whereby the dispensing points are linked to a computer, which will record each sale.

To dispense a drink from an optical measure, a clean glass is held under the optic, the dispensing lever is pressed upwards with a finger and held there until a full measure is dispensed. The glass is then removed and the optic refills. Use only clean glasses, never refill a used one.

Thimble measures

These are government stamped in the UK and must be kept scrupulously clean. Care must be taken to ensure that these measures are filled to the top when serving spirits. See Figure 2.13.

Pourers

Pourers are used on the tops of opened bottles of such items as vermouths, cordials, spirits and sherries (see Figure 2.14). In a busy bar this saves having to remove the bottle cap and replace it every time a drink is served from the bottle.

Pourers should only be used on fast-selling items; the product is open to the air and will deteriorate, even when the pourers have hinged caps. Pourers should be washed regularly.

Syphons

Syphons are used for the service of soda water. They should be kept in a cool place. Before using a new syphon, release a little over a sink, as the pressure is sometimes too high.

There is another type of syphon in which soda water can be made by injecting carbon dioxide into fresh water. Cordials may be added to the water. These syphons are mainly for domestic use.

Figure 2.13 *Thimble measures*

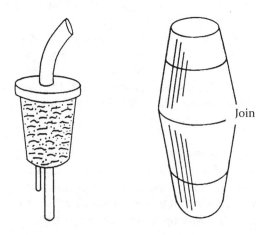

Figure 2.14 *A pourer*   **Figure 2.15** *Boston shaker*

Join

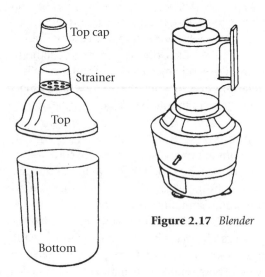

Top cap

Strainer

Top

Bottom

Figure 2.16 *Standard shaker*

Figure 2.17 *Blender*

Ice-making equipment

There are many ice-making machines on the market that are suitable for use in beverage sales and service. A machine should be chosen which will produce a sufficient quantity of ice for the needs of the operation. Cube ice is probably the most useful shape for beverages. Cocktail bars should have a crushed ice-making machine in addition.

Ice crushers

Electric or hand-operated ice crushers will crush ice cubes or pieces of ice. Crushed ice is used for *frappés* and other drinks.

Cocktail shakers

There are two types of cocktail shaker: the Boston Shaker (Figure 2.15) and the Standard shaker (Figure 2.16).

Boston shaker

This has two parts and is used in conjunction with a Hawthorn strainer (see later in this section). It is sometimes referred to as the professional shaker. It is the best type to use if the quantity to be mixed is large, but is equally good for a single cocktail. See Figure 2.15.

Standard shaker

This has three parts and a built-in strainer. It is shorter than the Boston shaker and is more suitable for smaller quantities. See Figure 2.16.

Blenders

Blenders are a type of liquidizer. They usually have two speeds, and may have an attachment for crushing ice. They should be washed out after use and dried. See Figure 2.17.

Always ensure the top is on the blender before switching it on.

Muddlers and spoons

A muddler is a stirrer, often made from plastic. It is served with long mixed drinks. Muddlers are often produced by drinks companies to carry advertising.

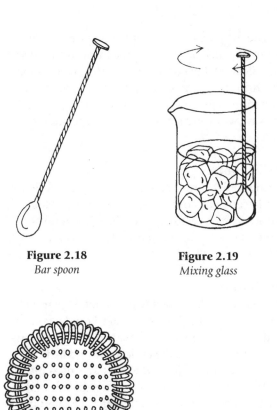

Figure 2.18
Bar spoon

Figure 2.19
Mixing glass

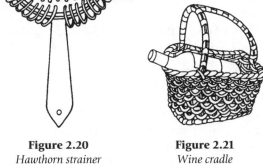

Figure 2.20
Hawthorn strainer

Figure 2.21
Wine cradle

A bar spoon is usually made from EPNS or stainless steel. It is sufficiently long to be used with a mixing glass. The handle should have a flat top for crushing, for example sugar lumps for an Old-Fashioned. See Figure 2.18.

Mixing glass

The mixing glass is used for stirred cocktails such as a Dry Martini. Rinse it out before use to ensure that there is no dust in it. Throw away the ice used

for each drink; never re-use the ice. See Figure 2.19.

Hawthorn strainer

The Hawthorn strainer is used in conjunction with the Boston shaker and the mixing glass for the service of mixed drinks and cocktails.

It is usually made of EPNS or stainless steel. It has a coil around the outside edge which will compress when pushed into a Boston shaker or mixing glass to form a perfect fit for the strainer. See Figure 2.20.

Wine cradles

Wine cradles or baskets were designed to transport bottles of wine on their sides from the cellar to the point of decanting without disturbing the sediment in them. See Figure 2.21.

Many establishments use them, incorrectly, to pour the wine at the table. Although they may look decorative on the table, they are not designed for the service of wine, especially if the wine has sediment in it. As the cradle is tilted backwards and forwards for service, the wine will wash up and down inside the bottle, disturbing the sediment and causing all but the heaviest particles to mix with the wine. The wine will become cloudy, and some will be wasted.

Decanters, carafes and water jugs

These should all be clean and highly polished in advance of service. Decanters come in various shapes, depending on the wine for which they are intended. Many establishments have all-purpose decanters. Decanters should have glass stoppers. Carafes must be marked with the size, and are restricted by law in the UK to 25 cl, 50 cl, 75 cl, 1 l, 10 fl oz and 20 fl oz.

Water jugs may have a lip on them to prevent the ice from coming out with the water. However, this type of jug requires more care when polishing to ensure that the lip is polished properly. Water jugs should not be filled more than three-quarters full, otherwise it will be difficult to pour from them without spilling some of the water.

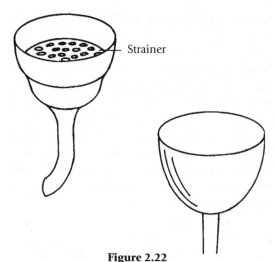

Figure 2.22
Decanting funnel and general-purpose funnel

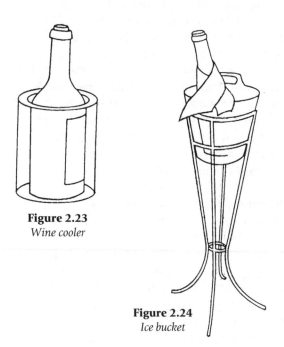

Figure 2.23
Wine cooler

Figure 2.24
Ice bucket

Funnels and strainers

Funnels are used in the bar and cellar to pour liquids from one container into another through a small hole. Strainers may be used with the funnels.

The most obvious example is the decanting funnel, which is usually made from silver, EPNS, stainless steel or copper. This funnel usually has a built-in strainer in it, but it is often used in conjunction with a piece of muslin. See Figure 2.22. Always wash and sterilize funnels and strainers after use.

Wine coolers
Wine coolers are insulated plastic cylinders which will keep wine cool for up to two hours. Most coolers do not actually cool the wine: it must be chilled in advance. Others do take small ice packs. See Figure 2.23.

Ice buckets
Ice buckets (also called wine coolers) are used to chill wines. If the bucket is placed on the table it should be put on a plate or salver to prevent condensation spoiling the table. It should be filled with a mixture of ice and water to cover as much of the bottle as possible. A clean napkin should be draped over the top of the bucket so that the customer can wipe the bottle if he wants to serve himself.

Ice buckets are usually made from EPNS, stainless steel or aluminium. See Figure 2.24.

Beer dispensing equipment

Manual beer pumps
Manual pumping is the traditional method of raising cask-conditioned beer. The pump is mounted on and under the bar counter with the handle extending above the counter. Carbon dioxide (CO_2) or nitrogen (N_2) may be fed into the top of the cask as the beer is withdrawn to prevent bacteria in the air from coming into contact with the beer and spoiling it. Where swan-neck taps are used for the dispensing of cask-conditioned beer, a clean glass must be used for each new drink; it is illegal in the UK to refill a customer's glass.

Free-flow or top pressure
This method is used to dispense keg beers and

occasionally to serve cask-conditioned beer. Cylinders of carbon dioxide and nitrogen are connected to the keg; the gas pressure raises the beer to the dispense point.

Electric cellar pump
This is used where long pipe runs or vertical lifts between the keg and the bar would necessitate using excessive pressure, which in turn would over-carbonate the beer. Only balanced CO_2/N_2 pressure is then necessary.

Beer meters
Beer meters may be used to dispense cask, keg or tank beers. They are government sealed and stamped in the UK and measure exactly half a pint each time the pump is operated. The Exemption Order 1965 allows these meters to be used with 'oversized' glasses. All these systems should be cleaned out regularly with beer pipe cleaner fluid (see later in this chapter).

In-line coolers
In-line coolers may be provided for the cooling of keg beer. The beer pipes go through the coolers, which are adjusted to the correct temperature for each beer. The coolers are either sited under the bar or shelving, or in the cellar.

Lager beer should be served at 48–51°F (9–10.5°C). Bitter beers should be served at 54–57°F (12.2–13.9°C).

A certain amount of heat is given off by these coolers, but they must not be used to dry towels or cloths as the air intake and vents may get blocked and a fire may result (see Chapter Eleven).

Cooling shelves
Cooling shelves are used to maintain bottles and cans of beers and minerals at the correct temperature for serving. They are discussed later in this chapter under 'Storage of beverages'.

Pressurized containers (kegs)
Kegs are supplied in various sizes according to the requirements of the brewery and the establish-

ment (keg sizes are given at the end of the chapter).

Kegs should be kept in a cool place, and must not be left outside in the sun.

The gas pressure of keg beer is predetermined by the brewery. The pressure is controlled from the CO_2 and N_2 cylinders, which are connected to the kegs for service, are pre-set on installation by the brewery or supplier, and should not require alteration. If there is a problem with the pressure, call in the service engineer.

Each beer has a specific pressure requirement. Do not try to use one brewery's connection equipment on another brewery's beers.

Pipe-cleaning bottle
This is described later in this chapter (see page 18).

Beer taps
These are used for the dispensing of cask-conditioned beers direct from the cask. In the past they were made of brass, but are now more commonly made from plastic as these are more hygienic. They must be brushed through and sterilized immediately after use and stored tidily in the cellar.

Shives and spiles
The shive is a wooden or plastic bung fitted in the hole in the top of a beer cask. A soft spile is hammered into the shive. There is a sealing plug in the centre of the shive, which is forced out into the cask by the spile. A hard spile replaces the soft one before service. See Figure 2.25.

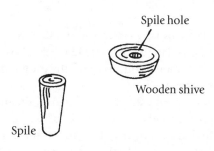

Figure 2.25 *Shives and spiles*

A metal 'spile' with an open and close valve is commonly used in place of the soft spile. It has a plastic drain tube which allows the beer forced out of the cask to be run off into a container, which is a much more hygienic system than using the soft wooden spile. When the beer has settled the valve is closed and generally replaced by a hard wooden spile.

Beer filters

Only filters which are used in conjunction with a filter paper should be used for beer. Filters must be used in conjunction with a filter paper, which is used only once. Suitable beer should be filtered back into casks which are at least half full, to avoid disturbing the sediment in the cask. After use, all parts of the filter including the spile tube must be thoroughly washed. Remove the bottom screw and replace it after cleaning. Sterilize the filter and put it away after use. This process must only be carried out with strict compliance to the relevant Health and Safety regulations.

Stillions or thrawls

Stillions or thrawls are stands on which cask-conditioned beers are 'stillaged' or 'thrawled' after delivery. They are placed in the positon for service, with the shive at the top and the tap hole at the bottom front. Spring-loaded automatic metal stillions are now more common and easier to use as they tilt the cask gradually as the beer is sold, whereas with fixed stillions the cask must be tilted by hand.

Tills

Bar tills are usually electronic and have till rolls incorporated in them. Some EPOS systems have the keys pre-programmed with the individual drink prices.

The till should always be cleared by the management before and after each service. A key is required to clear the till. The cash in the drawer should be checked. Both the till reading and the actual takings should be recorded in a book.

The till drawer *must* be kept closed between each transaction.

If a mistake of over-ringing is made it should be noted on the till roll; it should *not* be corrected by under-ringing another transaction. Some establishments require over-rings to be noted in a book and signed for by the bar supervisor or manager, but this is not common practice.

Skips

Plastic skips are placed in bars to hold empty bottles during service. Empty bottles should be placed in these skips, not thrown into them. Broken glass is very dangerous for the people who have to empty the skips at the end of service.

CLEANING EQUIPMENT AND MATERIALS

Equipment

Cloths
Various cloths are used in beverage sales and service:

Dish cloths must be kept clean. They should be washed out thoroughly, sterilized and then dried at the end of each service.
Swabs are another name for dish cloths or absorbent pads used for cleaning.
J cloths or other disposable cloths should be used where suitable (not on hot hotplates) and disposed of when worn.
Glass cloths should be made out of linen, not cotton, and they should be used to polish glasses. If glass cloths are used to dry glasses, ensure that they are changed when damp. An over-damp cloth may well stick to the glass and cause it to break. Never use a nylon cloth as it repels water.

Brushes
Brushes used for cleaning equipment should be kept clean and sterilized daily to prevent bacteria and dirt being transferred from one item of equipment to another (cross-contamination).

Mops
Woollen mops are still used in many establishments for cleaning floors but are steadily being replaced by the more hygienic squeegee mops. Ensure that both types are left clean and sterile after use.

Vacuum cleaners
Always disconnect the vacuum cleaner before attempting to attend to any problem which it might have.

Do not attempt to vacuum up bottle tops, wine capsules, tin tacks, nails or any piece of metal as these are likely to damage the vacuum cleaner.

Empty the dust bag before it becomes too full.

Ensure that the electric cable is sound, and that the wiring of the plug is checked regularly. Do not try to stretch the electric cable: use an extension lead.

Keep the brush or beater cylinder free from accumulated cotton, string, etc. If there is any smell of burning rubber, or should the sound of the vacuum cleaner change abruptly, switch off immediately and investigate. This is usually a sign that something is preventing the brush or beater cylinder from revolving.

Glass-washing machinery
Read and follow the manufacturer's instructions carefully. Ensure that the glass washer is emptied at the end of each service period. The practice of putting glasses as well as crockery through the washing-up machine must be avoided as the glasses will invariably come out of the machine smeared.

Materials

Water
Be very careful not to scald yourself or another person with boiling water. Take care, when cleaning cellar floors with very hot water, that other people do not get scalded.

Ensure that taps are fully turned off and that they are not left to drip. In winter a dripping tap may cause the waste pipe to freeze up overnight.

Soap
Soap is generally used for hand washing in beverage service areas. There must always be a tablet of soap (or liquid soap dispenser) and a nailbrush with all hand washbasins. (Hygiene Regulations: see Chapter Eleven.)

Detergents
Use detergents in a diluted form as directed by the manufacturer. Use the correct detergent and the correct quantity for the job as directed. *Never* mix two or more detergents together, as poisonous and even explosive fumes may be given off.

Care should be taken when handling detergents, particularly in their undiluted states. If any concentrated detergent, and in particular a caustic one, comes into contact with the eyes or skin, liberally rinse with water and obtain medical attention.

Never put detergents into a container which is marked as another product, or one which could be mistaken for another product. *Never* use a drinking glass or cup to measure a required quantity of detergent: use a special container. Store detergents out of reach of children and in a safe place.

When using detergents, wear goggles and rubber gloves if recommended to do so by the manufacturer's instructions.

Abrasives
Abrasive powders are used for removing stubborn stains and dirt. They should *never* be used on silver or EPNS, or other items which will scratch or mark.

Solvents
Care must be taken when using solvents. They must be used in the correct ratio for dilution as directed by the manufacturer. Use the correct solvent for the job.

Polishes

Before using a polish, ensure that the surface to be treated is clean and free from dust and dirt. If it is not, it should be washed thoroughly and dried before any polish is applied. Polish polishes: it does not remove dirt.

Bleach

As with detergents, care must be taken with bleach, especially in the undiluted state. It must be used diluted with water in the ratio as directed by the manufacturer.

If undiluted bleach comes into contact with the eyes or skin, wash off liberally with water. The same action should be taken if it is spilled on clothes.

PREPARATION OF BAR AND RESTAURANT FOR BEVERAGE SERVICE

Glassware

Polishing glassware

All glasses should be polished before they are placed in a bar or on a restaurant table for service. Dirty or smeared glasses are unhygienic and will also spoil the enjoyment of the beverage.

If there is any sign of a smear or dullness on the glass, hold it over very hot water (steam) and then polish it. This should produce a sparkling clean glass. If the glass still shows a smear or is otherwise soiled put it to be washed. *Never* breathe on a glass to remove smears or marks.

To polish a stemmed glass, open the glass cloth out and hold it in both hands. Hold the bowl of the glass in one hand with the glass cloth, the thumb inside the glass and the fingers around the outside; hold the base of the glass with the other hand with the cloth. Rotate the glass, polishing all the surfaces of the glass both inside and outside. Don't grip the glass too tightly, as this might cause the stem of the glass to snap where it meets the bowl. *Never* use a damp cloth to polish glasses as this will also probably result

in the glass being broken. If the glass is too small to put the thumb and cloth inside the bowl, just insert a small wad of the cloth and polish as before. Remember to polish the base of all glasses.

Always polish sufficient glasses for service.

Carrying empty glasses

During the *mise-en-place* or when transferring from one point to another, other than to the table, stemmed glasses may be carried upside down between the fingers.

When assembling the glasses in the hand, place them between alternate fingers of the upturned hand. Always ensure that the base of each glass is placed resting on the fingers as it is added to those in the hand, not on the base of other glasses; the glasses are then less likely to slip. Do not try to carry too many. Alternatively they may be carried upside down on a tray or salver.

When carrying empty glasses to the table, arrange them on a salver and place them on the table from the right of the customer in their correct position.

Setting glassware on the table

Always place the glasses on the table from the right-hand side of the customer when the customer is present (see Chapter Seven). During the *mise-en-place* of a restaurant, place the glasses upside down (unless just prior to service) on the table in their correct position.

Never place unpolished glasses on the table with the intention of coming back later to polish them. One or more are sure to be missed!

Ingredients

Fruit

Oranges and lemons should be cut in half lengthwise, sliced, and placed on a board or plate ready for service.

Some pieces of lemon zest should be prepared for Dry Martinis, dry vermouths and other drinks.

Frosting glasses

Frosted glasses are used for some cocktails and other special drinks to the requirements of the establishment. These are prepared by dipping the rim of the glass into a shallow dish containing lightly beaten egg whites, then into a shallow dish containing castor sugar. The sugar is sometimes coloured with vegetable colouring. Water is often used in place of egg white as this makes it easier to wash the glasses.

Crushing ice

If there is not a crushed ice-making machine, an electric ice crusher may be used. Crushed ice is quickly and easily obtained with this machine.

In the absence of both of these, crushed ice may be prepared by hand. Pieces of ice should be put into a clean cloth, which is twisted tightly. This 'bag' should then be placed on a solid table and banged with a heavy object (preferably wooden) until the ice is crushed.

Fresh fruit juice

This is prepared by taking washed/wiped fruit, usually oranges, lemons or grapefruit, cutting the fruit in half across the centre, and then placing each half into a bench fruit squeezer or pressing each half over the centre of a glass, plastic or stainless steel fruit squeezer (see page 5).

Stocks

Rotation

Fresh stocks of spirits, beers, minerals and liqueurs must always be placed behind the existing stocks in a bar to ensure that they are used in strict rotation.

For wines which are kept on racks, an ordered system of rotation must be practised. For example, at the end of each service move all the remaining bottles of each bin number to the left of the racks before replenishing with new stock.

Condition

Bottle fermentation beers and wines require time to settle prior to service, for example Worthington White Shield, and red wines containing sediment. Sufficient stocks must be prepared in plenty of time to ensure that this can happen.

White, rosé and sparkling wines, lagers and some other bottled beers are best kept in a refrigerated cabinet or on a cooling shelf. Ensure that there are enough of these items at the correct temperature for service.

Red wines are served at a higher temperature than that of the cellar or wine store where they have been kept. Sufficient stock should be made ready elsewhere (for example the dispense or service area) to give the wine time to come up to room temperature .

Replenishment

During a busy service it is sometimes difficult to replenish stocks which have run out in the bar or restaurant, and this may cause the customers to have to wait. They will probably then be presented with a drink in the wrong condition. While fresh stocks are being brought up, customers are waiting to be served. All this is business being lost. It is therefore vital that sufficient stocks are made ready before service.

Beverage lists

Beverage lists, like menus, are a prime marketing tool of any restaurant. They must be kept clean, well maintained and up to date. They must state clearly and correctly all the items which are available. There must be sufficient beverage lists ready for immediate presentation to customers. In a restaurant the list should be presented to the customer at the same time as the menu (see Chapter Nine).

Dirty and soiled lists present a scruffy image of the establishment to the customer.

STORAGE OF BEVERAGES

The wine cellar

The kind of grape, soil composition, vineyard location, climate, viticulture, vinification methods, hard work and just plain luck, all combine to produce the wine in the bottle; but all this effort can be negated if the wine is transported or stored badly.

Bottles of wine should be stored on their sides, labels uppermost. The cork is porous: it must be kept moistened by the wine, otherwise it will dry out and allow air to penetrate the bottle, which will spoil the wine.

Pasteurized wines with plastic tops and screw-top wine bottles are best kept upright. Wines in storage should be kept at an even temperature, preferably at 52–56°F (11–13°C). Wines which are being kept ready for service in a dispense area should be at the following temperatures: red wines at approximately 59–64°F (15–18°C); white, rosé and sparkling wines at approximately 50°F (10°C). The exact temperature will vary according to the origin and age of the wine. The wrong
temperature, too much light or a dried-out cork will probably spoil the wine completely or reduce its quality. Too much heat will age the wine prematurely and might cause it to maderize. A maderized wine loses its fruitiness and liveliness and takes on a cooked, toffee-like flavour. Red wines will begin to brown and white wines to darken in colour. Note that this can occur by lengthy storage in open racks in the restaurant. It can also be caused by poor transportation before you receive the wine. Too much light or a dried-out cork will cause the wine to oxidize. An oxidized wine changes colour in much the same way as a maderized wine and takes on a woody, sherry-like character. This can also occur due to lengthy restaurant storage or lengthy storage in an upright position. Particular care must be taken with clear glass bottles as the light penetrates more easily. Light is probably the most serious enemy of Champagne and sparkling wine causing the bubbles to disappear, the colour to darken and the taste to oxidize.

The ideal wine store or cellar will have little or no natural light, no draughts, no vibration, and little or no variation in temperature. It should be clean, hygienic, with no strong smells and easily and safely accessible. Although a damp cellar will not harm the wine, it will cause the labels to mould: but the use of a de-humidifier will prevent the mould occurring. If this is not possible and the wine is to be stored for a number of months or longer, lacquering the labels should prevent the mould affecting them. Wine bottles sealed with corks should be stored on their sides to ensure the cork remains moist and air-tight. It is however recommended that Champagne stored for eighteen months or more should be stood upright rather than on its side according to research carried out in 1996 by the Comité Interprofessionnel du Vin de Champagne (CIVC), but this is subject to debate and is not recommended by this author.

Spirits, liqueurs, syrups and cordials should always be kept upright on shelves. This will prevent any leakage caused by a damaged capsule. They are normally kept in a separate secure store.

The beer cellar

The temperature in a beer cellar should be maintained at 55–58°F (12.7–14.4°C), which is the correct temperature for the service of cask-conditioned beers. The best method of obtaining this temperature is by thermostatically controlled cooling and heating units, cooling the cellar in hot weather and heating it in winter. Beer cellars must be kept scrupulously clean and should be washed down at least weekly (see page 18).

Bottled and canned beers and minerals should also be stored at 55–58°F (12.7–14.4°C). A bottle-cooling shelf behind the bar is convenient for storing these items at the correct temperature in sufficient quantities for service. Bottled and canned lagers should be served chilled at about 48–50°F (9–10°C). Cooling shelves work more efficiently when they are kept full. This prevents them from icing up.

All beverage stocks must be used in strict rotation.

CLEARING AND CLEANING THE SERVICE AREA

Empty bottles, waste and ullages

Ullages are beverages that are not able to be sold, for example beer delivered in bottles which are empty or only partially filled, or wine which is unfit for service. These are kept for return to the supplier.

All empty returnable (deposit) bottles must be stored under lock and key and should be returned to the supplier when a delivery is made. Empty beer and mineral bottles are only returnable in full crates. These crates also carry a deposit, so they must be looked after. They must be counted before being returned to the brewery, and a credit note received for them from the delivery man (drayman).

Empty wine, spirit and liqueur bottles do not carry a deposit and are therefore either disposed of in a glass crusher or compactor, or boxed up neatly and put out for the recycling collector.

Equipment and service area

Equipment
Equipment must always be thoroughly cleaned after use and put away ready for service. When using it again it should be checked for cleanliness. Every piece of bar equipment should have its own set position, and all items must be put back in their correct places so that they are easily located when required.

Glasses usually require polishing, and other items such as funnels and mixing glasses should be rinsed out with water before use. Glasses should always be stored upside down in a bar, and on a plastic grid mat if on shelves. Extra stocks of glassware are best kept in the boxes in which they were delivered.

Stained decanters can be successfully cleaned by leaving them overnight filled with a mixture of hot water and a little washing-up machine powder. They must be very thoroughly rinsed out the next morning.

Work area
At the end of service the service areas must be left clean and tidy. Work and service tops must be wiped down with a damp cloth and washed with diluted detergent if necessary. The floor of the bar work area must be swept and then washed, preferably with a squeegee mop.

SECURITY OF CASH, STOCK AND EQUIPMENT

Floats should be checked when received and placed in the till. The drawer of the till should be kept closed between transactions. At the end of service the till should be read by a member of the management team, the cash should be counted and the total recorded, and then locked in a safe. The till key should not be left either in the till or in the bar.

Stock should be kept in a locked store or cellar and issued by a member of the management team only on receipt of a signed requisition. Requisitions should be made out as in Figure 2.26. The line closing off the requisition will prevent any unofficial additions being made. Never leave an open unused line on a requisition.

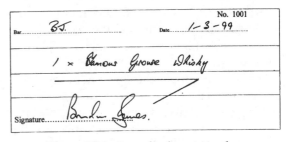

Figure 2.26 *A completed requisition form*

A day-to-day stock control system should be in force for items such as wines. When deliveries are being received there must be a responsible person present to count the stock in and to check it with the delivery note. All items being returned, empty or otherwise, must be noted on a credit note.

Equipment should be locked away out of service hours, where possible, and an inventory of the equipment should be taken on a regular basis. Any equipment found to be out of order, damaged or missing at any time should be reported to the management.

Bars should have a security grille or screen in position when the bar is not in use. Only a restricted number of persons should hold a key to the grille.

HANDLING AND CHANGING BEVERAGES

Cask beers

Cask-conditioned beer is the traditional beer. It contains finings when delivered to an establishment. The cask should immediately be placed in the beer cellar on a stillion or thrawl, and scotched in a position with the bung hole at the top and the tap hole facing outwards. If an automatic stillion is available, the cask can be placed directly on to it.

The temperature of the cellar should be 55–58°F (12.7–14.4°C).

A soft (porous) spile should be banged into the centre of the shive in the bung hole at the top of the cask within eight hours of delivery. If the beer begins to 'work' and a light froth appears on the top of the spile, leave the soft spile in until it stops working. If the beer is quiet, or the frothing has stopped, a hard spile should be used to replace the soft one.

The keystone plug in the tap hole (or keystone bush) should then be wiped clean and a clean sterile tap hammered in with a rubber mallet. It is best to knock the tap into the cask with one solid blow, as this is less likely to disturb the sediment. The tap should be partially open to prevent air being forced into the cask and disturbing the sediment. Check the clarity, smell and flavour of the beer before connecting it up to the dispensing beer pipes.

The hard spile which is now in place must be loosened before service, otherwise it will be impossible to draw any beer, and it should be tapped back again after service to keep it air-tight.

A small quantity of beer should be drawn off from the pipes before opening each day. This can be returned to the cask through a filter.

Sometimes mixed gas, nitrogen gas (N_2) and carbon dioxide (CO_2) top pressure, is used to eliminate air coming into contact with the beer in the cask as the beer is drawn off. In this case the gas spigot is screwed into the spile hole.

When approximately three-quarters of a cask of beer has been used it should be carefully tilted forward to enable most of the beer to be served. This action is not required with an automatic stillion. At the end of service remember to tap the hard spile back in.

Keg beers

Keg beers are ready for service on delivery. They are connected up to a mixed gas cylinder and service beer pipe. A gas-reducing valve and a pressure gauge are attached to the pipes. Standard beers are forced by a mixture of 40% nitrogen and 60% carbon dioxide gas, Cream flow beers are forced by a mixture of 70% nitrogen and 30% carbon dioxide gas.

The pressure is set at the time of installation and should be checked frequently. The beer supplier will state what the correct pressure should be. Too much pressure over-carbonates the beer, causing it to 'fob', that is to be too gassy and difficult to serve. Too low a pressure causes the beer to be flat. Many dispensers have a flow adjuster on the tap, which can be hand adjusted during service. This will regulate the size of the head on the beer. Before changing a keg, switch off the gas supply.

Tank beers

The directions and instructions received from the supplier must be followed.

Bulk minerals

Bulk minerals come in two forms – pre-mixed and post-mixed.

Pre-mixed minerals are in a cylinder, usually of size 4 gallons or 20 litres. The mineral is ready for use in a similar way to a keg beer, and is dispensed through a free-flow tap or gun on the bar top.

Post-mixed minerals require an installation linking the water supply to the gas cylinder and the syrup cylinder, which is of a similar size and shape to that used for the pre-mixed minerals. The water, syrup and gas are brought together as required and dispensed through a free-flow tap or gun on the bar. Some suppliers seal their syrup containers to prevent adulteration, dilution or substitution with another brand. Other suppliers provide syrup in 5-litre plastic containers, which are poured into the stainless-steel cylinders. The quality of the post-mixed type of mineral is dependent upon the quality of the local water supply.

When changing a bulk mineral container, switch off the gas before disconnecting.

Wine in the box may be dispensed by carbon dioxide pressure in a similar manner, the box being in the beer cellar or bar.

Mixed gas

Nitrogen/carbon dioxide gas is available in 7 lb, 14 lb and 28 lb cylinders. The cylinders should be kept in a cool place, fixed to a wall in an upright position.

It should be remembered that gas expands with a rise in temperature. However, the cylinders are equipped with a safety bursting disc, which will break if the pressure inside the cylinder becomes too great: this will cause a noisy release of all the remaining gas. If the cylinder is not properly secured to a wall it may be propelled round the cellar during this release. After release there would probably be a high concentration of gas in the cellar atmosphere, and this might be dangerous for somebody entering the area, as the gas would have replaced the oxygen in the air.

Optics

Optics should be washed out regularly. The stoppers should be checked to ensure that they are sound or are not allowing liquor to ooze out of the join between stopper and bottle.

Separate optical measures should be kept for the different drinks, especially strongly flavoured ones. Special optics suitable for aniseed-flavoured drinks are available.

After the last complete measure has been sold from a bottle on optic, it should be changed. When changing a bottle on optic, the optic and bottle should be released from the holder by grasping the optic and bottleneck with one hand and releasing the spring button securing the holder with the other hand. This hand should then be used to grasp the empty bottle. The empty bottle with the optic still attached should be stood upright on a work surface and the optic should be removed. Any small amount of liquor left in the optic will have run back into the bottle and this should be poured into the new bottle. The optic should then be placed into the neck of the new bottle firmly and the whole inverted. It should be placed back into its holder, taking care to hold the optic in one hand and the full bottle in the other.

Government-stamped optical measures (UK) must never have their seal broken as this would make them illegal to use. This does not apply to non-stamped optics such as free-flow and cordial optics.

CLEARING AND CLEANING THE CELLAR AREA

Equipment

Kegs, casks and gas cylinders may or may not carry a deposit but are expensive equipment. They should be stored in a secure place. They must be returned to the supplier on the next occasion a delivery is received; the items must be recorded on a return slip.

Empty cask-conditioned beer containers should have a hard spile knocked into the shive, and the tap hole should be sealed with a cork.

Gas cylinders are given a five-year check-up, so it is most important to use them in strict rotation and to return empty ones as soon as possible after use to allow the supplier to have them maintained correctly.

Empty bottles should be sorted out and packed into their respective crates, either at the end of a service or during the preparation time on the morning of the next day. The crates should then be stacked in a secure area ready for collection by the drayman.

Walls, floors and ceiling

The walls and ceiling of a beer cellar should be whitewashed or painted in a light colour at regular intervals. The atmosphere of a beer cellar encourages moulds to grow on the walls and ceiling, especially if the cellar is naturally damp. This will increase the chance of cask-conditioned beer becoming infected. In addition the cellar will acquire an unpleasant musty smell. Unnecessary wetting should therefore be avoided and ventilation should be provided as far as possible. The cellar cooling air vents and intakes must be kept free of dust and dirt and any filters cleaned or replaced when necessary. It is best to have such a system on a maintenance contract. If this system should fail, call in the installation or maintenance company.

The floor of a beer cellar must be kept clean and tidy at all times. The floor should be scrubbed and washed down at least once a week and where possible dried afterwards. While the floor is still damp a little diluted bleach or chloride of lime may be sprinkled over the floor: this will inhibit the growing of mould. Do not use strong-smelling disinfectants – they may spoil the beer.

No equipment must be left lying around on the floor, as this could prove to be a hazard to safety.

Drainage

The drains, gulleys and sump (if any) must be kept clean and fresh. If there is a sump, it must be scrubbed out at least once a week using bleach and chloride of lime. Ensure that the sump pump filter and grating are kept clean and in position.

Rubbish

Rubbish must not be allowed to accumulate or be left lying around: it can be a hazard to safety by being an obstacle to free passage or a possible fire risk. All rubbish must be properly binned outside the building in an area especially constructed for this purpose (and which can be cleaned and washed down), compacted in a compactor, or burnt in an incinerator.

CLEANING AND MAINTENANCE OF BEER-DISPENSING EQUIPMENT

Taps, pipes and pumps

Unsatisfactory or insufficient cleaning and maintenance of beer-raising equipment can result in extra waste beer through fobbing, unclean and hazy beer, and breakdowns within the system. The pipes should be cleaned weekly.

Manual beer-pump systems are cleaned by disconnecting the beer pipes from the cask tap and draining off any beer into a bucket. The pipe end should then be put into a bucket of clean water, which is drawn through the system by operating the manual pump. The pipe end is then put into a plastic or stainless steel bucket of correctly diluted cleaning fluid, which is drawn through the whole system and left to stand for 30 minutes or as directed by the cleaning fluid/powder manufacturer. This is then well flushed out by drawing from a bucket of clean water. The pipe is then reconnected to the cask and beer is drawn through again, pushing out the water which is still in the pipe. The beer is then checked for appearance, smell and flavour. The manual pumps themselves should be dismantled and cleaned internally on a monthly basis.

Pressure systems are cleaned by first switching off the gas and disconnecting the connector head from the keg. Clean cold water should be put into a plastic cleaning 'bottle' provided by the brewery or supplier, which is then attached to the pipes by the connector head. The gas is switched on and water is drawn through the system by opening the serving tap, catching the beer and water in a bucket or other container. The pipes are disconnected from the water bottle and reconnected to another cleaning bottle containing diluted cleaning fluid. This is then drawn through the system and left to stand for 30 minutes or as directed by the cleaning fluid/powder manufacturer. The pipes are then connected to the clean water bottle again and the system is thoroughly flushed out to remove all trace of the cleaning fluid. The pipes are now reconnected to the keg of beer and beer is drawn through, expelling the clean water. The beer is then checked for appearance, smell and flavour.

Large installations usually have a cleaning 'ring main' with cleaning 'tees' situated on the walls round the cellar. This is then connected to a large plastic cleaning container containing the cleaning fluid. The beer pipes are connected to these tees and cleaned as for the pressure system described above. The cleaning fluid manufacturer's instructions must be strictly adhered to.

The dispensing taps should be wiped down after every service period and the drip-trays below them emptied away and washed. Never return the beer, collected in these drip trays, back into a cask or keg: this would contaminate the rest of the cask.

Cold shelves

When a cold shelf is beginning to show signs of icing up it should be switched off and completely emptied of bottles. When the ice has melted, any water which has not run down the drain pipe should be wiped up. The cold tray should be washed down and a little warm water poured down the drain hole. The tray should be dried and switched on again and the bottles wiped and replaced.

Refrigerated shelves become prematurely iced up if the cold shelf is not kept filled up or if the temperature is set too low.

In-line or flash coolers and Python systems

In-line coolers are cleaned internally as a matter of course when the pipes are cleaned. At the same time, the outside of the coolers should be wiped down and any air intakes or outlet louvres wiped

clean. Ensure that the intake and outlet louvres are kept clear. Do not dry teatowels by draping them over the outlet.

Other equipment

The corks, pegs and spiles used for cask-conditioned beers should be kept in plastic bags in the cellar tidy.

All items of equipment such as beer taps, dipsticks, beer filters, jugs and buckets must be washed and sterilized immediately before and after use.

All items of cleaning equipment, such as brushes and dish cloths, should be washed out after use and dried. They should be put away when not in use.

SIZES OF BOTTLES, CASKS AND KEGS

Beer and cider bottles

Nip	180 ml
Bottle	275 ml
	330 ml
Pint	568 ml
Litre	1 litre

Mineral bottles

Baby	113 ml
Split	180 ml
	330 ml
Litre	1 litre
Litre and a half	1.5 litres
Non-returnables	various sizes

Beer casks

Pin	4.5 gallons
Firkin	9 gallons
Kilderkin	18 gallons
Barrel	36 gallons
Puncheon	54 gallons
Butt	108 gallons

The puncheon and butt are now rarely used.

Beer kegs

The sizes of kegs are dependent on the brewing company but some common sizes are:

UK	USA
9 gallons	58.6 litres
10 gallons	30 litres
11 gallons	20 litres
18 gallons	
22 gallons	
36 gallons	

Spirit bottles

The standard bottle size for spirits is 70 cl, half-bottles 35 cl, litres and 1.5 litres. Miniatures, quarter-size and half-size bottles are also available, usually for off-sales. There is no standard capacity for miniatures, but these are normally between 3 cl and 5 cl.

Wine bottles

The standard size for a wine bottle is 75 cl and 37.5 cl for a half-bottle.

Some wines are available in 1-litre, 1.5-litre and 2-litre bottles. Some quality wines are also sold in magnums (1.5 litres or two-bottle size). Some high-quality Bordeaux wines, which are intended for keeping, are bottled in impériales, which hold approximately 6 litres or eight bottles.

For the range of Champagne bottle sizes see Chapter Five.

CHAPTER THREE

Wine Production and Selection

DEFINITION OF WINE

Wine is the alcoholic beverage obtained from the juice of freshly gathered grapes, the fermentation of which is carried out in the district of origin according to local tradition and practice. Wines may be red, white or rosé, and still or sparkling (Figure 3.1).

Still wine

Still wines are produced from black and white grapes in a fermentation, which is allowed to complete naturally. Still wines may be divided into light and heavy wines.

Light wine

Light wine is the official name for a natural unfortified wine. It is also used to describe one lacking in body and low in alcoholic content. The light wines of the world are described in Chapter Four.

Heavy wine

Heavy wine is an official term for fortified wines. They are defined in the EU as liqueur wines and are made by adding grape spirit (brandy) to wine during or after the fermentation. If it is added during the fermentation it has the effect of stopping it, leaving the remaining sugar in the wine; this produces a sweet fortified wine, for example port. The fortification can be added after the fermentation has been completed, in which case dry or sweet wines may be produced, for example sherry. Apart from sherry, the majority of fortified wines are sweet. Fortified liqueur wines are described fully in Chapter Five.

Vin de liqueur

Vin de liqueurs (e.g. Pineau des Charente) are produced by adding grape spirit to unfermented grape must (see p. 130). Vin de liqueurs are also known as *Mistelles*.

Sparkling wine

Sparkling wines are produced by allowing the natural carbon dioxide produced during a fermentation to be retained in the bottle, or by the addition of carbon dioxide at a later stage. Champagne and the production methods for sparkling wine are described in Chapter Five.

THE PRODUCTION OF WINE

A number of factors contribute to the quality of wines:

1　The grape
2　The soil

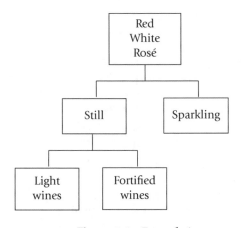

Figure 3.1 *Types of wine*

3   Climatic conditions, location and aspect
4   Viticulture
5   The process of vinification
6   Other factors which are loosely termed the 'luck of the year'
7   Storage (see Chapter Two)

The grape

Many varieties of grapes are used to produce wine. They are all based on the grafting of the scions of European varieties of the species *Vitis vinifera* on to American rootstocks *Vitis rupestris, Vitis riparia* and *Vitis berlandieri* (Figure 3.2). Grafting began in the nineteenth century because the louse *Phylloxera* attacked European rootstocks, and the practice has continued. Further outbreaks have occurred in California. The first of these occurred in the 1980s and they have continued into 2003. A mutation of the original *Phylloxera* called *biotype B* has attacked vines grafted onto AXR1 rootstocks with devastating results. This rootstock was considered to be immune to *Phylloxera* and was used extensively, but has proved to be extremely vulnerable. The only option is to remove the vines and burn them.

Alsace has traditionally marketed its wine under the name of the grape variety used in its production. This method of labelling is now very common, especially for wines from the Americas, South Africa, Australia, New Zealand and some East European countries.

Germany has always identified the name of the grape or grapes used in its better-quality wines, and many parts of the lesser wine areas of France have followed suit.

The following sections set out some of the better-known grape varieties/cultivars. Although the character of the wine produced from these grapes will vary from region to region, the classic base usually remains, so the best-known wines produced from these grapes have been listed.

New students of wine and also many experienced students look for specific characteristics by which they might identify a grape variety. In an attempt to assist the reader in this area some general characteristics of a number of varieties have been listed, but it must be realized that these will

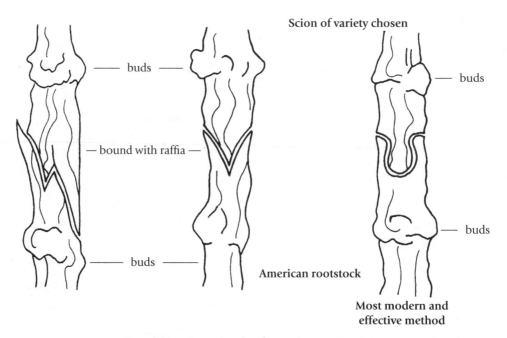

Figure 3.2 *Examples of grafting techniques*

not be present in every wine made from the stated varietal. They will change to a greater or lesser degree depending on the country, district, soil, wine-maker and quality of the year.

White grape varieties
Albariño   Grown extensively in the Rias Baixas region of north-west Spain where it produces highly aromatic dry wines with a ripe peach and lemon zest character, and fresh acidity. Also grown in the Vinho Verde region of northern Portugal under the name *Alvarinho*.

Chardonnay   This is the classic white grape of Burgundy and Champagne producing wines full of flavour and a crisp acidity. It is grown throughout the world's wine-growing regions and thrives particularly well on soils rich in calcium. Lemon, green apple, melon skin and butter are associated with Old World wines; lemon, pineapple, charentais melon, exotic fruits with New World ones. Many Chardonnays are matured in oak; this adds toastiness, butterscotch, vanilla, cinnamon or coconut, or a combination of a number of these aromas and flavours depending on the type of oak used.

Chasselas   The Chasselas is grown in the Loire valley, producing Pouilly-sur-Loire, and in Switzerland to produce Fendant.

Chenin Blanc   This grape is grown extensively in the middle Loire regions of Anjou and Touraine. It is renowned for producing Vouvray and Saumur still and sparkling wines, the dry and medium wines of Savennières and the sweet wines of Coteaux-du-Layon. Loire wines made from *Chenin Blanc* have high acidity, a minerally/chalky character with an aroma of lemon, baked apple, honey and wet wool, and a taste of lemon, baked apple and honey. It is now grown widely in Australia, California, South Africa and South America. In South Africa it is also known as *Steen*.

Gewürztraminer   The wines are usually medium dry, spicy, full of fruit with a highly perfumed bouquet. The Alsace wine of this name is the best known. It is grown in Australia, Austria, California, Chile, Germany, Italy, New Zealand, Oregon, South Africa and Washington State.

Marsanne   A major white variety in northern Rhône, it is also grown in the south of France, California and Australia. It produces strong coloured, full-bodied dry white wines often with a light marzipan character.

Müller-Thurgau   Used extensively in Germany, Austria and New Zealand producing wines which are slightly fuller than the Rhine Riesling, to which it is closely related.

Muscadet or Melon de Bourgogne   The sole variety used in the production of Muscadet in the Loire valley. It produces crisp, dry, acidic wines.

Muscat   There are three main varieties of the muscat grape, *Muscat Blanc à Petits Grains*, *Muscat of Alexandria* and *Muscat Ottonel*. Between them they produce a range from the dry Muscats of Alsace to the sweet liqueur and VDN wines of Samos. Muscat-de-Beaumes-de-Venise and Asti are two of the best-known wines from this varietal. Muscat is used in many blended wines. On its own it has a raisin-like flavour and bouquet. Muscat d'Alsace is an exception in that it is a dry wine.

Pinot Blanc   Probably best known as an Alsace variety, but is grown widely in Austria and Germany – where it is known as *Weissburgunder* – Italy – where it is known as *Pinot Bianco* – eastern Europe, California and Canada. Its characteristics vary considerably from country to country but generally it is dry with a good level of alcohol. It is often confused with Chardonnay both in the vineyard and in the glass.

Pinot Gris   Closely related to the *Pinot Noir* it has a pinkish, light purple skin. As with *Pinot Blanc*, it is known as an Alsace grape, and is classified there as a noble variety. It is grown in Austria and Germany where it is known as *Rülander*, although the Italian synonym *Pinot Grigio* is also used. It is grown extensively in northern Italy as well as in eastern Europe, California and Oregon. The wines are normally dry with floral notes, a white peach and light apricot flavour, coupled with some spiciness, particularly in Alsace. Under the synonyms *Malvasia* and *Malvoisie*, it produces sweet wines in a number of countries.

Rhine Riesling   This classic white grape of Germany produces very high-quality Rhine and Mosel wines, and top-quality wines in Alsace and Austria. It produces some of the finest late-harvested sweet wines and is grown extensively throughout the wine-growing countries. Rieslings grown in Germany usually display a mineral quality with pear, yellow/green apple, white peach, some citrus, floral and honey notes. Old Rieslings have a petrol character. Many of the so-called Rieslings grown in countries other than France and Germany are not the Rhine Riesling: the name is often applied to lesser grape varieties.

Sauvignon Blanc   Dry, fresh wines which are usually at their best within five years. Sancerre and Pouilly-Fumé are good examples of these light dry wines. They have a bouquet of blackcurrant leaves or wood, and a slight gooseberry taste; they are also described as grassy. Blended with the Sémillon grape it produces dry white Graves and the very sweet Sauternes and Barsac. New Zealand Sauvignon Blanc often has a canned asparagus character, while in Australia and Chile this is less apparent. Californian Sauvignon Blancs are also called Fumé Blancs and have a softer more scented aroma.

Sémillon   This grape attracts the fungus *Botrytis cinerea* (giving *pourriture noble* or noble rot) and is blended with Sauvignon to produce Sauternes, Barsac and white Graves. It is extremely successful in Australia and New Zealand where it is often

blended with Chardonnay and is producing good dry wines in California, South Africa and Chile where it is often blended with Chardonnay or Sauvignon Blanc. A full-bodied dry wine, it has a fat waxy character and a light aroma of citrus, melon and fig. Besides producing dry white wines, it is being used in Australia and California to make late-harvested or Botrytis-affected sweet wines of high quality. Some areas of France are now using Sémillon as a single grape variety.

Sylvaner (Silvaner)   Grown in Germany, Alsace and some eastern European countries, it is probably at its best in Franconia and produces good wine in Switzerland under the name Johannisberger. Sylvaner wines are less elegant than Rieslings, and have a softer finish.

Trebbiano   The major white grape variety grown in Italy, which produces fresh light white wines and is often blended with one or more other varieties. It is used in the production of Soave, Orvieto, Frascati and a very small quantity (2 per cent) is permitted in *Chianti*. On its own it produces a dry white wine. It is another name for Ugni Blanc, which is used for Armagnac and Cognac production.

Viognier   This is the grape responsible for Condrieu and Château Grillet in northern Rhône. It is now being grown in the Languedoc-Roussillon region of France and in California and Australia. The wines are a deep yellow in colour, highly aromatic with strong peach and apricot aromas and flavours. Wines from the warmer climates are high in alcohol.

Black grape varieties
Cabernet Franc   Blended with other grapes, it is used to produce claret (red Bordeaux). It also produces the rosé wine Cabernet d'Anjou and the red Chinon and Bourgeuil in the Loire Valley. It has black fruit, bell (green) pepper, stemmy and earthy characters, and less firmness than Cabernet Sauvignon.

Cabernet Sauvignon   The classic grape for red Bordeaux, for which it is blended with one or more of Cabernet Franc, Merlot, and sometimes Petit Verdot, Malbec and Carmenère.

It provides the backbone to all the great wines of the Médoc and usually produces wines high in acid and tannin which will mature with age. It is also a major varietal throughout the temperate and warm wine-producing regions particularly in eastern Europe and the New World countries. It has blackcurrant/cassis, blackberry fruit aromas and flavours with cedar box/wood shavings, mint (New World, usually Australia), eucalyptus (New World, usually California), Christmas pudding dried fruits (South Australia) and bell (green) pepper when less ripe. Mint is also discernible in some of the Bordeaux wines.

Carmenère   One of the original Bordeaux vines, which is still allowed for these AOC wines, is being planted by one or two growers there. It is, however, a major variety in Chile where it produces wines with a deep colour and juicy black fruit characters.

Gamay   Gamay is the single varietal of Beaujolais. The wines are light coloured, light bodied and soft, with aromas and flavours of strawberries and cherries with a low tannin content. Those produced by the *macération carbonique* method have a bubble gum/ boiled sweet character. Gamay is also grown in the Loire.

Grenache Noir   The second most widely planted grape variety. This is a major varietal of Spain and the South of France, in particular the Southern Côtes du Rhône. It is the most important grape used in the blend for Châteauneuf-du-Pape and the sole varietal used for Tavel rosé and Lirac. The wines have black fruit, violet perfume, peppery characters, with a good alcohol content and often a slightly 'sweet' flavour. It is also grown in California, Australia and other hot countries.

Malbec   Besides being one of the lesser Bordeaux varietals, this grape is grown extensively in the Loire (here known as Cot) and Cahors, and many other areas of France. It is a major varietal in Argentina and Chile.

Merlot   This is the most widely planted black grape in Bordeaux, is very important in the Médoc blends and is the major varietal used in St Emilion and Pomerol wine production. It is an everincreasing varietal in California and Australia, and is widely grown in Australia, New Zealand, Italy, South Africa and Switzerland. The wines have soft lush blackberry, blackcurrant and plumy flavours and a velvety texture. The New World wines have additional jammy, peppery and often minty notes.

Meunier   One of the three permitted grapes used for Champagne.

Nebbiolo   The most important red variety in Piedmont, Italy, where it is also know as *Spanna*. It produces Barolo and Barbaresco, and is used blended in many other wines. Characteristics include rose, prune, chocolate, truffle, hot tar and asphalt. The wines tend to brown quickly.

Pinot Noir   This is the classic grape of red Burgundy and Champagne. It is the single variety of AOC Côte d'Or wines and is also one of the three permitted grapes for Champagne. It is grown world-wide, in particular in Australia, Austria, California, Hungary, New Zealand and Switzerland. The wines are light in tannin, have aromas and flavours of raspberries, strawberries, red and black cherries, and when mature take on an old cabbage/ barnyard character.

Sangiovese   The most planted red grape in Italy. It is the main ingredient in the Chianti blend and is a major ingredient in a large number of highquality wines. It has cherry and cherry pit aromas and flavours and tends to brown early. Under the name Brunello it produces such wines as Brunello di Montalcino and Torgiano. It is now being grown in California with some success.

Syrah (Shiraz)   Syrah is the main red varietal of the northern Côtes du Rhône, producing Côte Rôtie, Hermitage, St Joseph and Cornas. It is an important grape in the Châteauneuf-du-Pape blend and the most widely planted red varietal in Australia. It is widely planted in South Africa, and is found throughout the hotter wine-growing regions including California. The wines are power-ful and full-bodied, with concentrated flavours. Black pepper, raspberry, mulberry, rubber, liquorice, chocolate and leather are common characteristics and when mature wet leather and game aromas and flavours are often present.

Tempranillo   This is the principal grape varietal used in the production of Rioja and Navarra and Ribera del Duero wines. It is an important varietal in Argentina and is one of the top varietals used in Port production under the name *Tinta Roriz*. The wines are full-bodied, with aromas and flavours of red fruits, particularly strawberries, raspberries and cherries.

Description of the grape
The grape is made up of four main parts (Figure 3.3).

1   The *pulp* produces the grape juice known as *must* in France and *mosto* in Italy and Spain. In the resulting wine, the juice provides the water content and the fruit flavours which come from the sugars and acids. It also supplies the sugar required for the fermentation process.
2   The skin of black grapes provides the colour and tannin in red wine. On the outside of the skin of a mature grape there are between 10,000 and 100,000 yeast cells, the over-whelming majority of which are 'grape yeasts' with a small proportion of *saccharomyces cere-visiae*. The latter will quickly develop and ferment the must into wine while the other yeasts die off.
3   The pips are not crushed in the vinification process, as they contain oils which are very bitter and which would spoil the wine.
4   The stalk is usually removed by an *égrappoir*

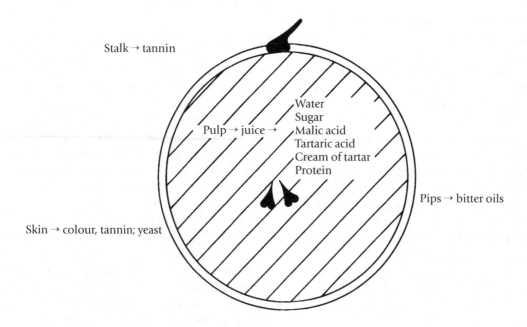

Stalk → tannin

Pulp → juice →

Water
Sugar
Malic acid
Tartaric acid
Cream of tartar
Protein

Pips → bitter oils

Skin → colour, tannin; yeast

Figure 3.3   *The grape*

before the grapes are crushed or pressed. Previously the stalks were left on the grapes for red wines, and this increased the tannin content of the wine. The characteristics of the wine will vary according to the variety of grape used and the vinification process.

The soil

The vine will grow in any type of soil. However, it has been found that where it has to struggle for its existence in agriculturally poor soil it produces better wine grapes, because the vine will push its roots downwards, enabling it to pick up many more trace elements and minerals (see Figure 3.4).

Deeper roots make the vine less likely to be affected by severe winters. An example of this occurred in 1984–85, when, during the coldest winter recorded in the last century, the ground in Chablis was frozen to a depth of one metre from the surface. Although this is a dormant time for the vine, it does need to take in a certain amount of moisture. Thus, although damage was done to some of the younger vines, the majority survived.

Deep roots also enable vines to withstand long dry spells. However, in the very hot summers of 1975 and 1976 the water level in the soil fell below the roots of many of the younger vines, particularly in parts of Spain, causing them to die.

The topsoil should be well drained and fairly light. High-quality wines may be associated in particular with limestone (calcareous) and sandy/gravel soils, but good drainage is the most important factor.

Climate and location

Vines grow best at latitudes of 30–50° north and 30–50° south. The most northerly vineyards of mainland Europe are now at Saala-Unstrut and Sachsen in Germany at 51.5° north. South-west England is on 50–51° north, but because the German vineyards are situated in a large land mass away from the coast, they usually experience more hours of sunshine than the vineyards of England. The Ahr district of Germany is on the same latitude as south-west England but the vineyards are sited on south-facing slopes as are the vineyards of

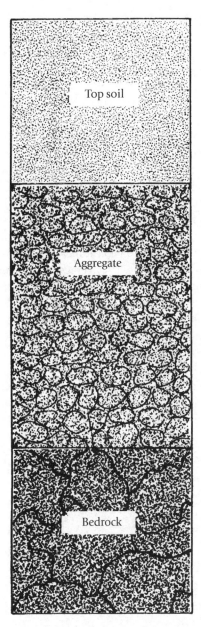

Figure 3.4 *Soil structure at Château Giscours in the Médoc*

the Mosel and northern Rhine; this causes the vines to receive more concentrated rays from the sun. The rivers raise the ambient temperatures one or two vital degrees; and in some cases, as in the Mosel and parts of the Rheingau, light is reflected from the rivers.

27

The Rheingau in Germany (see Chapter Four) has an excellent aspect, benefiting from the south-facing slopes, the reflected sun from the river Rhine and Mosel, and the mist rising from the river early on summer mornings, allowing the vines to take in moisture through their leaves (Figure 3.5). Moreover there are often trees at the top of the slopes; these improve the humidity and, together with the slopes behind the vines, help to shield the crop from the cold north and north-east winds. At this point the river is very wide, and the expanse of water moderates any changes in temperature.

Climatic conditions are probably the most important factor in viticulture – next, of course, to the variety of grape. The average yearly temperature must not be below 10°C; the ideal average is 14°C.

Of all the climatic conditions, frost is the most feared. Frost in late spring will damage the new shoots, thus reducing the size of the crop. 1991 experienced a particularly severe frost which affected Northern Europe and many other wine areas. Various methods of combating the effect of late frosts are used. In Germany, Champagne and Chablis and parts of California, oil stoves known as smudge pots are set between the rows of vines to heat the air, but these are particularly environmentally unfriendly. It can cost as much as $1,800 (£1,200) per week to protect 5 hectares of vines in this way. Another method is to spray the vines with water; the cold air will freeze the water, forming a coating of ice. This method is called *aspersion*. The ice remains at freezing point (0°C) during frosts, protecting the vine from air at lower temperatures. This is a process which has to be repeated. Large propellers are also used to disturb the air, as frost will only occur in still conditions. It is now thought that grass and vegetation produce a small amount of humidity, which will attract frost, so recently vineyard owners have been keeping their rows of vines free from weeds!

Cold or wet weather at flowering time may cause *coulure*, which is the non-pollination of some of the blossoms, causing the grapes either to fall off or never to develop. Although this can greatly reduce the size of the crop, it will not affect the quality of the other grapes. *Millerandage* is another result of cold, wet weather at flowering time causing poor fruit set, preventing some of the berries

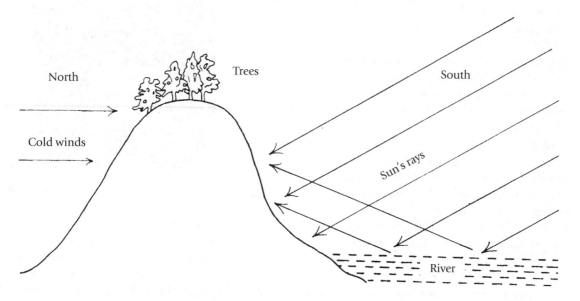

Figure 3.5 *Climate and location: the Rheingau and Mosel-Saar-Ruwer*

from developing. There are therefore uneven sizes of grapes in a bunch, reducing the yield.

The ripening period in the northern hemisphere is from June to September, and in the southern hemisphere from November to February. A lack of sunshine during this period will produce grapes short of sugar. Too much rain towards the end of the ripening period will swell the grapes, raising the water content too much and thus weakening the resulting juice. Hail will damage the vines, sometimes seriously, and will split the grapes, causing unwanted moulds to form and the grapes to spoil. Heavy mists or rain at harvest time can ruin the whole year's work, preventing the grapes from being picked at the correct time; grey rot may attack the grapes, rendering them useless. If the winter is not cold enough, many diseases and pests will survive and produce problems in the following year.

Depending on the variety of grape, it is generally accepted that 85 to 100 days of sunshine are required from flowering to harvest. Rain puts the moisture into the grapes, while the sun ripens and sweetens them. A shortage of sunshine usually results in grapes high in acid and low in sugar; too much heat produces grapes high in sugar and low in acid, giving 'flabby' wines.

Viticulture

Before giving consideration to the vinification of wine, a mention must be made of the importance of viticulture – the growing of grapes for the production of wine. This requires deep study for full understanding, and it will only be touched on here. The type of pruning plays a large part in the quantity and thus the quality of the grapes produced. The methods of pruning are defined for each district and region by the applicable wine authority, for example in France by the Institut National des Appellations d'Origine (INAO). The vines and the soil must be looked after throughout the year, necessitating up to eighteen visits to each vine in some districts for pruning, training the vine, spraying, hoeing or ploughing, picking and fertilizing. In all regions governed by wine

laws a top limit is put on the amount of hectolitres permitted to be made per hectare. This may vary from district to district and from year to year.

Vinification

Some wineries will hand-sort the grapes on a table, selecting only sound grapes. This process is called *triage*. The vinification process is illustrated in Figure 3.6. The figure shows the essential difference between white and red wine production. For white wine, the grapes (white and/or black) are pressed immediately after harvest, and only the juice goes for fermentation. Sufficient yeasts are run off with the juice for fermentation to take place. By contrast, for red wine the fermentation begins with the skins still present in the must; this practice is called *cuvaison*. The running wine (*vin de goutte*) is usually removed from the skins after a few days when sufficient colour and tannin have been extracted. The skins and other material are then pressed, and the resulting wine (*vin de presse*), high in tannin and colour, may be added to the *vin de goutte* depending on the style of wine required. The dry skins and pips, and also the stalks recovered from the early part of the process (the whole is called the *marc*), may be wetted, fermented again and distilled to produce a brandy of the region (for example Marc de Bourgogne in Burgundy), or used as a fertilizer. The *marc* from pressing for white wine is treated similarly (see Chapter Six). Unfermented must contains perhaps 24 per cent sugar, together with malic acid, tartaric acid, cream of tartar, protein, tannin and colouring matter. After fermentation, the fermented must contains typically 11 per cent alcohol and 0.2 per cent sugar, together with carbon dioxide, malic acid, cream of tartar, protein, tannin, colouring matter and glycerol. The alcohol formed in the production of wine is ethyl alcohol or ethanol (C_2H_5OH). The alcohol percentage will depend on the sugar content of the must and variety of yeast:

grape sugar (glucose) ethyl alcohol   carbon dioxide
$$C_2H_{12}O_6 + \text{yeast} = 2C_2H_5OH + 2CO_2 + \text{heat}$$

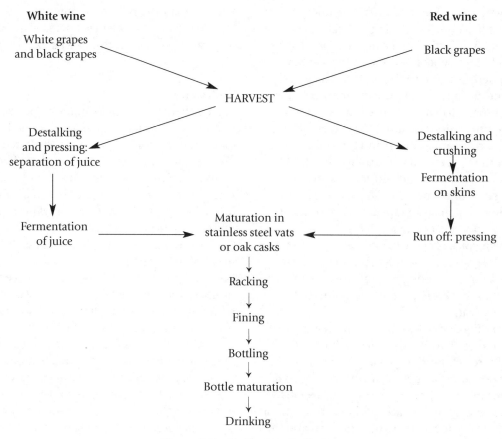

Figure 3.6 *Vinification of still wine*

As stated previously, there are myriad yeasts and moulds (bacteria) on each grape. If the wine yeasts and moulds are allowed to develop, the wine will be ruined. These yeasts will die when the alcoholic content reaches 4 per cent alcohol by volume (abv), whereas the yeast *saccharomyces cerevisiae* will live and continue to develop to between 16% and 18% abv.

Converting the must into wine
Both the wine yeasts and the acetobacter, which is a wine-spoiling mould, are aerobic – that is, they require oxygen to live. *Saccharomyces cerevisiae*, however, is anaerobic – that is, it develops in the absence of oxygen. By adding sulphur dioxide to the unfermented must, the wine maker is able to prevent the development of the unwanted yeasts

and wine-spoiling moulds. The sulphur dioxide takes up any oxygen in the must and forms a film over the top, preventing any oxygen from getting through. This process is referred to as *sulphuring* the wine. *S. cerevisiae* will cause fermentation to take place, quickly raising the alcoholic content above 4% abv and thus killing the unwanted yeasts and bacteria. Many wine makers kill off all yeast and add their own cultured yeasts.

Temperature is an important factor in the fermentation process, as *s.cerevisiae* will operate only between 10°C and 30°C. It is essential to reach 4% abv as soon as possible to ensure the destruction of the unwanted yeasts and acetobacter, but after this a slower fermentation will produce better-quality wine. Many wine makers, particularly those in hot climates, cool their fermentation vats either by using double-skinned stainless steel vats with cold water circulating between the two skins or by running cold water over the vats. This temperature control has been especially important in the improvement of the quality of wines from countries such as Spain, South Africa and the USA. In cooler climates the reverse is sometimes the case. If the weather is bad and the temperature low during the fermentation, the vats may have to be heated.

Malolactic fermentation

This fermentation takes place after the alcoholic fermentation, and sometimes not until the spring following the harvest. It is the conversion of malic acid into lactic acid and a little carbon dioxide. If this takes place in the bottle it will make the wine slightly sparkling (*pétillant* or *spritzig*) and cause a small amount of sediment to form. Sometimes it will force the cork out of the bottle. This fermentation is usually carried out in vats or casks, either by the wine maker creating favourable conditions for this to occur, or by natural methods.

Malic acid is harsh and this process causes the wine to soften.

Macération carbonique

This is a modern system of controlling the speed of the fermentation. Whole grapes are put into the fermenting vat, which is sealed and is fitted with a valve, which allows the carbon dioxide to escape when a certain pressure is reached within the vat. The whole berries ferment causing them to burst and to give off carbon dioxide. This method of fermenting under pressure causes the colour pigment to be extracted very quickly, enabling the skins to be removed after a short time. This keeps the tannin content low and helps the production of a fast-maturing wine. Gamay grapes are frequently fermented by this method. Beaujolais Nouveau and Touraine Primeur are produced in this way. Wines produced by this method have a 'pear drop' aroma.

Macération pelliculaire or Prefermentation maceration

This is the process of leaving the grape skins in contact with the must for a few hours prior to fermentation to extract a little more flavour. This is practised for white wine production particularly in the Loire. The colour for rosé wine is obtained by the same method, and lasts between 12 and 24 hours.

Cuvaison

The maceration of the grape skins (pomace) in the fermenting juice during red wine production, to extract colour, tannin and other constituents from the skins.

Pigeage

The process of punching down the cap (pomace) to drown the aerobic bacteria and to assist the cuvaison process.

Remontage

The process of pumping the fermenting juice over the cap (pomace) during the cuvaison.

Batonnage

The process of stirring the lees with a stick or paddle to increase the flavour extraction. This is practised with some lighter-flavoured white wines such as Muscadet.

Soutirage or Racking

This is the transfer of wine from one container to another leaving the lees behind.

THE MAIN CHARACTERISTICS OF WINE

Appearance and colour

Wine can be red, white or rosé. Whatever its colour, sound wine must be clear. If it is cloudy, either it contains sediment and has been shaken up, in which case it should be left to rest for 24 hours before decanting and serving, or there is something wrong with it. In both cases the wine should not be served.

As explained in the previous section, red wine is produced from black grapes, the skins of which are allowed to be present for all or part of the fermentation process. The colour ranges from deep purple through the various shades of red to brown. Young red wines are usually purple, old wines are reddish-brown. The outer rim of the wine (*robe*) should be looked at to ascertain if there is any rim variation (Figure 3.7). This will enable the connoisseur to judge the age of the wine. A purple rim usually indicates a youthful wine, and an orange or brown rim an older wine.

White wine can be produced from black grapes, white grapes or a blend of the two. The red colouring pigment is contained in the skins of black grapes and not in the pulp or juice; therefore if black grapes are pressed and the juice is run off the skins straight away, white wine will result. White wine varies in colour, from almost colourless through the shades of yellow to gold. Some of the younger wines have a greenish tinge to them, while some of the older wines turn brown with age.

Rosé wine is made in several ways. The classic method is to commence the fermentation as for red wine, to remove the partly fermented juice from the skins after the correct degree of color-ation has been achieved, and then to continue the fermentation off the skins. Another method is to blend a small quantity of red wine with a large quantity of white wine. A third method is to blend black and white grapes, with the fermentation taking place on the skins of the black grapes.

Pelure d'oignon is a term used to describe some rosé wines which have a russet-brown tinge similar to that of an onion skin. It is also used to describe some old red wines, which have acquired this colour with ageing.

Bouquet
The bouquet is the smell of the wine. It is very important in judging the characteristics and quality of a wine. It is generally accepted that (other than the label) the smell of a wine is the best indicator of its origin, its content, its quality, its age and its character. Wine should always smell like wine: or, in tasting terminology, 'clean'. If the wine smells of vinegar, any decayed vegetables or cork, then there is something wrong with it.

Taste
The taste of the wine confirms the impressions formed by the wine's appearance and bouquet. The first thing to be confirmed will be the sweetness or dryness of the wine. This is followed by the acidity, the fruitiness or vinosity, the tannin content (which often helps to indicate the age of red wines), and the 'weight' or 'body' of the wine in the mouth, which indicates the alcoholic content. Figure 3.8 shows the functions of the various parts of the tongue in detecting the characteristics of wine.

Ageing potential
Some wines, for example Beaujolais and Muscadet, are made for early drinking, which means that the wines will not improve with keeping for a long time: 'Old is not necessarily good.' These wines are made from grape varieties which produce wines full of fruit, low in tannin and early maturing. Red wines, which are produced to age, contain tannin; this is a preservative, and it falls out of the wine as it ages. Wines in this category

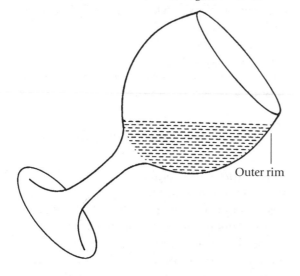

Outer rim

Figure 3.7 *Method of ascertaining variation in colour*

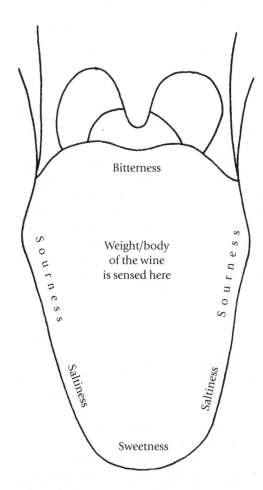

Figure 3.8 *Functions of parts of the tongue in detecting characteristics of wine. Tannin is sensed by a dryness round the gums and the sides of the mouth*

are best from 'good' years – that is, years in which all the variable factors that contribute to quality combine to form an outstanding wine.

Full bodied or light bodied

Wines which are high in alcoholic content, that is 13% abv upwards, are classed as full bodied. The alcohol causes the wine to weigh heavy on the palate. The wine is also full in flavour. Light-bodied wine is usually below 13% abv alcohol and is lighter in flavour.

Sweet or dry

Sweet wine has a high sugar content. The sugar may remain in the wine after the fermentation has finished, for example Sauternes, or it may be added in sufficient quantity to produce a sweet wine. *Chaptalization* – named after Dr Chaptal who developed this process – is used to increase the sugar content prior to fermentation so that a higher alcoholic level can be obtained. It is practised in cool regions and in poor vintages but is banned in many of the hot regions. Sweet wines are also produced by adding alcohol early during the fermentation which arrests the process before much of the sugar is used up (VDN wines, see p. 130), or by adding grape spirit to unfermented must to produce vin de liqueur or Mistelle (see p. 130)

Dry wine is low in sugar. This is usually arrived at by allowing the fermentation to use up the grape sugar (and any added sugar) in the fermentation.

TASTING

Wine is tasted by the customer to ensure that it is in good condition, and at the correct temperature. The sommelier tastes wine for these two reasons plus others. He/she will want to assess the quality, whether it is ready for drinking, will improve with age, or is passed its best, and how the wine will react with different types of food. An analysis of the wine may also be required to enable the sommelier to describe the wine to customers or attendees at wine-tasting events.

Condition of the wine

The wine is tasted to assess whether it is as it should be or whether the wine is off, e.g. contaminated by a faulty cork, faulty wine production or poor storage. Contamination can result from unhygienic practices or faulty equipment used during wine production, or bottling processes resulting in tainted or musty smells and flavours, or over-oxidized or maderized characteristics.

Oxidation is not necessarily a fault as it is a normal part of the maturation process. It is a feature of sherry production and a number of other wines, but for the majority it is a fault. Generally it is caused either by allowing too much air to come into contact with the wine during production, maturation or bottling, or through over-lengthy storage. It has a sherry-type smell to it.

Maderization has a similar smell and flavour plus a cooked characteristic. It is caused by the wine being subjected to too much heat, either during its production/maturation or storage. Many wines stored in south-facing rooms during hot summers without temperature control, or in the windows of wine stores, have been ruined in this way. Wines transported in non-refrigerated containers in hot climates are often similarly affected. Madeira correctly has these characteristics as its production includes heating as part of the process, and it is from this wine that the term originates.

Temperature

Temperature has quite an effect on the taste of wines. The old adage, which advocated serving red wines at room temperature and white, rosé and sparkling wines at cool or cold temperatures, was based on sound principles. There are always exceptions to every rule but with the advances in wine technology and production methods there are now many more exceptions, and average room temperatures are now higher than when this guide was proposed. Warmer temperatures increase the perception of the aromas, fruit, sweetness and alcohol, but decrease the perception of acids and tannins. Cooler temperatures increase the perception of acids and tannins but decrease the aromas, fruit, sweetness, alcohol and volatile aromas.

Quality

Sommeliers responsible for purchasing wines will need to determine the quality of wines, and whether they need time to reach their best condition, are ready now or past their best. Quality wines have a good balance between the acids, tannins, fruit and alcohol. A good-quality wine will linger on the palate after it has been swallowed. A low-quality wine may have a pleasant taste in the mouth, but immediately it is swallowed the taste will disappear. Wines require a good acid balance to enable the flavour to linger on.

Suitability with food

Sommeliers must have the ability to assess which foods the wine will best accompany.

Analysis of wine (sensory evaluation)

The sommelier may need to do this when a wine has been returned by a customer to determine whether there is a fault, and the nature of the fault if there is one. In sommelier competitions, wine-tasting examinations or when judging wines at shows, this is carried out 'blind' (with no knowledge of the origin or name of the wine).

Becoming an expert wine-taster requires tasting a great many wines and years of experience.

Basic tasting techniques

The most suitable sizes of glassware for tasting are 10–12 oz (30–35 cl) with an ample bowl and tapering slightly towards the top. This will enable it to be tilted for examination, for the wine to be agitated by swirling it in the glass and for the bouquet to be concentrated as it is sniffed at the top. By swirling the wine around in the glass more of the esters and alderhydes (the smells) are released. The glasses must be spotlessly clean, highly polished and with no detergent odour. 75 ml (2.5 oz) is an ample quantity of wine for tasting. This will allow the glass to be tilted (Figure 3.7) to enable the hue (colour) of the wine and any rim variation to be studied without spillage. The tasting room should have good natural light by preference, and must have clean, fresh air, untainted by cigarette smoke or other odours.

Appearance

The wine is studied for its clarity, brightness, any evidence of gas, colour (hue), colour intensity, and any rim variation. The brightness of the wine may be an indication of whether it has been filtered or not and is usually described in descending order as star-bright, day-bright, bright followed by degrees of cloudiness. Deep-coloured red wines may be opaque. This is not normally a fault and will probably be due to the amount of concentration of the extraction. This is more likely in young full-bodied red wines.

The colour of white wines will generally range from almost colourless to yellow and gold, but can be amber or even brown if the wine is very old. A deep yellow or golden colour may indicate the wine is from a hot climate, has a high extraction and/or is an older wine. Some younger white wines have a greenish tinge or hue, which may indicate the wine is from a cooler climate, while some wines will turn amber with age.

The colour of red wines will generally range from a light strawberry/cherry red, purple through to a deep ruby, and from garnet to brown. Young red wines are usually purple and either show no change in colour from the centre to the rim, or show a lighter purple or pink; older red wines show a change of colour to orange or even brown developing first at the rim. Evidence of gas in a still wine should be noted as it can indicate that the wine is young, fresh or in some cases out of condition. In sparkling wines the quality of the bubbles will probably indicate the quality of the product (see p. 113)

The viscosity of the wine is the final point of appearance to assess. This refers to the consistency of the wine, which is identified by the thickness of the 'tears' on the inside of the glass. The thicker the 'tears', the higher the alcohol content, sugar content, or both. If light or sheeting 'tears' are observed, the wine has a low alcohol content. This is assessed by swilling the wine in the glass and observing the thickness of the 'tears' and the speed at which they fall.

Be warned that a dirty or greasy glass will distort the result. At the same time as viscosity is assessed in red wines, it can be noted whether the 'tears' are colour stained. Colour in the 'tears' would indicate a high extraction and/or a hot/good vintage. At this point an opinion on the possible origin of the wine and the age and quality of the vintage will have been formed, but no more than this.

Smell/Nose (bouquet)

The next stage of the assessment is probably the most important, that of nosing or smelling the wine. This is best achieved by swirling the wine round the glass which will release the esters and alderhydes making it easier to detect the bouquet of the wine. All wines should smell clean or like wine, if they do not then there is a fault. The most common fault is a corky wine which is caused by the cork being contaminated by Trichloroanisole (TCA). The wine will smell mouldy or of damp cardboard and, once smelled, will never be forgotten! Another similar contaminate giving a mouldy taint to the wine is Tetrachloroanisole (TeCA) which is caused by a contaminated atmosphere in the cellar rather than a faulty cork. (For more information on contaminations read Ribéreau *et al.* (2000), *Handbook of Enology vol. 2*, Wiley, Chichester.) Other faults are mainly due to poor hygiene, infected wood in a cask or vat, oxidation, maderization, or poor wine making.

The correct smells identified in wine may be similar to fruits, vegetables, nuts, herbs, spices, flora, earth, minerals, tar, oak, cedar, leather, honey, caramel, chocolate, coffee, chemicals, meat/game, or simply grapes. The strength of the smells may suggest whether the wine is of a New World or Old World style. New World style wines tend to have a 'forward fruit' or fruit-driven nose, with the bouquet 'climbing' out of the glass, whereas Old World style wines tend to have a more subtle, complex and less aggressive nose. These aromas will assist in identifying the grape(s), origin, climate, vinification method and quality of the vintage. There are also other important smells such as those indicating oxidation, maderization and the use of wood in the fermentation and/or maturation processes. At this point the grape varietal is usually identified.

Taste

Finally the wine is tasted, and the flavours considered in relation to the appearance and the bouquet, confirming or refining the information previously gathered.

Sweetness/dryness is assessed first; dry, off dry, medium, medium sweet, sweet; acidity and tannin assessed low through to high; the strength or power of the fruit; soil or mineral flavours; other flavour characteristics from low through to high. The balance of the wine (e.g. fruit:acid:tannin: alcohol) and the length of the finish. If the flavour remains on the palate for a long time, the wine is said to have a long finish and is of high quality. If the flavour disappears as the wine is drunk then it is said to have a short finish and is of low quality.

Once the fingerprint of the wine has been established and the jigsaw completed, the taster is in a position to form an educated conclusion on the grape(s) used, the climate, geographical origin and country, age/vintage, quality and name.

At the end of a tasting other than a 'blind' tasting, conclusions on the wines value for money, and which foods it would be suitable with, are often arrived at.

QUALITY CATEGORIES: THE LABEL

France

Vin de table and vin de pays (VdP)

Vin de table (table wine) is the lowest category of wine. It is meant for everyday drinking; it is not produced to be laid down as it does not improve with age. Some *vins de table*, after passing a tasting panel, can become the *vin de pays* of the region in which it was produced. *Vin de pays* (VdP) is a local or country wine and of a level superior to *vin de table*. VdP is the lowest official category recognized by the French government. There are five regional VdPs, approximately fifty VdP departments and close to a hundred VdP zones. The five regional VdPs are:

- Vin de Pays du Jardin du France
- Vin de Pays des Comptés Rhodanienes
- Vin de Pays des Comté Tolosan
- Vin de Pays d'Oc
- Vin de Pays Portes de la Méditerranean

VdP should not be confused with *vin de paille*, the best of which is produced in Hermitage and the Jura (see Chapter Four).

Vin délimité de qualité supérieure (VDQS)

This is an official category of French wine, and was introduced in 1949. It is a grading applied to wine in France, which cannot obtain an *appellation contrôlée* (see next section). The area of production, types of vines permitted, production method, alcoholic content and yield are all subject to regulations. VDQS wines account for less than 5 per cent of French wine. It is generally accepted as being just below AC standard. Many wines which were previously VDQS have obtained AC status.

Appellation contrôlée

Appellation (d'origine) contrôlée (AC or AOC) may be applied to quality French wines which achieve certain standards and comply with regulations laid down for each area, region or district. The controls are organized by the Institut National des Appellations d'origine (INAO). AC is a guarantee of origin of the wine, and the various *appellations* ensure other standards such as types of vine or vines permitted, yield, production methods, alcoholic content and character of the wine. There are similar control systems in all EU countries, and many non-EU countries have introduced their own controls based on the AOC of France. These are explained in the relevant chapters. In some regions there are a number of ACs which could be applied to the wine. The Pauillac commune in the Haut-Médoc district of Bordeaux provides an example (see Figure 3.9).

Appellation Pauillac Contrôlée (1 on figure) This AC guarantees that the wine originated from the commune and meets the standards laid down for wine from the commune. The same wine can be declassified and marketed under many other ACs, as follows.

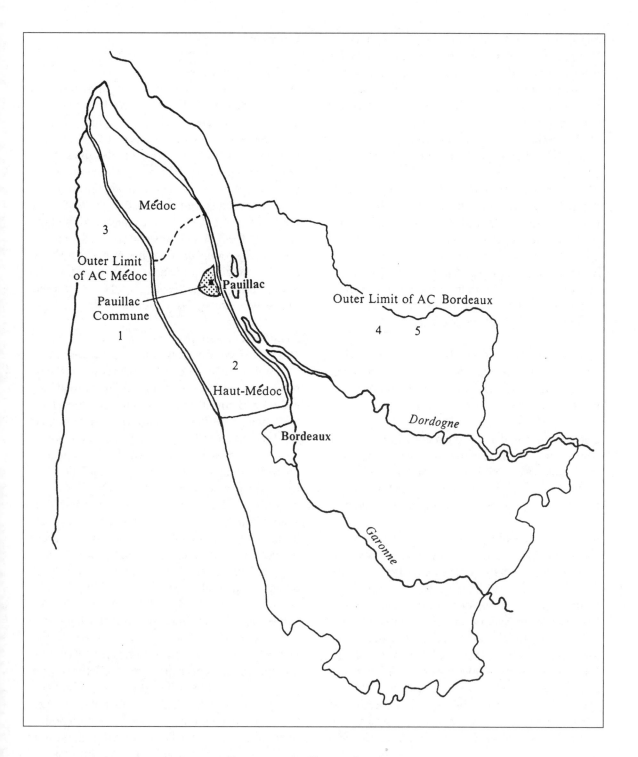

Figure 3.9 *Appellations of Bordeaux*

Appellation Haut-Médoc Contrôlée (2 on figure)
This guarantees that the wine originated from the Haut-Médoc and meets the requirements of this AC, which are slightly less specific than for *Appellation Pauillac Contrôlée*. The wine may be blended with wine from other communes in the Haut-Médoc. If the wine cannot meet these requirements, the following ACs are still available.

Appellation Médoc Contrôlée (3 on figure)   This is the highest AC for wines from the Bas-Médoc which is north of Haut-Médoc. The requirements are also different for this AC.

Appellation Bordeaux Supérieur Contrôlée (4 on figure)   This signifies that the wine comes from Bordeaux and has 1% abv above the legal minimum for that style of Bordeaux wine.

Appellation Bordeaux Contrôlée (5 on figure)   This guarantees that the wine originated in Bordeaux. It is the lowest AC available to a wine produced in Bordeaux.

Note   A wine which has the name of the château, commune or district on the label must originate from that place even though it may carry a lower *appellation* and does not therefore reach some of the other requirements of the higher *appellations*.

In some regions of France the AC may be given to groups of vineyards or even individual vineyards. The smallest vineyards in France to have their own AC are Château Grillet in Condrieu, Northern Côtes-du-Rhône, Romanée-Conti in the Côtes-de-Nuits, and Coulée de Serrant in Savennières.

Some regional ACs are less definitive in their locations. For example, in the Loire valley the AC for Muscadet wine defines the grape variety (Muscadet or Melon) which has to be grown within the specified region. The highest AC for Muscadet wine is Appellation Muscadet Sèvre-et-Maine Contrôlée, which is a district within the Muscadet region.

Germany

Tafelwein (table wine)
This is the lowest category of German wine. When this is made entirely from grapes which have been grown in Germany, it is sold under one of five *Weinbaugebiete* or wine regions (see Chapter Four); these wines are German table wines, *Deutscher Tafelwein*, and may state the vintage. When the wine is blended with wine from other EU countries it is sold as *Tafelwein, EU Tafelwein* or *Tafelwein aus Ländern EWG. Landwein* is a higher-grade *Tafelwein*, which must be sold as either *trocken* (dry) or *halbtrocken* (medium dry). There are fifteen regions for *Landwein*, and these are different from both the *Tafelwein* and *Qualitätswein bestimmster Anbaugebiet* regions.

Qualitätswein bestimmter Anbaugebiet
This is the second-highest quality of the four categories of German wine. The official controls include measuring the amount of sugar in the must at harvest time, chemical analysis of the wine and a taste test. There are thirteen *Anbaugebiete* (regions) specified for QbA (see Chapter Four), and a QbA wine must state on the label from which of these regions the wine originates. There are other regulations to which these wines must conform to be allowed to put the QbA classification on the label. These wines are permitted to be chaptalized. The name of the *Bereich* (district), *Grosslage* (collective) or *Einzellage* (vineyard) may be shown, plus the vintage (see Chapter Four). Each QbA wine must be approved by a governmental laboratory and tasting panel within its district of origin. The *Amtliche Prüfungsnummer* (control number) which each label then carries is in five sets; for example: 2 607 030 07 96. The first set identifies the examining panel (in this example the [2] represents Bernkastel), the second block [607] identifies where the wine was bottled, the third [030] is the official number of the bottler, the fourth [07] identifies this as the seventh bottling of the year, and the final number [96] is the year the wine was tested. This number is often, but not always, one year after the wine was made.

Qualitätswein mit Prädikat
These wines are of superior quality. There are six *Prädikat* (distinctions or degrees of ripeness) which indicate details of the harvesting of the grapes and the sugar content of the grapes. No QmP wine is permitted to be chaptalized: all sweetness in the wine comes naturally from the grape. The harvesting of these grapes must be authorized by the local wine authorities, and minimum must weights (sugar content of the juice) are laid down for each district. These wines may only originate from a single *Bereich*. The label for these wines may show the same details as a QbA wine in addition to the *Prädikat,* and must show the *Anbaugebiet.* The six *Prädikat* are as follows:

Kabinett   Wines with this attribute are the least sweet of this category. Before 1971 this name was used by the vineyard owners to indicate wines specially selected for their own use, but was spelt *Cabinett.*

Spätlese   This wine is made from late-gathered grapes which have been left on the vine to ripen. These wines are a little sweeter and more expensive.

Auslese   This wine is made from selected bunches of grapes which have been left on the vine and allowed to become over-ripe. Some will have been attacked by *botrytis cinerea* to give *Edelfäule* (noble rot). These wines are sweeter and often produce a faint honeyed nose (bouquet). They should be used as dessert wines. The grapes for both Spätlesen and Auslesen wines can be picked only after a minimum of one week has passed following the main harvest.

Beerenauslese   This *Prädikat* means that specially selected berries (grapes) chosen from the ripest bunches, which have been affected by *Edelfäule,* have been used to make the wine. It is only made in outstanding years, and the quantity produced is very small and extremely expensive. It is very sweet, usually with a strong honeyed nose, and is a dessert wine.

Trockenbeerenauslese   This literally means dried-up selected berries (grapes). Wine with this *Prädikat* is made only in exceptional years when *Edelfäule* has affected the grapes and they have been left to shrivel up on the vine. There is very little quantity, and it is an exorbitant price. It is strictly reserved for use as a dessert wine.

Eiswein   Made from over-ripe grapes unaffected by *edelfäule* which have been left on the vine until caught by the frost, then picked at 18°F (−8°C) or colder and pressed to separate the frozen water from the very sweet juice. This *Prädikat* may only be used for wine produced from grapes which reach the must weight (sugar content) levels required for *Beerenauslese* or higher.

VDP Accord 2002
From the 2002 vintage a three-rank system or quality nomenclature was introduced in Germany. At the highest level are *Grosses Gewächs* (great growths) and *Erstes Gewächs* (1st growth Rheingau only) categories, at the next level *Klassifizierte Lagenweine* (from a classified site) and at the third level *Gutsweine* (estate house wines/proprietary name) and *Ortswein* (from a village or region). (See p. 72 and Appendix 9.)

Italy
The Italian wine law of July 1963 introduced three categories of Italian wine: *Vino da Tavola* (VDT), *Denominazione di Origine Controllata* (DOC) and *Denominazione di Origine Controllate e Garantita* (DOCG). The 1963 law was updated in 1992 creating new sub-zones of the present DOC zones, and introducing a new category, *Indicazioni Geografiche Tipiche* (IGT). It also allowed for wines to be declassified to a lower category if they did not meet the required standards, similar to the cascade system operated in France. For example, a DOCG wine of a sub-zone could be downgraded to the zonal DOCG and then down to a sub-zonal DOC category and so on down to *Vino da Tavola*.

Vino da Tavola (VDT)
This is simply table wine and is the lowest category of Italian wine.

SALES AND SERVICE FOR THE WINE PROFESSIONAL

Indicazioni Geografiche Tipiche (IGT)
This is intended to be equivalent to *Vin de pays* of France and the Landwein of Germany.

Denominazione di Origine Controllata
DOC wines have controlled origin, grape varieties, methods of production, yields and characteristics of the district of origin. The first wines were granted DOC status in May 1966. These regulations – which have to be complied with – are intended to be similar to the AC regulations of France, but in some respects they are not quite so stringent. Since 1992 DOC wines must pass a laboratory and tasting examination.

Denominazione di Origine Controllata e Garantita
This category incorporates all the DOC controls and, in addition, guarantees the quality. Generally these wines have a lower yield per hectare and are of a high quality. All DOCG wines must be passed by a laboratory and tasting examination.

Spain

On entry to the EU Spanish wine law has been brought into line with the other European member countries. The Instituto Nacional de Denominaciones de Origen (INDO) administer the law. In each DO there is a Regulating Council (Consejo Regulador), an administrative growers' committee which enforces the law. There are five categories.

Vino de Mesa (VdM)
This is the lowest-category table wine and may not be sold under a region or vintage.

Vino Comarçal (VC)
A slightly higher-quality table wine which may be sold under a region and vintage.

Vino de la Tierra (VdlT)
This is the next level upwards and is a similar classification to the VdP of France and IGT of Italy. These wines are from a local region with a specific local character but do not yet satisfy the DO status.

Denominación de Origen (DO)
DOs are quality wines subject to regulations similar to the French AOC laws.

Denominación de Origen Calificada (DOC or DOCa)
DOCa is the highest classification for Spanish wine. At the time of going to print, only Rioja has obtained this. It was awarded on 9 April 1991.

European Union

Vin de qualité produit en régions déterminées (VQPRD)
This is an EU wine category, meaning quality wine produced in specific regions. The AC wines and VDQS wines of France qualify for VQPRD, but few put it on the label. The DOCG and DOC wines of Italy may also use this classification. The QbA and QmP wines of Germany may use QWPSR, and the DO and DOCs of Spain may use VQPRD on their labels, indicating the same thing.

Other information on the wine label

Vintage and non-vintage
'Vintage' with a date refers to the year in which the grapes were harvested. On its own it can also mean the gathering of the grapes. In France *millésime* and *récolte* are both terms on the label meaning the year of the vintage; in Spain *vendimia*, *cosecha*, or sometimes *año* plus the year, is used; and in Italy *vendemmia*, or sometimes *annata* plus the year.

There is a vintage every year, but the wine is not always sold under that year, particularly if it was a bad one. In this case the wine is usually blended with other years and sold as non-vintage wine (NV).

Bottling

French bottling terms include the following:

Mise en bouteille au château   This means simply that the wine was bottled at the château named on the bottle. This is commonly used for Bordeaux wines and wines from other areas, which have châteaux, like the Loire valley. The first château bottling was at Château Lafite in 1793.

Mise en bouteille au domaine   Mise du domaine These terms are used when the wine has been bottled on the estate or domaine. They are used very often for quality Burgundy and Rhône wines and for wines of other areas that do not have large integral estates such as are found in Bordeaux. The estate may be made up of a number of vineyards in different communes but all under the same ownership.

Mise en bouteille dans nos caves   This means bottled in the cellars. The cellars are usually those of the *négociant,* who will be named.

Mise en bouteille par Xyz   Simply means bottled by the company or person Xyz.

Terms of other countries meaning 'estate bottled' include:

Erzeugerabfüllung, Gutsabfüllung (Germany)
Messo in bottiglia nel'origine or *imbottigliato del produttore all'origine* (Italy)
Embottelado or *engarrafado de origen* (Spain)
Engarrafado no origem (Portugal)

Sweetness and dryness

	Dry	Medium	Sweet
France	*sec*	*demi-sec/ demi-doux*	*doux*
Germany	*trocken*	*halbtrocken*	
Italy	*secco*	*amabile/ abboccato*	*dolce*
Spain	*seco*	—	*dulce*
Portugal	*séco*	—	*adamado/doce*

Colour

	Light red	Red	Dark red
France		*rouge*	
Germany		*Rotwein*	
Italy	*chiaretto*	*rosso*	*nero*
Spain		*tinto*	
Portugal	*clarete*	*tinto*	

	White	Rosé or Pink
France	*blanc*	*rosé*
Germany	*Weiswein*	*Schillerwein, Weissherbst, Rotling*
Italy	*bianco*	*rosato*
Spain	*blanco*	*rosado*
Portugal	*branco*	*rosado*

Sparkling wine and fortified wine
The appropriate terms are covered in Chapter Five.

Ordinary wine
Ordinary wine is rarely bottled. In France it is called *vin ordinaire,* in Italy *vino ordinario,* and in Spain *vino corriente.*

CHAPTER FOUR

Wines of the World

The wine-producing countries of the world are shown in Figure 4.1. They are grouped at latitudes 30°–50°C north and south.

FRANCE

France remains the foremost country in the world in its diversity and experience of wines. The harvest is also large; for example, in 1994 (which was a small vintage) it produced 53.6 million hecto-litres, with only Italy producing more; but over 40 per cent of the French wines were of *appellation contrôlée* standard.

France's wine-producing regions are as follows (see Figure 4.2).

Main regions
Alsace
Bordeaux
Burgundy
Champagne
Loire
Rhône

Lesser regions
Bergerac
Pécharmant
Monbazillac
Cahors
Côtes de Duras
Gaillac
Jura
Jurançon
Limoux
Madiran

Languedoc/Roussillon
Provence
Savoie

Alsace

The region of Alsace stretches from Strasbourg in the north to Mulhouse in the south (Figure 4.3). It runs along the eastern slopes of the foothills of the Vosges mountains close to the German border. It is subdivided into the Bas-Rhin and the Haut-Rhin, although this has little significance for the sommelier or the customer, as the wines are not sold under these names. Riquewihr and Ribeauvillé are the best-known vineyard towns, and Colmar is the business centre for Alsace wines.

Although wines have been made in Alsace since the fourth century, the wines as we know them today only go back as far as 1945. Alsace has been occupied by Germany for some of its history and it was not until the end of the Second World War that the vineyards were replanted with the noble grape varieties which are used now. Germany had previously allowed only lesser grape varieties to be grown in Alsace, in order to protect its own fine wine industry.

The wines are made by very natural methods and are not so highly fined or filtered as, for example, German wine. The majority of Alsace wine is still white wine, but there is a little *vin rosé, vin gris* and *vin rouge*, all made from the Pinot Noir grape. There is also some *méthode traditionnelle* sparkling wine.

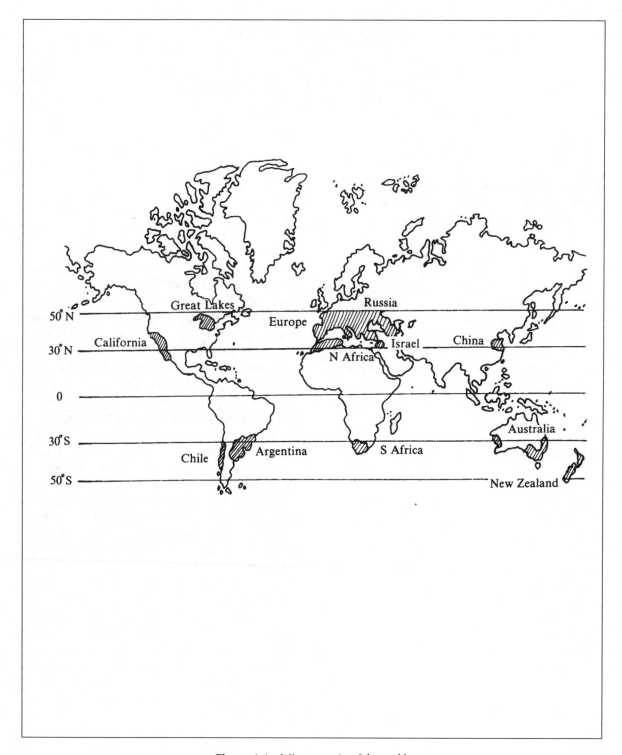

Figure 4.1 *Wine countries of the world*

Figure 4.2 *France*

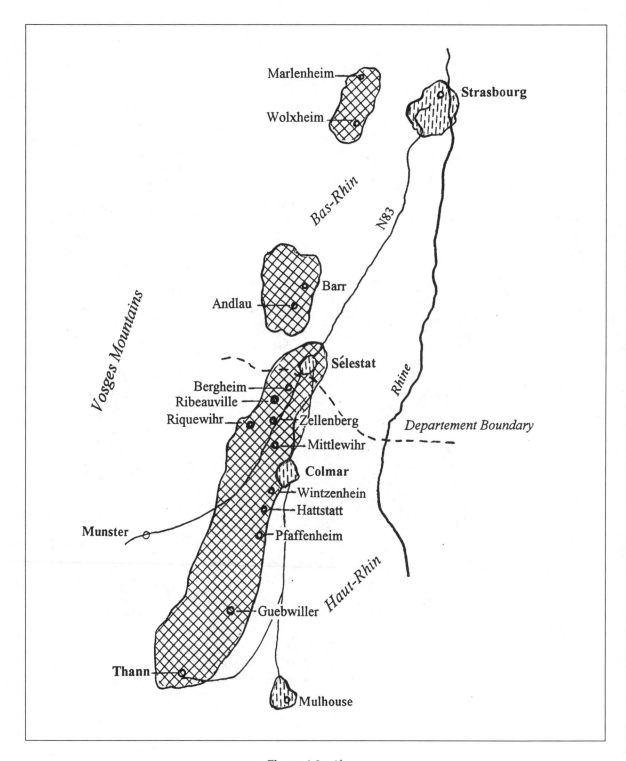

Figure 4.3 *Alsace*

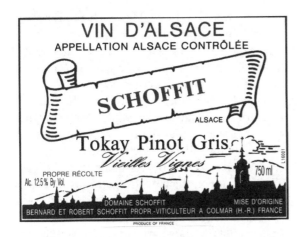

Alsace grapes, Muscat, Riesling, Gewürztraminer and Pinot Gris.

AC Alsace Crémant　This is the *appellation* for the sparkling wine which is fermented in the bottle as for Champagne. All the grape varieties of Alsace are permitted except for Gewürztraminer and Chasselas. Pinot Blanc is a good and common base for Crémant d'Alsace; Riesling will give the strongest flavour. It is sold in Champagne-style bottles.

Grapes and wine characteristics
The wines of Alsace are traditionally sold under the name of the grape rather than the name of a vineyard, although some do state the origin on the label as well. Wines which are sold under the Grand Cru *appellation* are permitted to show the name of the vineyard on the label. If the wine is sold by the grape name, the wine must by law be made from 100 per cent of that grape, with the exception of Pinot Blanc which may contain some of, or be totally made from, Auxerrois.

Riesling　Perhaps the best Alsace wine, very dry with a steely character, a good strong fruity nose, and fuller-bodied than German Rieslings. It is an excellent complement to hors-d'oeuvres, oysters

Classification
AC Vin d'Alsace and *AC Alsace* are the same. This AC has a minimum alcoholic content of 8.5% abv and must be made from one of the permitted grape varieties or a blend of two or more.

There are also ACs for each of the permitted grape varieties. These are Riesling, Gewürztraminer, Pinot Gris, Muscat, Sylvaner, Pinot Blanc (Klevner or Clevner), Pinot Noir, Chasselas (Gutedel). Aux-errois is permitted but it is interchangeable with Pinot Blanc and is usually labelled as such.

AC Edelzwicker is a blend of two or more of these.

AC Alsace Grand Cru　This classification was introduced in 1983 and there are currently about 54 vineyards entitled to this classification. These wines must have a minimum of 11% abv and be made from one of the four permitted varieties of and fish dishes. The best Rieslings are grown on granite.

Gewürztraminer   These wines are lower in acid and high in alcohol. They have a full, powerful fruit-bowl and flowers-of-the-field bouquet. They are dry and spicy with a strong mixed ripe-fruit and touch-of-grapefruit flavour – the most distinctive bouquet and flavour of all the Alsace wines. They are excellent with pâté de foie gras, strong terrines, and will stand up to dishes such as quails' eggs with spinach, and smoked mackerel. They will enhance fatty meats such as roast duck, goose and pork when a white wine is requested, are an excellent accompaniment to hot spicy dishes, and are superb on their own.

Pinot Gris   Prior to 1993 this wine was also called Tokay d'Alsace. There are now two AOCs, Alsace or Vin d'Alsace Pinot Gris and Alsace or Vin d'Alsace Tokay Pinot Gris. It has a citrus/spicy bouquet, is medium to full bodied, slightly 'sharp' yet smooth and dry. Good-quality Pinot Gris wines have the potential to age well.

Muscat d'Alsace is not widely planted in Alsace and relies on good years to produce a good wine. Its bouquet is grapey and it is less spicy than Gewürztraminer and Pinot Gris. The wine is dry with a musky flavour and is an excellent aperitif wine.

Pinot Blanc or Klevner   Dry, well-balanced wine, suitable whenever white wine is requested. As stated previously it is often blended with Auxerroise and is used as the base of many *crémant* wines. Although thinner than many other Alsace wines, it is much under-valued.

Sylvaner   As is usual for this grape variety the wine is dry, light and fruity, but softer than the others named. It is best when young and is used widely as local wine.

Pinot Noir   High in fruit, low in tannin, much lighter in body than Pinot Noir wines from Burgundy. This wine is made by leaving the maceration of the must on the skins for three to four days, and the stalks are usually left in to give some tannin to the wine. At its best it has a red cherry/raspberry bouquet with taste to match.

Chasselas   Wine produced from the Chasselas grape in Alsace is rarely sold as such and is not exported because it is not as high quality as the other exported Alsace wines. It is normally used locally for house or carafe wines. No new plantings of this varietal are permitted.

Klevener de Heiligenstein   Klevener is the Alsace name for the savagnin rosé grape, which is slightly less pungent and spicy than Gewürztraminer and is grown in the village of Heiligenstein.

Late Harvest Wines   The German practice of leaving the grapes on the vine in a good year with a warm autumn to allow the grapes to become over-ripe may be followed.

Vendange Tardive (late harvested) may be added to the label. This wine is generally sweeter but does not have to be. It is of a very high quality, high alcohol and has an excellent honeyed bouquet. These wines are good value for money. Only the Riesling, Gewürztraminer, Pinot Gris and Muscat varietals may be used for these wines.

Sélection de Grains Nobles   This is one stage further and can be likened to the Beerenauslese process in Germany and only the same grape varietals are permitted. The grapes are left on the vine to become over-ripe with some of them being attacked by *botrytis cinerea* to give *pourriture noble* or noble rot. The wines in this category will be sweet wines of high quality and are subject to strict regulations. The decree to permit VT and SGN wines was passed in 1984.

Alsace wines are shipped in slender flutes (tall green bottles, as for Mosel wines); they are usually suitable for drinking between one and four years old; they are dry and exceedingly fragrant. All of them have at least a slight spiciness about their bouquet and flavour.

Bordeaux

The best-quality wines of this region (see Figure 4.4) are produced from blends of grapes. The main black grape varieties are Cabernet Sauvignon, Cabernet Franc, Merlot, Malbec and Petit Verdot. The first three are the major varieties and the blend is often referred to as the Bordeaux blend. The

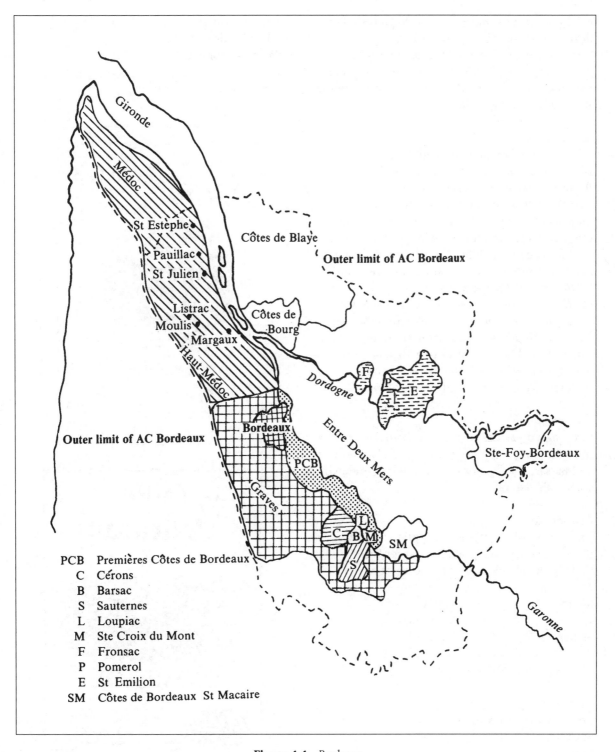

Figure 4.4 *Bordeaux*

Merlot is the most widely grown red grape in Bordeaux. The main white grape varieties are Sauvignon, Sémillon and Muscadelle. The red wines of Bordeaux are known in English-speaking countries as claret, the white wines simply as white Bordeaux or Bordeaux *blanc*.

Red Bordeaux
After the initial fermentation on the skins the wine is run off into vats which are now stainless steel in the top châteaux, then into casks called *barriques* (225l) which are usually made from *limousin* oak. Only a percentage of the casks are new. Throughout the next few months the wine continues a very slow fermentation in the *chai* or barrel hall where it is racked off into fresh casks every three months. During this period the wine is blended, a process which is called *assemblage*. After one year it is moved to the second year *chai* or part of the *chai* where it completes its oak maturation. A *chai* is a single-storey building for storing *barriques*. The wine is usually bottled after two years and matured in bottle until ready for drinking.

White Bordeaux
Sweet and dry wines are made in Bordeaux; the most famous are the sweet wines from Sauternes and Barsac. The top dry and sweet wines undergo some oak maturation.

Classification
An example of the AC system applied to a Bordeaux wine has been given in Chapter Three. The top-quality districts of Bordeaux are:

Médoc	Barsac
Graves	St-Emilion
Sauternes	Pomerol

The lesser-quality districts are:

Cérons
Premières Côtes de Bordeaux
St Croix du Mont
Loupiac

Entre-Deux-Mers
Ste-Foy-Bordeaux
Lalande de Pomerol
Fronsac
Côtes de Bourg
Côtes de Blaye

Médoc

This district is subdivided into two: Haut-Médoc and Médoc. These two *appellations* may only be used for red wines. The Haut-Médoc produces all the top wines of this district and for these top wines the Cabernet Sauvignon grape predominates. It comprises sixteen communes, the top six of which are Pauillac, Margaux, St-Estèphe, St-Julien, Moulis and Listrac. Each of these six communes has its own *appellation*.

The wines are made from a blend of two or more of the following: Cabernet Sauvignon, Cabernet Franc, Merlot, Malbec, Petit Verdot and Carmenère. The Cabernet Sauvignon is considered to be the top grape in the Médoc, with the

Merlot a close second. A blend of Cabernet Sauvignon, Cabernet Franc and Merlot is often referred to as the Bordeaux blend. The tendency with Médoc wines is to concentrate on the 61 wines classified in 1855 (Appendix 1) and to forget the rest. These wines were graded into the five growths (*crus classés*) on the basis of the prices they had achieved during the previous few years. There are, however, many excellent wines unofficially classified as *cru bourgeois*, which are sometimes as good as some of the *crus classés* wines. It is expected that a legal *cru bourgeois* classification will be introduced in 2003. In 1973 Château Mouton-Rothschild was deservedly upgraded from *second cru* to *premier cru*. The classifications of Bordeaux wines are given in Appendix 1.

The red wines of the Médoc vary in quality but they are all made from the grapes listed above. Most of them have a predominance of Cabernet in them, but the actual percentage varies from château to château. The main cause for the differences in the wines is the soil, the best coming from well-drained soil with plenty of stones in it, close to the Gironde. The wine is usually left in oak casks until it is one and a half to two years old, fined, then bottled. The top châteaux make wines in good years which will continue to improve in the bottle for twenty years upwards. They have a high tannin level, strong flavour and good acid content, which will mellow over the maturation period. The bouquet of these wines is often said to resemble blackcurrants, cedar wood, pencil shavings and often a wet leaf or wet soil character. Throughout the Médoc many wines are produced, and a large number of these are made to be ready for drinking within five years.

Graves AC

Best known in the UK for its dry white wines made from the Sauvignon and Sémillon grapes, it also produces some very fine red wines from a blend of Cabernet Sauvignon, Cabernet Franc and Merlot. These red wines are produced in the northern half of the Graves district. The finest red Graves is Château Haut-Brion, which was classified in 1855 in the first growth of the Médoc. Red Graves are slightly drier than the Médoc wines. The Graves wines were classified in 1959. Fifteen châteaux were classified, six for red and white wines, seven for red wine only and two for white wine only (see Appendix 2). In 1987 a new AC of Pessac/Léognan was created. It includes all the 1959 classified growths and covers 25 per cent of the Graves area, taking in ten communes.

Sauternes/Barsac ACs

The Sauternes district produces some of the very best of the world's sweet white wines. The best Sauternes are made from grapes which have been attacked by *botrytis cinerea* (giving *pourriture noble*). Sauvignon, Sémillon and Muscadelle are the varieties used. Eighty per cent of the vines are Sémillon and it is these which are left on the vines to be attacked by noble rot. This is a minute fungoid growth which causes the grapes to shrivel up, reducing the water content, thus increasing the percentage of sugar, and imparting a honeyed bouquet to the finished wine.

There are five communes in the district: Sauternes, Fargues, Bommes, Preignac and Barsac. Wines produced in the commune of Barsac can be sold under the AC of either Sauternes or Barsac. The wines of Barsac, like those of Sauternes, are luscious and sweet with a tremendous concentration of flavour and colour. The alcohol must be 13% abv for these ACs. The best of these wines are matured in cask for up to three years. They are then matured in bottle for as long as 30 to 40 years. They must be kept away from light and in cool surroundings, otherwise the wine will become oxidized or *maderisé* (maderized) – i.e. slightly bitter, like Madeira.

The 1855 classification graded the top châteaux into three growths. Château d'Yquem was graded alone as the *premier grand cru* or first great growth; eleven others were made first growths, and another thirteen second growths (see Appendix 3).

St-Emilion AC

This district produces red wines of superb quality. The wines are blended from Cabernet Sauvignon, Cabernet Franc, Merlot and a small quantity of Malbec. However, the predominant grape is the Merlot followed by the Cabernet Franc. The Merlot grape produces a softer wine, which will mature quicker than the Cabernets, so these wines are usually expected to be ready for drinking a little earlier than their counterparts in the Médoc.

There are eight communes entitled to the AC St-Emilion, and there are a further four which can add St-Emilion to their names, which are called the satellite *appellations*. They are Montagne, Lussac, Puisseguin and St-Georges. An order was passed to classify these wines in 1954. This first classification in 1955 established three categories – *premier grand cru classé, grand cru classé* and *grand cru* – and was completed in 1958. This classification was revised in 1969, 1985 and 1996 (see Appendix 4). Unclassified wines of AC quality are sold as AC St-Emilion.

Pomerol AC
Adjacent to St-Emilion, this district produces similar red wines, with the Merlot and Cabernet Franc grapes being the most important. Merlot is the most widely grown, forming as much as 80 per cent or more of the blend with the two Cabernets. It is slightly softer than St-Emilion and is often ready for drinking after five years, with the best maturing up to twelve to fifteen years. The wines are of a high quality and have a slight truffle smell. Three of the top châteaux are Pétrus, Le Pin and Vielle Château Certan.

Lalande de Pomerol AC
This district is larger than Pomerol and is situated to the north of its better-known neighbour. These red wines are good without reaching the quality of Pomerol.

Cérons AC
Cérons is situated betwen Graves and Sauternes and is a commune of Graves but has its own AC. Its dry red and white wines may be sold under the Graves AC but the sweet wines are sold under the Cérons AC.

Loupiac and Ste-Croix-du-Mont ACs
These two districts are across the Garonne to Sauternes and Barsac, and produce similar but lesser sweet white wines. These must contain some botrytized grapes.

Premières Côtes de Bordeaux AC
This long, narrow district following the northern bank of the Garonne produces styles of wine related to those on the southern bank of the river. Red wines are produced in the north (nowhere near the quality of those produced in the Médoc), medium-dry to dry wines in the centre, and sweet white wines in the south opposite Cérons, Barsac and Sauternes.

Entre-Deux-Mers AC
This is the largest district of Bordeaux and produces a large quantity of ordinary quality red and white wines, the white wines varying from sweet to dry, the majority being dry.

Ste-Foy-Bordeaux AC
This small district is situated on the extremity of the Bordeaux *appellation* boundary in the north-eastern corner of Entre-Deux-Mers bordering Bergerac. It produces sweet and dry white wines and a small amount of red wine.

Fronsac and Canon Fronsac ACs
Fronsac produces fruity red wines in the style of Pomerol and St-Emilion, of a slightly lower quality. The predominant grape is Merlot blended with Cabernet Franc and a little Cabernet Sauvignon.

Bourg and Blaye AC
Bourg and Blaye both produce red and dry white wines of average quality, but Blaye specializes in dry white wine while the district of Bourg is best known for its red wines, made mainly from the Merlot. The wines from these districts have improved tremendously and are of average to good quality.

Burgundy
The Burgundy region is long and narrow, spreading through the four *départements* of Yonne, Côte-d'Or, Saône-et-Loire and Rhône (Figure 4.5). The districts of Burgundy are:

Chablis (Yonne)
Côtes de Nuits (Côte-d'Or)
Hautes Côtes de Nuits (Côte-d'Or)
Côte de Beaune (Côte-d'Or)
Hautes Côtes de Beaune (Côte-d'Or)
Côte Chalonnaise or Région de Mercurey (Saône-et-Loire)
Côte Mâconnaise (Saône-et-Loire)
Beaujolias (Rhône)

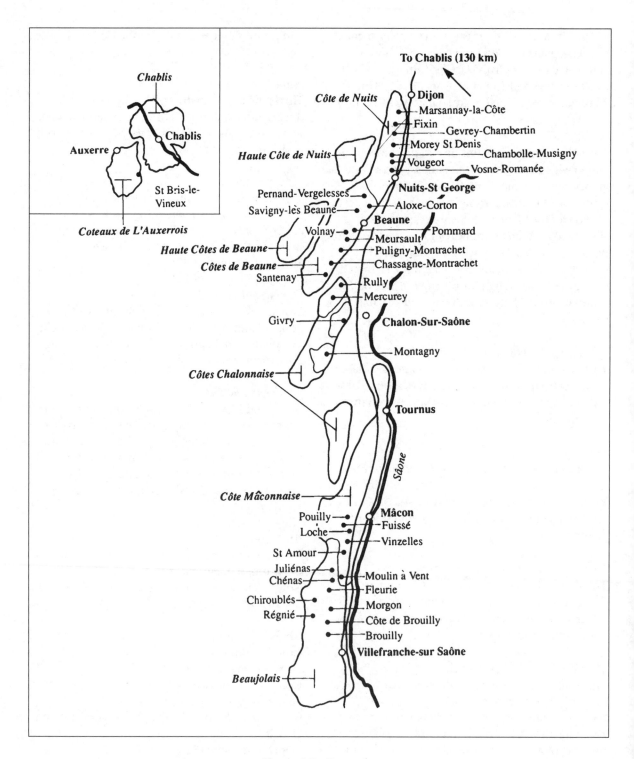

Figure 4.5 *Burgundy*

The method of classifying Burgundies is a complicated one, but it is sufficient to know that some vineyards and plots are classified *grands crus* and others *premiers crus*. The wines made in these places still have to meet the criteria laid down by the INAO. The quality wines of Burgundy are sold under the name of the *climat* (vineyard), commune, or under the name of the district AC, for example Mâcon. Lower-grade wines can take the AC Vin de Bourgogne, or Bourgogne Grand Ordinaire, which are both regional ACs. Other ACs are *AC Bourgogne Passetoutgrains* (red and rosé 9.5% abv), a blend of a minimum of one-third Pinot Noir and the rest Gamay; and AC Bourgogne Aligoté (white, min. 9.5% abv), made from the Aligoté grape with up to 15 per cent Chardonnay permitted.

A further complication in Burgundy is caused by people owning very small parcels of land within vineyards, so that *négociants* are necessary to buy up wines and to blend them to make sufficient quantities to market. The wine is often very dependent on the *négociant*, so the name of the *négociant* on the label is most important.

Chablis

This district is situated 130 km north-west of Dijon round the town of Chablis. The extremely calcareous soil mixed in with clay and known as Kimmeridgian is probably the single most important factor contributing to the quality of the wine. It produces the dry white wine called Chablis, and this is classified a white Burgundy. There is just one grape variety permitted for Chablis – the Chardonnay.

There are four ACs for Chablis:

AC Grand Cru Chablis (min 11% abv)   This comes from only seven vineyards which are situated on a south-facing slope in a small area immediately north and north-east of the town of Chablis: Les Vaudésirs, Les Clos, Les Grenouilles, Les Preuses, Bougros, Valmur and Les Blanchots. The names of these vineyards may be included in the AC.

AC Chablis Premier Cru (min 10.5% abv)   This comes from 40 vineyards but there are only twelve major vineyards. Some of the best of these are Mont de Milieu, Montmains, Vaillons, Montée de Tonnerre, Vaudevey and Fourchaume. The name of the vineyard may also be included on the label.
AC Chablis (min 10% abv)   This is a good wine from a large number of classified vineyards.
AC Petit Chablis (min 9.5% abv)   This is the lowest AC for Chablis, but still a quality wine. All Chablis are dry white wines, and are an excellent accompaniment to oysters, crab, lobster, smoked salmon, and other shellfish and fish dishes.
Sauvignon de St-Bris AC
This comes from a small cluster of villages southeast of Chablis, about 13 km from the town of Chablis. It is made from the Sauvignon grape, and is a dry white wine similar in style to the Sauvignon

wines from the central vineyards of the Loire. *Irancy* is a red wine made in a small area within the Sauvignon de St-Bris district. It is made from the Pinot Noir and César grapes and sold under the Bourgogne-Irancy AC.

Côte de Nuits
This district forms the northern part of the Côte d'Or. It is approximately 19 km long and rarely exceeds 0.5 km wide. It runs along the eastern-facing slopes of a range of hills from Fixin in the north to Corgoloin in the south. The Côte de Nuits produces almost all red wines from Pinot Noir. They are of a very high quality and are much sought after. They are full-bodied and full of fruit, but require some years (depending on the vintage) to become perfectly balanced.

Between Dijon and Fixin there is a village called

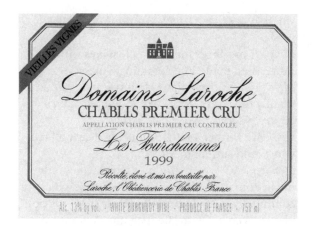

Marsannay where good-quality rosé wine is produced under the AC Marsannay-la-Côte (and AC Bourgogne Rosé de Marsannay) and made from Pinot Noir. AC red and white wines are also produced.

Some of the best ACs in the Côte de Nuits are:

Climats AC	Commune AC
Le Chambertin, Charmes Chambertin	Gevrey-Chambertin
Clos de la Roche, Clos de Tart, Bonnes-Mares (small part) Clos St-Denis Clos des Lambrays	Morey-St-Denis
Le Musigny, (Musigny also produces a little white wine), Bonnes-Mares	Chambolle-Musigny
Clos-de-Vougeot	Vougeot

Richebourg, La Tâche, Romanée-Conti
Grands Echézeaux   Flagey-Echézeaux

The Grands Crus of the Côte d'Or are listed under Appendix 5.

Côte de Beaune
This district runs south-west from just south of Corgoloin to just south of Chagny. It meanders along the slopes of the hills and has nearly double the amount of land growing vines to that of the Côte de Nuits. Red and white wines of excellent quality are produced using the Pinot Noir for red and the Chardonnay for white wines. The red wines are generally slightly lighter in colour and body than the Côte de Nuits wines. They do not usually continue to improve with age for as long

as the Côte de Nuits reds. The white wines are dry, and are outstanding with great depth of fruit and flavour.

Some of the best ACs in the Côte de Beaune are:

Climats AC	Commune AC
Corton (red, some white),	Aloxe-Corton
Charlemagne (white)	
Le Montrachet (white),	Puligny-Montrachet
Chevalier-Montrachet (white),	
Bâtard-Montrachet (white)	

Commune AC
Ladoix (red and white)
Aloxe-Corton (red and white)
Pernand-Vergelesses (red and white)
Savigny (red, some white)
Beaune (red, some white)
Pommard (red)
Volnay (red)
Meursault (white, some red)
Puligny-Montrachet (white, some red)
Chassagne-Montrachet (red and white)
Santenay (red, some white)

There is also the AC Côte de Beaune Villages (only red wines).

Hospices de Beaune

Nicolas Rolin and his wife opened a home for the old and infirm in 1443. Funds were needed so local vineyard owners were canvassed and an auction was set up from which a percentage of the sales would go to the upkeep of the Hospices. The auction takes place on the third Sunday of each November of the current year's wines. There are now 34 cuvées owned by the Hospices. All the wines (together with the Marc de Bourgogne, see Chapter Six) sold at this auction have the words 'Hospices de Beaune' on the label.

Région de Mercurey/Côte Chalonnais

Starting from below Chagny down to north of Tournus, the vineyard area of this district is only small. It has five village/commune *appellations*:

Rully AC produces mainly white wines which are more often made into sparkling wines.
Mercurey AC, immediately below Rully, produces mainly red wines, some of good quality and similar in style to Côte de Beaune reds.
Givry AC, further south, producing nearly all red wines, and similar to Mercurey.
Montagny AC, which produces white wines only, is made from the Chardonnay grape. These wines are continually being improved and are now very popular and can be of excellent quality. Any wine over 11.5 per cent alcohol can be labelled Premier Cru.
Bouzeron AC produces dry wines from the Aligoté grape with up to 15 per cent Chardonnay.

Mâconnais

This area runs from just above Tournus to below the Pouilly-Fuissé vineyards, a distance of 48 km. In the main, average quality red and white wines are produced. Some excellent Chardonnays are produced below the town of Mâcon around Pouilly and Fuissé; the sub-soil at this point is limestone which produces grapes with a high level of acid. The other Mâcon white wines are adequate without being world beaters and are sold under either Mâcon Superior, Mâcon Village (43), or Mâcon plus the name of the village, for example Mâcon Lugny, Viré-Clessé. Viré and Clessé are two villages in Mâcon which received their own joint *appellation* in 1998.

Pouilly-Fuissé AC is the shining star of white Mâcon wines. The name of the best commune Fuissé is appended to the village of Pouilly for the *appellation*, which includes the commune of Solutré. Pouilly-Vinzelles and Pouilly-Loché are two less good *appellations*. St-Véran is a relatively modern AC for wines just outside the Pouilly villages down to Beaujolais and is often a good-quality white wine.

Most of the Mâcon red wines are made from Gamay grapes and are sold either under Mâcon Superior, Mâcon Village or Mâcon plus the name of the village.

Note The Chardonnay grape takes its name from a small village just south of Tournus, and the Chasselas grape from the small village of that name, also in the Mâconnais close to Fuissé.

Beaujolais

Similar in size to the Mâconnais, Beaujolais has far more land under vines and accounts for nearly half the viticultural area of Burgundy AC wines. There is an indeterminate border between the southernmost part of the Mâconnais and the northern extremity of the Beaujolais district. Granite hills start in the extreme north, from which comes the very best Beaujolais, known as the *crus* Beaujolais. Two of the *crus* Beaujolais villages are geographically in the Mâconnais.

The red wines of Beaujolais are made from the Gamay grape, and Beaujolais *Blanc* from the Chardonnay.

The ten *crus* Beaujolais, all red wines are:

St-Amour
Juliénas
Chénas
Moulin-à-Vent
Fleurie
Chiroubles
Morgon
Brouilly
Côte de Brouilly
Régnié

These are all *appellations* that can be used on the label.

AC Beaujolais Villages (reds 10% abv, whites 10.5% abv.) Alternatively, AC Beaujolais plus the name of the village of origin may be used. There are 39 villages allowed to produce wine under this AC, all of which are in the northern half of the district in the granite hills.

AC Beaujolais Supérieur (reds 10.0% abv, white 10.5% abv)

AC Beaujolais (reds 9% abv, white 9.5% abv) These two AC are used for wines from anywhere in the district.

Beaujolais Nouveau (AC Beaujolais) This light red wine is made by the *semi-macération carbonique* method, which may be described as whole berry fermentation in closed vats filled with carbon dioxide gas. This system extracts flavour and colour quickly under pressure produced by the carbon dioxide given off by the closed fermentation with very little tannin. The wine is virtually a rosé wine with a purple tinge to it. It is light and fruity, and is at its best when served cool. It is released for sale on the third Thursday in November. The *macération carbonique* process is used in the production of a large amount of ordinary Beaujolais.

The very small quantity of Beaujolais Blanc often sold under the St-Véran AC is made from Chardonnay grapes.

La Confrérie des Chevaliers du Tastevin

This is the Burgundy wine brotherhood which has its headquarters in the Château de Clos de Vougeot. It was set up in 1933 and concerns itself with maintaining the high standards of Burgundian wines and their promotion. Some wines have a seal on the bottle to show that they have been passed by the *Confrérie* tasting panel.

Burgundy wines with food

The dry white wines of Burgundy are noted for being greatly suited as an apéritif or as an accompaniment to shellfish and other fish dishes, as well as to lightly flavoured entrées such as chicken vol-au-vent and escalope of veal. Some of the buttery oak styles will enhance much stronger dishes. The red wines are admirable with most medium-strength meat dishes and are suited for continuation with the cheeseboard.

The Côte d'Or Burgundies generally need some bottle age to make them ready for drinking, but the length of time will vary from vintage to vintage and wine to wine. For example, many 1992 reds were ready for drinking in 1996, whereas the 1990 wines required further ageing as they were still improving.

Beaujolais *crus* are often at their best after five years and sometimes longer, but the lesser Beaujolais are best drunk young, after one to three years.

The great white wines vary. Chablis ACs are often ready after two or three years, whereas the more concentrated and more powerful Grand and Premier Cru Chablis will require another three years or so. Top Côte de Beaune whites generally require five years or more to reach their peak, while top vintages such as 1998 and 1999 might take eight to ten years. It is a matter of taste with white Burgundies; the wines definitely change their character as they age, becoming almost buttery and nutty.

Champagne

The Champagne region and its wines, and the methods used for producing sparkling wines in general, are covered in Chapter Five.

Loire

The Loire is probably the most diverse wine region in the world, but it is certainly not given the respect that some of its wines deserve. The River Loire is 960 km long, rising in the Massif Central in the south of France and running north close to the west side of the Rhône wine region and the Beaujolais district of Burgundy. It flows a further 140 km to where its own celebrated Central Vineyards begin at Pouilly and Sancerre, and then on through Orléanais, Touraine and Anjou to the sea beyond Nantes (Figure 4.6). The region owes its existence to the river, which keeps the air temperature a few degrees higher. The warmest part of the Loire is in the Touraine where some very good red wines are produced. The soil varies considerably along its length and there are more than a dozen grape varieties being grown there. The region is susceptible to late frosts in the spring, and heavy hailstorms in the summer.

During the last few years modern wine-making techniques have become more widespread, caus-

ing the general standard to rise dramatically. The outstanding vintages of 1995 and 1996 have also improved the image. To obtain more flavour in the white wines, *macération pelliculaire* or cold soak (see p. 31) is practised by a number of producers. The sources of the Loire and the Allier, which is one of its tributaries, are in the foothills of the Massif Central, level with and 16 km west of Beaujolais. The Côte du Forez VDQS is the first wine district producing red and rôse still and sparkling wines for the Gamay grape. The only AOC is the red wine of the Côte Roannaise (since 1996) from the Gamay, and a little Pinot Noir.

The main districts of the Loire, with their sub-districts, are as follows:

Central Vineyards Pouilly-sur-Loire, Sancerre, Menetou-Salon, Reuilly and Quincy.
Touraine Cheverny, Vouvray, Montlouis, Bourgueil, Chinon and Coteaux du Loir.
Anjou Anjou, Saumur, Savennières and Coteaux-du-Layon.
Nantais Muscadet, Muscadet de Sèvre-et-Maine, Muscadet Côtes de Grand-Lieu, Muscadet des Coteaux de la Loire and Coteaux d'Ancenis.

These districts between them produce nearly every style of wine: dry crisp white wines from Muscadet, Sancerre and Pouilly; rosé wines from Anjou; sparkling and still dry wines from Anjou, Touraine, Vouvray and Saumur; sweet wines from Vouvray and Coteaux-du-Layon; full-bodied red wines from Saumur, Chinon and Bourgueil.

Central Vineyards
Pouilly-sur-Loire The best wines are made entirely from the Sauvignon grape and can be sold either as Pouilly-Fumé, Pouilly Blanc Fumé or Blanc Fumé de Pouilly. The other AC wine is made from the Chasselas grape and is called Pouilly-sur-Loire. Do not confuse these wines with Pouilly-Fuissé, which is produced in the Mâconnais from the Chardonnay grape.
Sancerre is known for its excellent dry white wines, again made entirely from the Sauvignon grape.

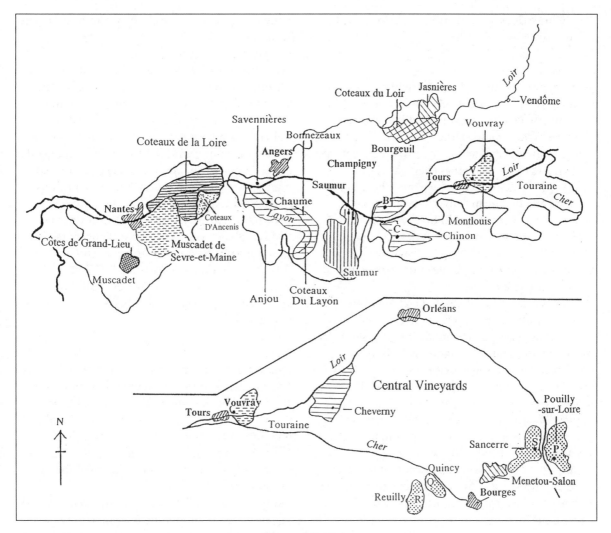

Figure 4.6 *Loire*

However, 25 per cent of the Sancerre production is red and rosé wines, which are made from the Pinot Noir grape.

The white wines from the two sub-districts of Pouilly and Sancerre are best drunk young (up to five years old), but are often at their best after two years. They are steely, citrousy and usually have a bouquet resembling the green wood or leaves of the blackcurrant bush or of fresh cut grass; this is not to be confused with the blackcurrant bouquet and taste of wine made from the Cabernet Sauvignon grape. The Sancerre rosé wines are best up to

one year old and the reds between two and four. *Menetou-Salon* is a small area adjoining Sancerre producing reds, whites and rosés.

Quincy is situated west of Bourges on the west banks of the River Cher. The only AC wine is made from the Sauvignon grape. The red and rosé wines are classified Vin de Pays.

Reuilly is south-west of and close to Quincy. It produces Sauvignon Blanc white wines. Red and rosés from Pinot Noir and Pinot Gris are made at AC level, although the quality is very variable. Quincy and Reuilly are lesser districts of the Loire and their white wines are similar but inferior to those of Pouilly.

Touraine

This province produces light red, white and rosé wines under the regional AC of Touraine. Within Touraine there are some smaller districts which produce higher-quality wines.

Cheverny and *Cour-Cheverny* are two villages at the eastern end of the Touraine. They were both upgraded to ACs in 1993. The white Cheverny must be blended from Sauvignon Blanc, a maximum of 15 per cent Chardonnay, and Chenin Blanc; the reds are a blend of Cabernet Franc, Pinot Noir, Gamay and the Cot (Malbec). Cour-Cheverny is white wine made entirely from the Romorantin grape.

Vouvray is a delimited district of eight communes. The wines are made entirely from the Chenin Blanc grape, which can be made into dry, semi-dry or sweet wine, and still, slightly sparkling (*pétillant*) or sparkling wine (*mousseux*) made by the *méthode traditionnelle* (see Chapter 5). The wines are very fruity and are generally made to be at their best within five years, but some of the best sweet wines continue to improve for many years. It is well known for the Tufa sub-soil.

Montlouis   This AC is situated south of the river facing Vouvray. Dry, semi-dry, sweet and sparkling *méthode traditionnelle* wines are made from Chenin Blanc.

Loir Valley

Twenty-five miles north of Tours on the Loir, a tributary of the Loire, there are two ACs.

Jasnières AC wines are dry whites made from the Chenin Blanc. The vines are on a steep south-facing slope, but the grapes have difficulty in ripening. Picking often does not begin until November.

Coteaux du Loir AC produces red wines from Cabernet Franc, Gamay, Cot (Malbec) and Pinot d'Aunis; white is from Chenin Blanc and rosé from the Grolleau.

Three of the best-known and best-quality AC Loire red wines come from the western end of the Touraine.

Bourgueil and Chinon

Bourgueil and *St-Nicolas-de-Bourgueil ACs* are to the north of the river and *Chinon* to the south. These two sub-districts produce red wines from the Cabernet Franc grape with up to 10 per cent Cabernet Sauvignon. St-Nicolas-de-Bourgueil is best drunk young and slightly chilled, Bourgueil is equally good drunk the same way but will also mature over a longer period, and both produce AC rosé wines. Chinon produces mainly red wine with some rosé and a small amount of dry Chinon Blanc from the Chenin Blanc grape. The reds can again be drunk young and chilled, but their full potential may require six or seven years' maturity. The best of these wines are full of fruit and have a slight taste of raspberries, while others have an earthy palate.

Anjou

This is another large district producing red, white and rosé wines under the regional AC of Anjou. The best of the dry and sweet whites are made from the Chenin Blanc grape, and the best of the reds and rosés from Cabernet Sauvignon and Cabernet Franc, although there is quite a quantity of Gamay grapes grown and sold under the AC Anjou-Gamay.

Anjou is probably best known for its rosé wines. The best are sold under the Rosé de Loire AC which is dry. It is made from the Cabernet Sauvignon, Cabernet Franc, Grolleau, Gamay, Pineau d'Aunis and Pinot Noir, but this accounts for only about 13 per cent of the total AC rosé produced in Anjou. The rest are the sweeter versions, produced mainly from the Grolleau, which have given Anjou rosé a bad name. Cabernet-d'Anjou-Rosé is made only from Cabernet grapes, while the majority are sold as AC Rosé-d'Anjou or Anjou Rosé and made from the same grapes as Rosé de Loire, with the Cot replacing Pinot Noir. The best of the red wines are sold under the AC Anjou Village, a recent *appellation*, the others under Anjou and Anjou Gamay.

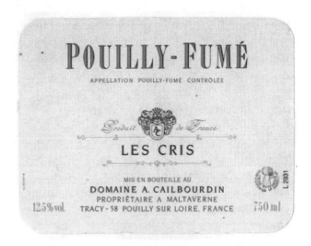

There are three sub-districts in Anjou, which produce very individual wines.

Saumur   This sub-district has an abundance of limestone caves and produces still and sparkling dry white wines of very good quality from the Chenin Blanc plus a maximum of 20 per cent Chardonnay and Sauvignon Blanc. The sparkling wines are often made by the Champagne method. There are two ACs for the *méthode traditionnelle* sparkling wines. Saumur d'Origine is the main one but surprisingly the more restricted and higher-quality sparkling wines are Crémant de Loire AC. Saumur is known for its Tufa sub-soil, which predominates round the town of Saumur. The rosés are made from the same grapes as for Anjou and the best would again be sold as Rosé de Loire. Saumur Rouge is the basic AC but under the AC Saumur-Champigny from Cabernet Sauvignon, Cabernet Franc and the Pineau d'Aunis grapes, a wine of quality is produced. It is drunk young and chilled although some are made to last and will mature well up to six to ten years, the best coming from Champigny just south of the town of Saumur.

Coteaux du Layon   This area produces red, white and rosé wines, much of the rosé wines being sold as Anjou Rosé or Rosé de Cabernet. The white wines of *Coteaux du Layon* may be sold as either demi-sec, moelleux or, this being the sweetest, liquoreux. The outstanding wine of this sub-district is its sweet white dessert wine made from the Chenin Blanc, which in a good year will be equal to Sauternes, Barsac and the *Auslese* wines of Germany. Two outstanding vineyard areas producing these sweet wines are Quarts de Chaume and Bonnezeaux, which have their own *appellations*. There are two other ACs, Coteaux du Layon-Chaume and Coteaux du Layon Villages. Six villages are considered to produce superior wines and may add their name to the Village AC. These are: Beaulieu-sur-Layon, Faye d'Anjou, Rablay-sur-Layon, Rochefort-sur-Loire, St Aubin de Luignés and St Lambert-du-Lattay.

Haut Poitou   This is a small region south of Saumur and Touraine just north of Poitiers producing red wines from Cabernet grapes and white wines from Sauvignon grapes. It received its AOC in 1989.

Savennières is a commune on the north of the river just south of Angers; it has its own AC plus Savennières-Coulée-de-Serrant and Savennières-Roche-aux-Moines. The soil is quite different from that of the surrounds, and it produces a very fine dry, white wine from the Chenin Blanc grape, which requires many years to reach its maturity.

Nantais

Nantais has four AC areas, Muscadet, Muscadet Coteaux de la Loire, Muscadet Côtes de Grand-Lieu and Muscadet Sèvre-et-Maine. The main wine from this region is Muscadet, named after the grape from which it is made. This is the local name for the Melon de Bourgogne grape. The best of this wine comes from the AC Muscadet Sèvre-et-Maine, and the next best are Muscadet Côtes de Grandlieu, and AC Muscadet Coteaux de la Loire. Sometimes these wines are sold *sur lie*, which means they have been matured on their fine lees over the winter following the harvest, imparting an extra flavour and light 'prickle' to the wine. Muscadets are at their best young and fresh, and admirably complement shellfish and other types of fish.

   There are two significant VDQS wines produced in the Nantais. *VDQS Gros Plant du Pays Nantais* is named after the *Gros Plant* (*Folle Blanche* grape) and is a wine of much lower quality. It is dry and tart, and most of it is drunk locally. The *VDQS Coteaux d'Ancenis* covers red and rosé wines from the Gamay, a small quantity of dry white from the Chenin Blanc and a very small quantity of sweet white wine from the Malvoisie grape.

Fiefs Vendeens   VDQS is situated south of Muscadet and covers dry red, white and rosé wines, the red and rosé being the best.

Rhône

From Vienna in the north to Avignon in the south there is an abundance of excellent vineyards, producing mainly red wines with some white, rosé and sparkling wines. The region falls into two distinct parts (Figure 4.7). The Northern Rhône is a narrow strip located on steep granite hillsides following the course of the Rhône. There is a gap of 40 km

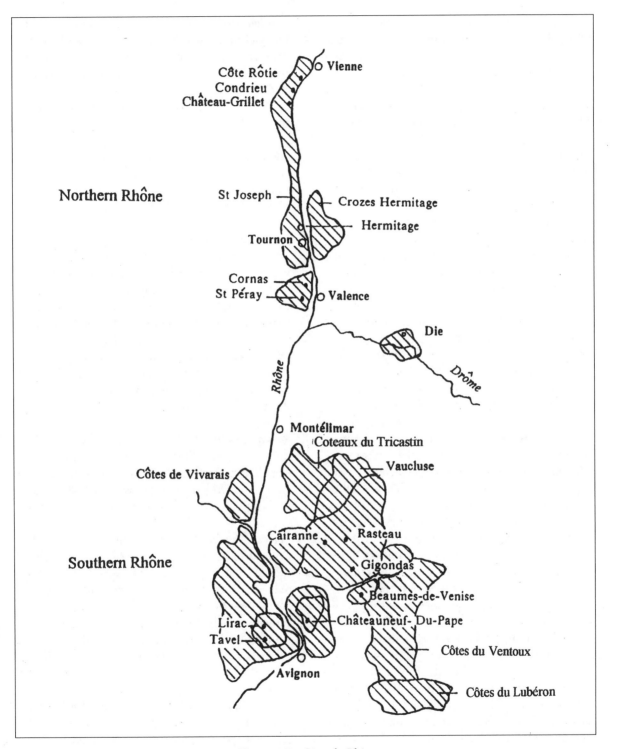

Figure 4.7 *Côtes-du-Rhône*

between this and the bottom half of the district, which is spread out over flatter countryside and a wider area. The Southern Rhône can be affected by the *mistral* – a very strong, cold wind. The Syrah grape, known as the Shiraz in other parts of the world, is the only black grape of the Northern Rhône, although this is sometimes blended with one or more white varieties. The Viognier is the major white grape of the north, and, along with the Rousanne and Marsanne, is permitted to be blended in the red wines. The northerly red wines, for example Côte Rôtie, St- Joseph, Crozes-Hermitage, Hermitage and Cornas, improve in bottle often up to ten years, but they are usually drunk too young. They all have their own ACs. The best of these are the Côte Rôtie and Hermitage. The classic white wines of Condrieu and Château-Grillet (one of the smallest ACs in France), and made from the Voignier, are usually at their best when drunk young. They are golden in colour, dry and spicy. The white wines from Crozes Hermitage and St-Joseph are produced from a blend of roussanne and marsanne grapes. St-Péray produces white wine and a heavy sparkling wine made by the *méthode traditionnelle*. Die, which is a small area to the east of the main district on the river Drôme, produces a light dry sparkling wine from the Clairette grape. This has been legally changed from Clairette de Die Brut to Crémant de Die in 1999, and a sweeter wine from the muscat grape sold as Clairette de Die Tradition. This is made by a local version of the *méthode traditionnelle*.

The Southern Rhône district is dominated by *Châteauneuf-du-Pape*, but there are a great many other wines produced in this sub-district. There are many permitted grape varieties, with Grenache, Syrah, Cinsault and Mourvèdre being the most important black grapes. The wines are usually blended from a number of grape varieties. Much of the wine is made into *AC Côtes-du-Rhône*, a light red wine, which is the basic AC. A Côtes-du-Rhône *primeur* is also produced. The *AC Côtes-du-Rhône-Villages* which may have the name of the village attached, is a considerably better product. *Gigondas AC*, upgraded from *Côtes-*

du-Rhône-Villages has a maximum of 80 per cent Grenache grapes in its red and rosé blends, and a minimum of 15 per cent Syrah and Morvèdre in the reds. The red wines are well respected and similar in style and alcoholic strength (12.5% min.) to Châteauneuf-du-Pape. The rosés are good quality and dry.

Vacqueras AC, up-graded like Gigondas, produces similar wines from similar grapes, with a minimum 50 per cent Grenache in the red and rosé blends. A very small quantity of dry white is made.

Muscat de Beaumes-de-Venise AC wines take their name from the village of Beaumes-de-Venise. The wines are naturally sweet and are produced by adding grape spirit (brandy) to the fermentation to arrest it (as in port production). This ensures that plenty of unfermented sugar remains in the wine, producing a sweet wine of 14–15% abv, which has tremendous fruit and flavour. These Côtes-du-Rhône VDN wines are dessert wines suitable to be served with the sweet course or drunk on their own.

Rasteau produces red, white and rosé wines sold under AC Côtes-du-Rhône-Villages, but the Appellation Rasteau Contrôlée wines are naturally sweet red fortified wines known as VDNs which can originate from Rasteau, Sablet and Cairanne.

Côtes du Ventoux AC is a large district between the Côtes-du-Rhône AC and the Côtes du Lubéron AC. Red, white and rosé wines are produced. The reds, which are lighter than normal Rhône wines, are the best of these, followed by the rosés. *Tavel* is a strong dry rosé wine of 11–13% abv which is more of a *pelure d'oignon* (onion skin) colour. *Lirac* produces a similar rosé wine, plus red and white wines.

The *Châteauneuf-du-Pape* sub-district takes its name from the ruined summer palace of a fourteenth-century Pope. The wines are nearly all red, being made from blends of up to thirteen grape varieties but with Grenache being the most important. Much, but not all, of this area is covered in 'pudding stones' – large, smooth, rounded stones which help to drain the ground, act as storage heaters to warm the vines at night, and also prevent the soil underneath from drying out. These wines range from medium to strong, are robust, and high in alcohol (minimum 12.5% abv). The wines from the best estates have crossed keys embossed in the glass of the bottle and sometimes require up to twenty years to reach maturity. These wines are frequently drunk too young. Châteaux Beaucastel (a complex blend of 30 per cent Grenache plus most if not all of the other 12 permitted varieties) and Château Rayas (100 per cent Grenache) are considered to be two of the top estates.

All the Northern Rhône red wines and the Southern Rhône's Gigondas and Châteauneuf-du-Pape are high in alcohol and suitable for serving with roasts and dark meat dishes. Gigondas and Châteauneuf-du-Pape are also excellent with stronger dishes, such as game and strongly flavoured stews.

Coteaux du Tricastin AC is a small district situated just south of Montélimar which produces very good red wines produced from the Southern Côtes-du-Rhône grapes. A small quantity of very good rosé and a small amount of white wines of a lesser quality are also made.

Côtes du Lubéron AC This small region is situated 65 km to the east of Avignon and produces red, white and rosé wines. The red and rosé wines are made from the same grapes as southern Côtes-du-Rhône, with a quantity of Pinot Noir being used by some producers. The white wines are made from various grapes including Clairette, Grenache blanc, Roussanne, Ugni Blanc, Boubelenc and Vermentino.

Other wine-producing regions of France

Bergerac AC
The region is similar in size to Entre-Deux-Mers and is divided by the River Dordogne. Adjoining the Bordeaux region and made from the same grape varieties, its wines are predictably similar in style, and are improving in quality. In the north of the region, which adjoins St-Emilion, the wines are generally red, being made from Cabernet and Merlot grapes. In the south the wines are more often white and made from the Sémillon and Sauvignon, the same as for Sauternes. The Sémillon is the most common grape variety.

Pécharmant
An AC within the Bergerac region for an excellent red wine which ages up to ten years and is made from the Bordeaux red grapes, with Merlot predominating.

Monbazillac AC
A small region in the centre of Bergerac, producing wines similar to Sauternes but of a much lower quality. The opportunity for *pourriture noble* is present but rarely used.

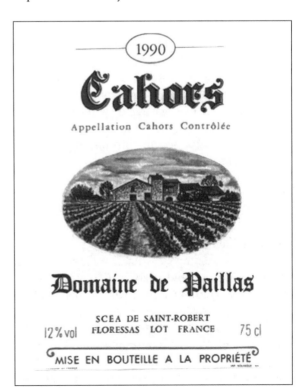

1990
Cahors
Appellation Cahors Contrôlée

Domaine de Paillas

SCEA DE SAINT-ROBERT
12 % vol   FLORESSAS   LOT   FRANCE   75 cl

MISE EN BOUTEILLE A LA PROPRIÉTÉ

Côtes de Duras AC

This is an extension of Entre-Deux-Mers to the east, producing a fuller style of wine. There are some good full, dry, Sauvignon wines being made.

Cahors AC

Situated south-east of Bergerac, on the River Lot, this small region obtained AC status in 1971. The wine is red and made from a minimum of 70 per cent Malbec with some Merlot and a little Tannat. They require up to five years or more to reach their best.

Gaillac AC

South-east of Cahors and north-east of Toulouse, Gaillac is a substantial size. It produces reds, mainly dry whites, rosés and two types of sparkling wine; *Gaillac Perle* is a pétillant and semi-sweet light sparkling wine which still contains yeast sediment. Although there are some Sauvignon and Gamay, the grapes used most are local varieties.

Jura

For such a small district a large number of different styles of wine are produced. Two of them are most unusual. One is the AC Château-Chalon, a *vin jaune* bottled in a squat, square bottle called a *clavelin*. It is made by leaving the white wine, produced from the Savagnin (Traminer) grape, in vats which are never topped up, for a minimum of six years. A *flor* settles on the wine as in sherry production, producing a *vin jaune* which is similar in many respects to an old sherry. The other is the *vin de paille*, which was originally made from grapes that had been laid out on beds of straw to dry before fermentation. They are now put on wire netting or wicker trays. (Switzerland is also known for its *vin de paille*, and a very small quantity is produced in Hermitage.) The wine is high in alcohol (14–16% abv) and very sweet, and gold to amber in colour. Both these wines are made only in good years. *Vin Fou*, a refreshing sparkling wine, is also made here. Local grape varieties are important here but Chardonnay and Pinot Noir are also

grown. Arbois is the main AC under which reds, whites and rosés are sold. Arbois Mousseux AC sparkling wines in this region must be made by the *méthode traditionnelle*.

Jurançon AC

This is situated further to the south-west again, in the French Pyrenees south and west of Pau. The grape varieties are the Gros Manseng and Petit Manseng, plus a few other local grapes which produce a distinctive *Jurançon Sec* and an excellent spicy sweet dessert wine high in alcohol.

Languedoc/Roussillon

These regions together are by far the largest producer in both cultivated area and quantity of wine. Until recently the quality of the wine was generally of an ordinary to poor standard. The number of vines has been considerably reduced, better-quality varieties have been planted and modern winemaking techniques have been introduced. The result is that better-quality wines are being made. Some good, and a few very good wines are produced, but most of these are non-*appellation*-permitted varietals and are therefore sold under *Vin de Pays d'Oc* the regional VdP, or one of the numerous VdP departments or zones.

Banyuls and *Banyuls Grand Cru AC*   These are the most southerly ACs in France and they are red, white, rosé VDNs (*vins doux naturals*). The red wines are very dark and sweet and made from 50 per cent Grenache for Banyuls and 75 per cent for the Grand Cru, which must also be matured 30 months before sale. Many of the top-quality Banyuls are aged ten to twenty years. There is a small quantity of red table wine made under the *Collioure AC*.

Corbières AC are sound wines, mainly red, with some rosé and a small amount of dry white wine. The AC is large and the quality is above the general standard of the Languedoc area in which it is situated. The predominant grape variety is Carignan, which is supported by many other local varietals.

Costières de Nîmes is in the eastern part of the Languedoc district bordering the Southern Rhône and produces similar style red wines. Dry rosés and a little dry white are also made.

Rivesaltes AC is situated in the centre of Languedoc/Roussillon. Rivesaltes AC produces 50 per cent of the *appellation controlée* VDN wines of France, which are either red, white or rosé and which are at their best after ten years. These wines are made from a blend of many varieties including Grenache Noir, Grenache Gris and Grenache Blanc.

Muscat de Rivesaltes AC is made from the muscat grape and is only white or rosé. It is far superior to the Rivesaltes AC and is best drunk young, up to three years old.

Maury is also situated in the Roussillon. Maury AC wines are red, white or rosé VDNs which are made mainly from Grenache and are similar in style to Banyuls. The table wines are sold under the Côtes du Roussillon Villages AC.

Blanquette de Limoux AC Limoux is south-west of Carcassonne. Still, semi-sparkling and sparkling white wines are produced, but it is the sparkling wines made from the Mauzac, Chardonnay, and Chenin grapes which are the best. The soil is heavy with limestone, and the wines are made sparkling by the *méthode traditionnelle*. Blanquette de Limoux is produced from a minimum 90 per cent Mauzac grapes and Crémant de Limoux from a maximum of 70 per cent Mauzac. The sparkling wines made from the Mauzac, Chardonnay, and Chenin grapes are the best.

Madiran AC

Situated in the French Pyrenees, it adjoins the south-western corner of the Armagnac region. It produces a strong full-bodied red wine made from a blend of up to 40–60 per cent *Tannat* grape with Cabernet Sauvignon and Cabernet Franc. A small amount of white wine, which may be sweet or dry, is also made.

Minervois AC

Mainly rustic- style red wines from Grenache, Syrah and Mourvèdre blended with a number of other varietals. Some dry rosés and a very small quantity of dry white wine are produced.

Fitou AC

Fitou is in two small parts within Corbières on the border with Roussillon. It produces strong dark wines from mainly Carignan and Grenache grapes.

Provence AC

Provence is noted for its large output rather than the quality of its wine, but the wines have been improved over the years with the introduction of more classic grape varieties and modern wine-making. Provence is best known for its rosé wines, much of it sold under the Côtes de Provence AC. Coteaux d'Aix-en-Provence is another large *appellation*, with AC Bandol producing the best of the reds with some rosé and white wine. AC Cassis also produces red white and rosé but is best known for its white wines.

Savoie

Savoie produces mainly white wines but also red and rosé under the *Vin de Savoie AC*, and sparkling wines under *Pétillant de Savoie* and *Mousseux de Savoie*. One other AC of particular interest is *Roussette de Savoie*, a good dry white named after a local grape varietal.

GERMANY

The main wine-producing region of Germany is situated in the south-west quarter of Germany (Figure 4.8). It is the most northerly wine region of Europe and crosses latitude 50°N, above which it is not normal elsewhere for grapes to fully ripen. However, it is in these borderline districts that some of the finest white wines are produced. Two new small areas have been recognized in the east since German unification and both of these are further north, above 51°N.

Many vineyards in Germany, particularly along the Mosel, Saar, Ruwer and Ahr rivers, and the Mittelrhein and upper sections of the Rheingau area, are on particularly steep slopes where they benefit from extra concentration of the sun's rays and reflected light from the rivers (see p. 28).

However, these slopes make working the vineyards extremely difficult. Therefore, to ease this problem and to improve accessibility to the vines *fleuberinigung* has been introduced whereby the vineyards have been re-allocated so that they are in neat blocks and the vines planted in lines up and down the slopes. Small roads built at various levels across the slopes make for easy access.

Wine categories and labelling

The wines are produced and sold under the German Wine Law, which came into force in 1971 and which has had a number of adjustments made to it since. The law set out the names under which wines can be sold and the terminology permitted for use on the wine label. The vineyard classification was excellent but the quality classification was based on the sweetness and ripeness of the grapes, which has caused innumerable problems. The wines are divided into four categories: *Tafelwein*, *Landwein*, *Qualitätswein bestimmter Anbaugebiete (QbA)* and *Qualitätswein mit Prädikat (QmP)* (see Chapter Three).

The five main *Weinbaugebiete* (regions) used for *Deutscher Tafelwein* are:

Rhein–Mosel (covers *Anbaugebiete* 1–8; see below)
Bayern (Anbaugebiet 9)
Neckar (Anbaugebiet 10)
Oberrhein (part of Anbaugebiet 11)
Albrechtsburg (Anbaugebiete 12–13)

Deutscher Tafelwein may only be sold under one of these *Weinbaugebiete*. There are twenty *Landwein* regions permitted, but these wines are rarely exported.

There are thirteen *Anbaugebiete* (wine-growing areas) for *Qualitätswein* (QbA and QmP):

1 Ahr
2 Hessiche Bergstrasse
3 Mittelrhein
4 Mosel-Saar-Ruwer
5 Nahe
6 Rheingau

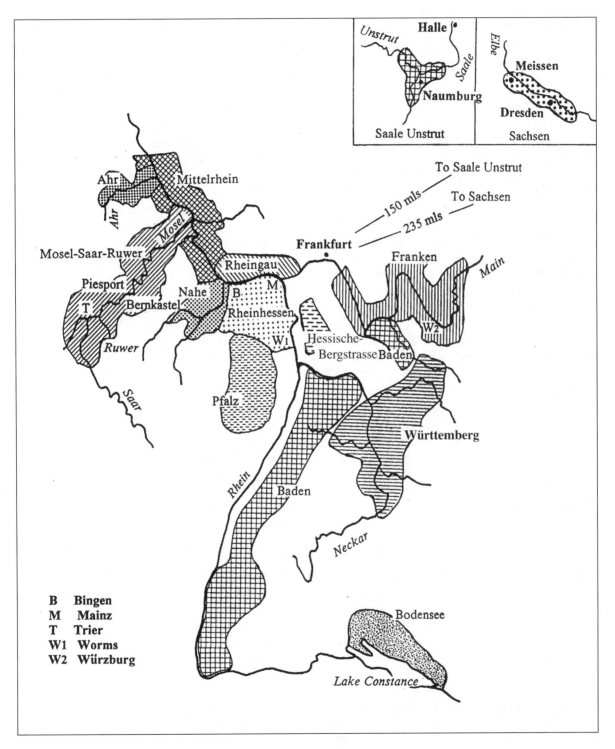

Figure 4.8 *German wine-growing areas*

7 Rheinhessen
8 Pfalz
9 Franken
10 Württemberg
11 Baden
12 Saale-Unstrut
13 Sachsen

All *Qualitätswein* (QbA and QmP) must bear one of these names on the label. The following may also appear:

Bereich   This is a district within an *Anbaugebiet* spanning many parishes and vineyards which all produce wine with similar characteristics, for example Bereich Bernkastel and Bereich Niersten.
Grosslage   This is the name for a collection of vineyard sites, for example Rosengarten for the vineyards surrounding Rüdesheim in the Nahe, Schwarze Katz for those surrounding Zell on the River Mosel, and Erntebringer for the vineyards round Johannisberg in the Rheingau.
Einzellage   This is an individual vineyard site. The names of these sites are only permitted to be used on the label of *Qualitätswein* bA and mP. An example is Maximin Grünhauser Herrenberg. The village of Maximin Grünhaus is situated in the *Grosslage* of Romerlay, which is part of the *Bereich* of Saar-Ruwer. This *Bereich* is in the *Anbaugebiet* of Mosel-Saar-Ruwer, which in turn is part of the *Weinbaugebiet* of Rhein-Mosel.

The majority of these quality wines are named after the *Bereich*, *Grosslage* or *Einzellage*, adding the letters -er; for example Bernkasteler.

The perception of German wine quality has been severely damaged through its mass-market wines but in earlier years it had a high reputation, which was built on the excellent quality of its white wines. There is an increasing quantity of red of improving quality being produced, particularly in Baden and Pfalz, but it is the white wines which will always be the finest. It is to these that the VDP Accord of 2002 is directed to bring them into line

with the 'Grand Cru' systems operated in other countries. The *Ernst Gëwachs* or first growth and *Grosse Gewächs* or Great Growth are to be applied to 75 plots in the Rheingau. These categories are intended to be at the same level as the Grand Cru of other countries. The label will state the vineyard site, grape variety and in the case of the *Grosse Gewächs*, a prädikat will be added. There will be a new logo (the number 1 plus a bunch of grapes) embossed on the bottle. The *Ernst Gëwachs* wines will be dry Riesling, and the *Grosse Gewächs* luscious sweet wines. *Grosse Gewächs* may also be applied to designated plots in the Rheinhessen, Nahe, Mittelrhein, Württemberg, Baden, Franken and Pfalz regions. Chaptalization is permitted for *Ernst Gewächs* but not for pradikät wines. The second category, *Klassifizierte Lagenweine*, is applied to wines from a classified site. They are wines from single sites, 'terrior driven', that impart a distinctive character to the wine. The third category *Gutsweine* and *Ortsweine* will be estate house wines bearing a proprietary name and/or a designated village or region. All VDP-approved wines will carry the VDP Eagle logo on the capsule.

Grape varieties

There are nearly 40 grape varieties permitted to be used in Germany. The most important of these are Riesling, Müller-Thurgau and Silvaner (Sylvaner). These are followed by Bacchus, Elbling, Gewürztraminer, Kerner, Morio-Muscat, Grauerburgunder (Ruländer or Pinot Gris) and Scheurebe. The most notable black grape for the red wines is the Spätburgunder (Pinot Noir), the next most planted is the Blauer Portugieser, and Dornfelder.

To name a single grape variety on the label, the wine must contain a minimum of 85 per cent of that grape.

Wine characteristics

The six *Prädikats* (degrees of ripeness) for QmP have been described in Chapter Three.

It was at Schloss Johannisberg in 1775 that the secret of *Spätlese* was first discovered. At harvest

time, a courier was sent to the Bishop at Fulda, then in charge of the vineyard, to obtain permission to harvest the grapes. The courier fell ill *en route*, and arrived back at Schloss Johannisberg so late that the crop seemed to be ruined as the grapes were 'rotting' on the vines. However, the grapes were picked and made into wine which, to everyone's amazement, resulted in the best ever produced. This was caused by the action of *botrytis cinerea* (*Edelfäule* or noble rot) on the grapes.

Auslese, *Beerenauslese* and *Trockenbeerenauslese*

are dessert wines and are unsuitable with most dishes other than perhaps sweets and cheeses. They are normally drunk on their own. German wines which are to be made into dry wines will be called *trocken*, and those to be made into semi-dry wines will be called *halbtrocken*. *Kabinett*, *Spätlese* and *Auslese* wines are sometimes produced in this way, e.g. Spätlese Trocken.

Rheingau

This small, but high-quality region is on the slopes of the hillsides overlooking the Rhine from just north of Assmanshausen to the confluence with the Main. The vineyards face south and receive extra sunshine reflected from the broad expanse of the river (see Chapter Three). They are protected from the cold north winds by the hills. The main grape variety (over 80 per cent) is the Riesling. Location, soil and grape combine to produce outstanding white wines. Schloss Johannisberg and Schloss Vollrads are two of the best single vineyards named after their estates. The villages of Johannisberg, Rudesheim, Rauenthal, Hattenheim and Hochheim are perhaps the best known. It was from Hochheim that the name Hock was derived. Assmanshausen is at the northerly end of the area nearest to the Mittelrhein. It is different from the other Rheingau villages as it produces more red wines than white wines; 60 per cent of the vines are Spätburgunder, and nearly 40 per cent are Riesling. Nearly all Rheingau wines are sold in the traditional elongated brown bottles.

In 1984 the Charta (pronounced carter) Estates Association was formed in the Rheingau. There are now nearly 50 estates which are members. It was founded to further the classic Rheingau Riesling style of a dry-to-off-dry wine made from 100 per cent Riesling. Wines are blind-tasted twice and may not be sold until 1st October of the year following the harvest. They may then carry the Charta seal of quality.

Rheinhessen

This is a much larger region situated opposite the Rheingau on the south and west sides of the Rhine, extending down from Bingen and Mainz in the north to just below Worms. The main grape variety is Müller-Thurgau, closely followed by Silvaner; these two account for two-thirds of the grapes grown in this area, with only about 8 per cent of Riesling. However, the very best wines are produced from the Riesling. There is an increasing amount of red wine being produced from the Spätburgunder (Pinot Noir) which is of good quality.

Liebfraumilch is the main wine produced in this area (see below) with Niersteiner Spiegelberg and Niersteiner Gutes Domtal (both *Grosslagen*) being the next in quantity. Nackenheim, Oppenheim, Nierstein and Dienheim all produce some good-quality wines. The majority are sold in the traditional elongated brown bottles.

Liebfraumilch

This is not an area or a place on the map. It originally came from the Rheinhessia from the vineyards around a small church near Worms called Liebfrauenkirche (Church of our Lady). Now it is a blended wine from the Rheingau, Rheinhessen, Pfalz or the Nahe. It may not now (since 1982) be a blend of wines from different areas; it must be a QbA wine from one of these four areas and must contain a minimum of 70 per cent of Riesling, Müller-Thurgau, Silvaner or Kerner. It is a semi-sweet wine, and is usually sold in elongated brown bottles.

Pfalz

Although the Rheinhessen is the largest wine-producing region of Germany in terms of vineyard area, the Pfalz (also known as the Palatinate), slightly smaller in vineyard area, is the largest producing region. It is situated on the western side of the Rhine, the best vineyards being found on the lower slopes of the Haardt hills along the Bundesstrase, which is called the *Weinstrasse*. The southernmost extremity of the Pfalz is the border with France, at a point just north of the Alsace wine-producing region. Müller-Thurgau is the most planted, followed by Riesling, Silvaner, Sheurebe. Spätburgunder and Dornfelder for red wines, are on the increase.

Pfalz wines vary in quality but the best are truly great, being fuller bodied than the Rheingaus and less soft than the Rheinhessen wines. The bouquet is particularly full, and these wines are probably the best suited to being drunk with a meal. The finest wines come from the villages of Wachenheim, Forst, Deidesheim and Ruppertsberg Bad Dürkheim and Kallstadt.

The majority of the wines from this area are sold in the traditional elongated brown bottles.

Nahe

This region is, as its name suggests, situated along the River Nahe which joins the Rhine just east of Bingen. The vineyards are planted with many varieties of grapes, but the Riesling is the most common, followed by Müller-Thurgau and Silvaner. These three account for 75 per cent of the plantings. The wines are therefore likely to be similar in style to the other Hocks; in fact they closely resemble the wines from Nierstein. Riesling makes the best-quality wines here.

The two most important towns are Bad Kreuznach and Schloss Böckelheim, the single Bereich name is Nahetal. Bad Kreuznach is the centre of the Nahe wine area both geographically and commercially. The wines of this area are becoming better known and respected. The *Grosslage Rudesheimer Rosengarten* should not be confused with the *Einzelagen* of that name in the Rheingau. Nahe wines are usually sold in elongated brown bottles.

Franken (Franconia)

The region of Franken is situated along the River Main from Hörnstein, which is east of Frankfurt to about 18 miles (25 km) west of Würzburg. Much of this area is on steep slopes overlooking the river, and south-facing slopes are often the only usable sites. The main grape variety is the Müller-Thurgau, followed by the Silvaner (which used to be the dominant variety), Riesling, Bacchus and Sheurebe. The Silvaner produces the best Franken wine. The majority of wine is dry white but as in other areas the Spätburgunder is an ever-increasing variety producing some good red wines for food.

The best wines are produced from the vineyards around Würzburg, which is the centre of the Franken wine trade. There are two outstanding vineyards – Stein and Leiste. Wines produced from the Würzburger Stein vineyards are permitted to be called Steinwein; other Franken wines are not.

Franken wines are medium dry to dry, full bodied and very suitable to accompany food. In good years *Prädikat* wines are made as in other areas. Franken wines are often sold in flat-sided flasks called *Bocksbeutels*.

Mosel-Saar-Ruwer

This region follows the Mosel and its tributaries the Saar and Ruwer from Koblenz, where it meets the Rhine, to the border with Luxembourg in the south. The vineyards are situated on very steep south-facing slopes, many of which are totally inaccessible to machinery. The soil contains large quantities of red slate which radiates heat on to the grapes during the day and night, helping to ripen them, increases drainage, and slows down the erosion of the soil from the steep slopes. It also adds its own character to the wine.

The most important grape variety is the Riesling, giving the highest-quality wines and 50 per cent of the total production. Müller-Thurgau is the next most important and is on the increase. It is interesting that about 40 per cent of the vines are the original European vines, not those grafted on to American roots, as *Phylloxera* appears to dislike the slate soil. The wines are traditionally low in alcohol, usually being between 8 and 10% abv, which gives them a lightness in the mouth; but the *trocken* and *halbtrocken* wines may reach higher levels. They are fresh and fruity medium wines with often more than a touch of acidity. They may have a slight prickle to them (*spritzig*), which is caused by a small amount of carbon dioxide gas being in the wine when it is bottled. This gives the wine a pleasant freshness. These wines are often at their best when young, up to three years old, with the *Spätlese* and *Auslese* wines lasting longer.

The best villages on the Mosel are in the Bereich Bernkastel (Mittelmosel). These are Piesport, Bernkastel, Graach, Wehlen, Zeltingen and Brauneberg. The best in the Bereich Saar-Ruwer are Maximin Grünhause and Eitelsbach on the

Ruwer, and Wiltingen Ockfen and Scharzhof on the Saar. Mosel-Saar-Ruwer wines are usually sold in elongated green bottles.

Ahr

This region on the River Ahr is a small one and is best known for its red wines, which account for 60 per cent of the total production. The Pinot Noir (Spätburgunder) and the Portugieser, both black grapes, are the main varieties. The red wines tend to be light and rather thin due to the northern latitude. High-class Riesling and Müller-Thurgau wines are sometimes made, but they are rarely exported.

Baden

Baden produces red, white and rosé wines. It is the third-largest German wine-producing region. It runs from Franken in the north, where the wines are almost identical to the Franken wines and which are permitted to use the *Bocksbeutel*, down through the Neckar valley and on to the main section from Baden-Baden to Basel. This part is separated from the Alsace wine area only by the River Rhine. Nearly all Baden wines come from large co-operatives. Many grape varieties are grown, but the Müller-Thurgau is the main white grape followed by the Spätburgunder (Pinot Noir). A limited amount of good-quality Riesling wine is made. The wines are fuller bodied and higher in alcohol than the wines from the more northerly areas.

Mittelrhein

The Mittelrhein region follows the north-eastern bank of the Rhine from Koblenz to the north of Linz, where the Ahr meets the Rhine. These vineyards are the steepest in the world. The Riesling grape accounts for over 75 per cent of the vines, and the next most important is the Müller-Thurgau. Much of this wine is used for making sparkling wine (Sekt).

Hessische Bergstrasse

This is a very small wine region of Germany, producing full-bodied white wines, 50 per cent from Riesling; Müller-Thurgau makes up most of the rest. *Trocken* and *halbtrocken* styles are common, but few wines from this region are exported.

Saale-Unstrut

This is one of two regions which are situated in the former GDR or Eastern Germany. It is Germany's most northerly region and is situated at the confluence of the Rivers Saale and Unstrut at Neumburg, some 50 km south-west of Leipzig. It is the second-smallest region with 447 ha under the vine. Müller-Thurgau is the most widely planted variety, and over 80 per cent of the wines are produced by two co-operatives.

Sachsen

This is the other former GDR region and is 135 km almost due east of Neumburg, around Dresden and Meissen. This is Germany's smallest region with just 311 ha of vines. There are also two co-operatives here producing a majority of the wine, but there are more small producers whose dry wines suggest that there is good potential for the future.

Sekt

Sekt is the name for sparkling wine in Germany. There are two types.

Deutscher Sekt is sparkling wine made from German grapes.

Sekt on its own describes sparkling wine made from imported wine, which may or may not be blended with German wine. The better *Deutscher Sekt* wines are usually made by the *cuve close* (Charmat) process (see Chapter Five). Sparkling wine is very popular in Germany. It is presented and bottled in a similar way to Champagne.

ITALY

Italy is second only to France in wine production, with each of its 20 regions (see Figure 4.9) producing wine. The majority is drunk in Italy. There has been a significant reduction in consumption per capita with a strong move towards red wine. Since the DOC laws of 1963, amended in 1992 by the Goria Law (see Chapter Three), there has been a steady reduction in the quantity of wine produced and a consistent increase in wine exported. During the 1990s there was a steady improvement in the quality of the wines, but there is a considerable amount of low-quality wine still being produced by those who rate quantity as being more important than quality. In most regions there are large numbers of small producers with many negociants and cooperatives. While there has been a considerable increase in the plantings of the standard French varietals, the indigenous red varietals such as Sangiovese, Nebbiolo and Barbera have more than held their own and are producing some excellent wines.

Valle d'Aosta

This, the smallest of the 20 regions, is situated between the north-west border of Piedmont, and the borders of France and Switzerland. It has one DOC, that of Valle d'Aosta, which accounts for 85 per cent of the production comprising red, white and rosé wines.

Piedmont

Piedmont produces a large quantity of medium- and high-quality red wines, the best being from the Nebbiolo grape which is also know as Spanna. There are also some excellent sparkling wines.

Asti DOCG (7.5–9% abv) is the largest DOCG and is made exclusively from the *moscato bianco* grape. Its sparkle (3.5–4 atmospheres, 52–60lbs psi) is produced by a single fermentation in a closed tank similar to the *cuve close* method.
Moscato d'Asti DOCG (max. 5.5% abv) is produced in the same way from the same grape but has a

lighter effervescence (1 atmosphere, 15lbs psi). The red wines are much heavier.
Barbaresco DOCG (12.5% abv) is made from the Nebbiolo grape and named after the village. It must be aged two years in oak or chestnut wood. After three years it can be called *riserva* and after four years in wood *riserva speciale*. The wines are very tannic and require a minimum of five years to become softer, but some winemakers are using modern techniques including less time fermenting on the skins to produce earlier maturing wines.
Barolo DOCG (12.5% abv)   A highly acclaimed strong, highly tannic, deep red wine made from the Nebbiolo grape. It must be aged a minimum of one year in wood plus one year in bottle. After ageing for four years it can be called *riserva* and after five years *riserva speciale*, although as with Barbaresco, earlier maturing wines are being produced by some winemakers.
Barolo Chinato DOCG (16.5% abv) is a fortified aromatized wine which is given the bitter flavour of quinine by steeping the bark of the chinchona tree in the wine and flavouring with herbs and cardamon seed.
Barbera (12.0–12.5% abv)   Named after the grape and in plentiful supply. It is sold under DOCs which have Barbera attached to a district – Barbera d'Asti, Barbera d'Alba and Barbera del Monferrato. It is usually dry with high acid and low tannins but can be slightly sweet. Some quality-minded producers are reducing the yield per hectare and this has shown a great improvement to the wine. After three years in wood it can be called *superiore* if it has 13 per cent of alcohol.
Brachetto/Brachetto d'Acqui DOCG is a light, but alcoholic, sweet (*frizzante*) sparkling red wine, made from the Brachetto grape. It has a strong strawberry and muscat flavour. Still dry red DOC wines are also produced from this grape.
Gavi/Cortese di Gavi DOCG wines are still, *frizzante* or sparkling dry white wines which at their best are crisp with considerable depth of flavour. They are made from the Cortese grape and may be labelled *Gavi di Gavi* if they come from the commune of Gavi.

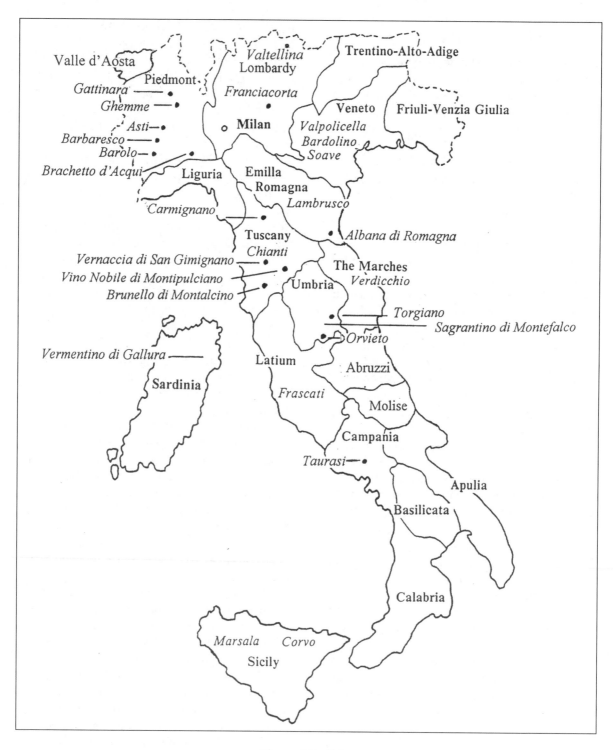

Figure 4.9 *Italy*

Gattinara DOCG (12% abv)   Named after the town and made from the Nebbiolo grape, very high-quality dry red wine, lighter in colour and less strong than Barolo. It is aged three years before sale, two of which must be in wood. A third year in wood makes it *riserva*. It often benefits from further ageing in bottle.

Ghemme DOCG is a dry red wine produced from a minimum 75 per cent Nebbiolo. The rest may be made up from Bonarda and Vespolina grapes. It is aged three years in wood plus one in bottle.

Lombardy

Franciacorta DOCG may only be applied to white or rosé (*metodo tradizionale*) wines. It is produced from Chardonnay, Pinot Bianco and Pinot Nero. Wines made exclusively from Chardonnay may be called *Blanc de Blancs*. The minimum age for N.V. wines must be 25 months from the vintage, of which 18 months are in bottle following the second fermentation, and vintage must be 37 months old, 30 of which are in bottle following the second fermentation. *Terre di Franciacorta DOC* is used for the white and red still wines. Probably the best-known red wine comes from the Valtellina which is situated on the River Adda close to the Swiss border and made from the Nebbiolo grape. The best are the *Valtellina Superiore DOCGs* which include the sub-regions of *Inferno*, *Grumello*, *Sassella* and *Valgella*. These wines are made from a minimum of 90% Nebbiolo grapes.

Trentino-Alto Adige

The general DOC is *Alto Adige*. French varietals are grown here producing light wines and are sold under this appellation. The most important red grape is the local *schiava*, which is used to produce *Santa Maddalena*, the most famous wine from the area. Wines with a named varietal on the label must contain a minimum 95 per cent of that varietal.

Veneto

Bardolino DOC (10.5% abv)   A light, red fruity wine made from a blend of four grapes, the three used for Valpolicella (see below) plus Negrara. *Bardolino superiore DOCG* and *Bardolino Classico superiore DOCG* (11% abv min.) are light red or rosé dry wines made from the Corvina, Molinara, Negrara and Rondinella grapes. *Bardolino DOC* may be dry red or rosé, still or sparkling.

Prosecco DOC (10.5% abv)   A white wine named after the grape, which accounts for a minimum of 85 per cent of the blend. It varies from dry to sweet.

Prosecco DOC (11% abv)   This is a dry white wine, *still*, *frizzante* or *spumante*. The *frizzante* and *spumante* wines are made by a form of the *charmat* method (see Chapter 5).

Soave DOC (10.5% abv)   Made from a blend of Garganega, Chardonnay and Trebbiano di Soave grapes, it is a dry white wine. Soave is probably the best-known and most plentiful Italian white wine but is spoilt by over-production. *Soave Superiore DOCG* will have been aged six months and will have a minimum of 11.5% abv. It is at its best when drunk young. *Classico* wines, which are of a higher quality, are produced in an inner delimited area. *Recioto di Soave DOCG* (14% abv) is an amber/gold, sweet desert wine made from semi-dried (*passito*) grapes which are the same as for Soave DOC. In good years these grapes can be affected by *botrytis*.

Torcolato is classified under the *Breganze DOC* and is made from semi-dried (*passito*) Vespaiolo grapes producing a golden dessert wine which has been aged in small oak barrels.

Valpolicella DOC (11% abv)   Produced from a blend of Corvina, Rondinella and Molinara. The best has a little more body than Bardolino, which uses a similar blend. It is by far the most plentiful of Italian red wines and is one of the best known. It becomes *superiore* after one year's ageing if it reaches 12% of alcohol. Like Soave it is at its best drunk young. *Classico* wines can again be produced in an inner delimited area.

Amarone della Valpolicella DOC (14% abv)   This is made from dried grapes (*vino passito*). The must is fully fermented out, producing a concentrated, high-alcoholic dry wine, which sometimes has a burnt character to it. *Recioto* wines are produced from dried grapes like *Amarone* but used to produce a semi-sweet wine, *Recioto della Valpolicella DOC*.

Emilia Romagna

This region is better known for quantity rather than quality.

Lambrusco DOC (11% abv) This is a sparkling wine, the majority of which is red or rosé. It can be either sweet or dry. The sparkling red sweet wine has gained popularity in the UK off-sales market, particularly among partygoers.

Albana di Romagna DOCG Being the first white wine to be awarded DOCG status in 1987 was a surprise to the majority of wine professionals. The wines are now mainly dry with a sweet style and are made from *passito botrytised* grapes. A DOC sweet sparkling wine is also made.

Tuscany

As with Piedmont and Veneto, Tuscany is recognized as a quality wine area which, at the time of writing, produces 6 of Italy's DOCGs and 37 DOCs. It is also the location of the new breed of wines known as the 'Super Tuscans', the most celebrated being Sassicaia. They were produced from grapes such as the Cabernets and Merlot which were outside the DOC regulations for the region. The use of some new oak and barriques was also introduced and this practice is spreading to other areas including the better Chiantis, and has helped to raise the quality.

Chianti DOCG (11.5% abv) Chianti is by far the best known of all Italian red wines and is produced in the following seven sub-regions: Chianti Colli Aretini, Chianti Colli Fiorentini, Chianti Colli Senesi, Chianti Colline Pisane, Chianti Montalbano, Chianti Montespertoli and Chianti Rufina. It is usually made from a blend of Sangiovese, Canaiolo Nero and up to 15 per cent Cabernet Sauvignon, with up to 10 per cent Trebbiano Toscano and Malvasia del Chianti (both white) still permitted. Less and less white grapes

are used and the law now allows Chianti to be produced from 100 per cent Sangiovese grapes. Chianti cannot be released for consumption prior to 1st March of the year following the harvest. If the wine is aged for a minimum of 26 months from 1st January following the harvest, and it has a minimum of 12 per cent of alcohol, it may be called *riserva*.

Chianti Classico DOCG (12% abv) This comes from a defined area of this name, which is in the middle of the Chianti region. Only 2 per cent of Trebbiano and Malvasia grapes is permitted in the blend but this is now rarely done. Up to 15 per cent non-local varieties (usually Cabernet Sauvignon and or Merlot) are permitted. *Chianti Colli Fiorentini DOCG* and *Chianti Rufina DOCG* are two other Chianti sub-zones. These three Chiantis cannot be released for consumption prior to 1st June of the year following the harvest. If they are aged for a minimum of 26 months from 1st January following the harvest, and they have a minimum of 12.5 per cent of alcohol, they may be called *riserva*.

Governo process The full title is *governo all'uso del Chianti*. It is a re-fermentation of racked wine with 5–10 per cent of must from grapes which have been dried up on *cannicci* or *castelli* (special wicker frames). This usually takes place before the end of the year of the harvest. It may be repeated in March or April, and this is called *rigoverno*. Governo is practised to start the malo-lactic fermentation and to increase the glycerol content, which makes the wine rounder and more refreshing with a slight prickle on the palate. This process is becoming less common.

Brunello di Montalcino DOCG (12.5% abv) One of the very best Italian red wines, made from the Brunello (Sangiovese clone) grape. It is a strong, dark red wine with plenty of tannin, and must be aged four years (two in wood) before sale. *Riserva* wines must be aged for five years. This wine definitely matures with bottle age.

Vino Nobile di Montepulciano DOCG (11.5% abv) The wine is usually made from a blend of Pugnolo Gentile (Sangiovese clone), Cannaiolo,

Mammolo, Trebbiano and Malvasia but these last two white varietals are now optional, and although the regulations state a maximum of 80 per cent of the Sangiovese clone, some producers are using 100 per cent. It is similar in character to Chianti and Brunello, if not quite as good as their best. It was the first wine to be given DOCG status (perhaps because it was one of the first to apply). It is, however, an outstanding wine. It must be matured two years in wood, and after three years in wood it may be called *riserva*. After four years it may be called riserva speciale. Many well-informed experts consider that this wine might improve with bottle age rather than an extended wood age.

Bolgheri DOC was introduced in 1994 mainly to

bring in *Sassicaia* which was made from Cabernet Sauvignon and Cabernet Franc. *Sassicaia* was the first single estate to be granted a DOC. These grapes were previously not permitted, so the wine had to be sold as Vino da Tavola even though it was the most expensive wine produced in Italy.
Sant'Antimo DOC   This was introduced in 1995 for the 1996 harvest in an attempt to bring other so called *Super Tuscan* wines into the *appellation* system. These are wines which have achieved outstanding prestige although produced from non-DOC grape varietals.

Other DOCG wines of Tuscany are the red *Carmignano* made from Sangiovese and Cabernet Sauvignon and the white *Vernaccia di San Gimignano* made from the Vernaccia grape and up to 10 per cent Chardonnay.
Vin Santo (14–17% abv)   There are a number of DOCs for this sweet (*passito*) wine produced in Tuscany.

Umbria
Orvieto DOC (12% abv)   Traditionally this was a sweet or semi-sweet (*abboccato*) white wine sold in a squat wicker-covered flask called a *pulcianella*. In recent years there has been a trend for drier and crisper wines. *Orvieto* is now more often made this way and sold in a Bordeaux-style bottle which is cheaper to make and easier to transport. It must be made from a minimum of 50 per cent Trebbiano grapes.
Torgiano DOC (red 12% abv, white 11.5 % abv) More red wine than white is made, and the red is made from a similar blend of grapes to the Chianti of neighbouring Tuscany. When aged three years it can be sold as *Torgiano Rosso Riserva DOCG*. The white wine is similar to a dry Orvieto.
Sagrantino di Montefalco DOCG is a dry red wine made from the Sagrantino grape. A sweet style is also produced from *passito* grapes (14.5% abv).

Latium
Frascati DOC (11.5% abv)   This is the best-known dry white wine from this area, produced

from Trebbiano and a small amount of Malvasia. A small quantity of semi-sweet, sweet and sparkling wines are also made. If the wine reaches 11.5 per cent of alcohol it may be called superiore.
Est! Est!! Est!!!di Montefiascone DOC (10.5% abv) This wine owes its reputation more to an event in 1110 AD than to quality. It is a white wine made from the Trebbiano grape and some Malvasia. It is similar to Orvieto but is of a lesser quality.

The Marches
Verdicchio dei Castelli di Jesi DOC (12% abv) is a white wine and by far the best-known wine from this region. Superiore wines must reach 12 per cent of alcohol. Lesser known but of better quality are the red DOCs of Rosso Conero, Rosso Piceno made from Montepulciano and Sangiovese grapes, but the production of these is in decline. There is a delimited part of this district, which is entitled to use Classico on the wine label.

Abruzzi
There are only two wines of any note, *Montepulciano d'Abruzzo DOC*, a good-quality red wine, and *Trebbiano d'Abruzzo DOC* which is surprisingly made from the white *Bombino* grape.

Campania
Campania is more famous for its volcano Vesuvius than for its wine, but there is plenty made here.
Vesuvio DOC (11% abv)   Red, white and rosé wines are made, the whites varying between semi-sweet and dry. Some sparkling and sweet fortified whites are also produced.
Taurasi DOCG (12% abv)   This very good, long-lived, tannic red wine made from the *Aglianico* grape must be matured for a minimum of three years, one of which must be in wood. *Riserva* wine requires a further year's maturing and 12.5 per cent of alcohol.

Apulia
This region of Italy produces more wine than any other. Although 24 DOCs have been granted,

nearly all of it is of a low quality. It is best known for its *trulli*, which are small prehistoric buildings, than for its wine.

Primitivo di Manduria DOC, the Primitivo grape, which is widely grown in this region, is related to the Zinfandel clones now grown in California. It is a highly alcoholic natural sweet or fortified wine, which can reach 18 per cent of alcohol in its fortified form.

Calabria

This area, known as the foot of Italy, is not renowned for its wines, although the Classico version of *Cirò DOC*, white from the Greco Bianco is of good quality. Red and rosé styles are also produced.

Sicily

Great changes in viticulture and vinification over the past twenty years have considerably improved the wines of Sicily. Wines bearing the letter Q meet official quality specifications (this also applies to Sicilian foods).

Marsala DOC is the best-known Sicilian wine. It is made mainly from white grapes but some red grapes are permitted. These fortified wines can be sweet or dry (see Chapter Five).

Sardinia

This island now produces some good-quality wines, most of which come from the co-operatives.

Cannonau di Sardegna DOC (12.5–13% abv) Cannonau is the name of the grape variety used; it is only found in Sardinia although it is considered to be closely related to the Grenache. The wine produced varies from strong rosé to deep red. The *riserva* wines have matured for a minimum of three years in wood. The *reservas* must have aged two years and have a minimum of 13% abv.

Vermentino di Gallura DOCG   Recently promoted to DOCG status, this is made from the white Vermentino grape.

Consorzi

There are many consorzi in Italy. These are voluntary organizations set up by the producers in many of the wine-producing regions in the 1930s, to protect quality and to help market the wine. They have now really been superseded by the DOC laws of 1963, but can still operate. In Chianti, for example, the best known is the Consorzio Chianti Classico, which has a neck label for the bottle of the Gallo Nero or Black Cockerel. This is only for Chianti, which is made from grapes grown in the Classico zone. The Consorzio Vino Chianti, with a cherub on the neck label, represents the Chianti zone. Baron Bettino Ricasoli developed the formula for the original blend of grapes used to produce Chianti.

The consorzi organizations do not offer any official guarantee of quality, but do exercise their own controls and marketing.

SPAIN

For many years Sherry was the only Spanish wine known to the wine-drinking public but in recent years Rioja, Cava, Ribera del Duera and Penedés have all become well known, while Sherry has been in decline. Since the 1960s Spanish wine has made enormous improvements due to modern wine-making equipment and technology, modern viticultural methods and the importation of quality grape varieties. This has resulted in quality wines being produced in areas where previously they were very ordinary. The new varietals have either been used to create completely new wines or been used in blends with the local varieties. The wines are now highly rated. Production and labelling is governed by the Instituto de Denominaciónes de Origen (INDO), which is controlled by administrative growers' committees or *consejos regulados*. There are 58 Denominaciónes de Origen DOs (as of 2002), many of which are unknown outside Spain. With a number of other applications made, it is expected that the number of DOs will continue to increase for a number of years.

The most important are:

Alella
Calatayud
Cariñena
Cava
Jerez
Jumilla
la Mancha
Málaga
Montilla-Moriles
Montsant
Navarra
Penedés
Priorato
Rias Baixas
Ribeiro
Ribera del Duero
Rioja
Rueda
Tarragona
Toro
Utiel-Requena
Valdepeñas
Valencia

In 1988 a new grading (DOCa) was announced and is a higher designation than DO. All DOCa wines must be bottled in the bodega of origin. The first wine to receive DOCa status was Rioja in 1991.

The Spanish wine law includes minimum requirements for ageing descriptions, although some DOs and DOCa stipulate longer periods in cask.

Joven, which has replaced *Sin Crianza*, means no cask ageing, or less than the legal minimum for *Crianza* wines.

Vino de Crianza　Red wines must be matured for two calendar years following the harvest, including a minimum of six months in *barricas* (225 litre oak casks). This means a 1997 vintage may be sold from 1st January 2000. White and rosé wines must be matured for one calendar year, of which

six months must be in *barricas*.

Reserva　Red wines must be matured for three calendar years following the harvest, including a minimum of one year in *barricas*. This means a 1997 vintage may be sold from 1st January 2001. White and rosé wines must be matured for two calendar years, of which six months must be in *barricas*.

Gran Reserva　Red wines must be matured for five calendar years following the harvest, including a minimum of two years in *barricas*. This means a 1997 vintage may be sold from 1st January 2003. White and rosé wines must be matured for four calendar years, of which six months must be in *barricas*.

Jumilla

This region, situated between La Mancha and Alicante, has in the past been known for its *Vinos de Mesa* (table wines), but since the middle 1980s, more emphasis has been placed on quality. The red grape Monastrell is proving to be most suitable for this region and is being used to produce some good-quality red wines.

La Mancha

This is the largest demarcated region in Spain (see Figure 4.10) and produces one-third of all its light wines. These are red, white and rosé, high in alcohol and have been used extensively for blending with other wines throughout Spain. Changes from the 1996 vintage have improved the wines, and good-value budget wines are being produced. The grape varietals are restricted to the Airen (most widely grown in the world), Pardilla and Macabeo for the white, and Cencibel (Tempranillo), Moravia, Garnacha, Cabernet Sauvignon and Merlot for red. An *Espumoso* was also authorized in 1996, which can be made from any of the above grapes, but Macabeo will be the most popular. A large amount is also still used for distillation into brandy and industrial alcohol. The region is better known for the quantity produced rather than for the quality of its wines, but with a regional parliament law being passed in 2000

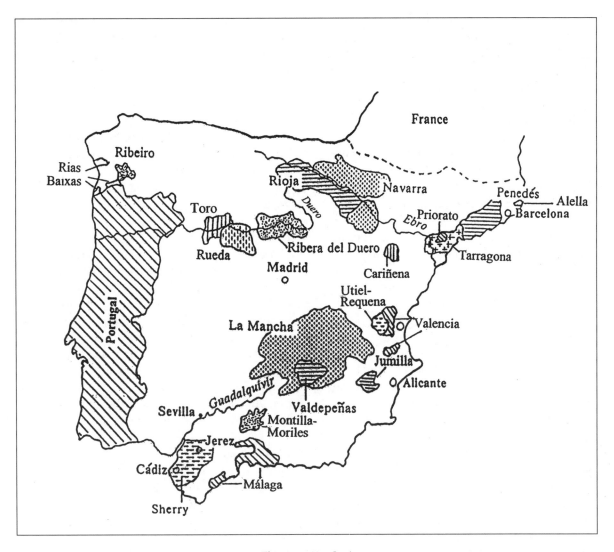

Figure 4.10 *Spain*

allowing estate wines of high reputation to apply for private DOs, the quality and DOs are expected to increase.

Montilla Moriles

Situated close to the Jerez region, it produces strong white wines similar in style to sherry and made from the Pedro Ximénez grape and blended by the Solera system (see Chapter Five). Although usually unfortified, the alcoholic strength is 15–20 per cent; the sweeter styles are the only

ones to be fortified. The dry styles are attacked by *flor*. The region gave the name *amontillado* to sherry, but cannot use this name for its own wines. Since the end of the 1980s a new style of wine has been made which is a young and fruity white wine for immediate consumption and sold as *Vino Joven* or *Jovenes Afrutados*.

Navarra

This region adjoins Rioja in the north, overlapping part of the Rioja Baja district. It produces 80 per cent red and rosé (rossado) and 20 per cent white. The rossados are highly rated but it is the red wines that are on the increase. There are five districts: Baja Montana, Ribera Alta, Ribera Baja, Tierra Estella and Valdizarbe. The most-planted grape variety is the Garnacha Tinta (Grenache) followed by Tempranilla, but Tempranilla and Cabernet Sauvignon are replacing the majority of the old Garnacha vines. Viura is the main white variety. The reds produced are medium dark wines high in alcohol, with some similarities to Côtes du Rhône wines. These are suitable to serve with pasta dishes, stews and roasts. *Crianza* wines may not be released until their third year, six months of which must have been spent in oak *barricas* plus some time in bottle.

Reserva and *Gran Reserva* wines follow the same maturation regulations as Rioja.

Penedés

Situated south of Barcelona, this region is divided into three based on height: Baix-Penedés (Low), Medio-Penedés (Middle) at 250–500 metres and Alt-Penedés (High) at 500–800 metres. The majority of the better-quality wines come from the Middle with some very good wines produced in small quantities in the Alt-Penedés. The best wines are white but there are some very good reds being produced. The region, and indeed Spain, owe the new-found quality levels of the wines to the late Miguel Torres, who introduced hygienic, controlled cool fermentation, new grape varieties and different vine densities. Penedés also has a very high reputation for sparkling wines, and in San Sadurní d'Anoia it has the centre of *Cava* production. There is a separate DO for Cava wines and the districts permitted, and the grapes for *Cava* are delimited. The majority of these are within Catalunia but cannot be sold as originating from Penedés grapes (see under Cava below). Of the wines of this region, 80 per cent are white, but red wine production is on the increase.

Priorato

This small region is 48 km inland from Tarragona.

The yield from the Garnacha and Cariñena grapes is extraordinarily low, producing strong dark red wines very high in alcohol, minimum 13% but as high as 18%. There are also some sweet white dessert wines, which are slightly maderized (*rancio*: bitter, like Madeira). Since the early 1990s Cabernet Sauvignon, Syrah and Pinot Noir have been planted on the slopes of the Priorato mountains and the banks of the River Montsant, producing highly priced red wines of a very high quality. Montsant is expected to receive its DO in 2002.

Ribera del Duero

Not to be confused with *Ribeiro*, which is very close to the northern tip of Portugal, this region is approximately 100 km west of the southern part of Rioja on the River Duero and produces red wines of good quality. It became better known due to *Vega Sicilia* which is one of Spain's most expensive wines, matured over many years in oak. A *crianza* wine from this region must have a minimum of one year in oak of its two calendar years of maturing. Another high-quality red wine is *Pesquera* made from the grape of that name.

Rias Baixas

Situated in Galicia in the extreme north-west of Spain on the Atlantic coast, the region comprises five sub-zones: *Val do Salnés, Condado do Tea, O Rosal, Soutomaior* and *Ribeira do Ulla*. The white wines are based on the albariño grape. Malo-lactic has either not been permitted or is only permitted in part. They are highly acidic and best drunk young up to three years old. Wines sold as *Rias Baixas* are produced from six permitted white varieties. Wines labelled *Rias Baixas Albariño* must contain 100 per cent albariño grapes, those sold under *Rias Baixas Condado do Tea*, a minimum of 70 per cent *albariño* and *treixadua, Rias Baixas O Rosal*, must contain a minimum of 70 per cent *albariño* and *loureiro*, but under the other three sub-zones they must contain a minimum of 70 per cent *albariño* grapes, with the remaining 30 per cent originating from the stated sub-zone.

Barrel Rias Baixas are wines which have spent three months in oak. *Red Rias Baixas* is produced from six listed red varietals.

Rioja

Named after the River Oja, this district is in the north of Spain astride the Rio Ebro. It is divided into three districts: Rioja Alta, Rioja Alavesa and Rioja Baja, in quality order. Red, white and rosé wines are produced. Red Rioja is made from Tempranilla, Garnacha, Graciano and Mazuela grapes, white Rioja is mainly from the Macabéo (Viura), plus Malvasia Riojana and Garnacho Blanca.

The red wines may be of outstanding quality. They are matured in oak casks in the same way as claret, taking on an oak bouquet and taste.

Riojas are bound by the same ageing minimums as other Spanish wines but the details are more specific.

Rioja Joven on the label means that the wine has not been matured in oak at all or for less than one year (red) and less than six months (white) and has spent some months in bottle. *Crianza* is wine released in its third year, one year of which must have been spent in *barricas* for red wines and six months for whites. *Reserva* on the label means that the wine has been matured in *barricas* for a minimum of one year for red and six months for white and rosé wines, plus a further two years in bottle or vice versa. *Gran reserva* on the label means that the wine has been made in an exceptional year, and has been matured in *barricas* for a minimum of two calendar years plus three calendar years in bottle. White and rosé *Gran reservas* spend a minimum of six months in barricas and three years in bottle. The *barricas* are oak and hold 225 litres.

White Rioja wines may be dry or medium sweet.

Red Rioja wines are excellent when served with strongly flavoured dishes such as game, casseroles and roasts, and will also complement spaghetti bolognese. Light dishes are likely to be overpowered by the strong flavour of these wines. The red wines generally benefit from being opened well in advance of serving.

Rueda

This mainly white-wine-producing region is found west of Ribera del Duero. The current DO regulations for this region were established in 1992. Rueda wines must contain a minimum 50 per cent of the local *Verdejo* grape, and the Rueda Superior 85 per cent. Other permitted varieties for blending with the *Verdejo* are the *Viura* and *Sauvignon Blanc*. The still wines may be either aged in oak for approximately six months or sold immediately, the Rueda Espumoso must be matured for a minimum of nine months and must contain a minimum 85 per cent *Verdejo*. It is made by the *método tradicional*. In 2001 red wines were classified under the DO. They are made from Tempranilla, Cabernet Sauvignon, Merlot and Garnacha.

Tarragona

Situated on the coast south of Penedés, this region produces DO graded Tarragona Classico Licoroso, sweet red fortified wines high in alcohol matured in oak for a minimum of twelve years, Tarragona Campo red for immediate drinking, Falset red which is good for ageing, dry white and rosé wines.

Valdepeñas

This region is immediately south of La Mancha. It has a yellow/red to white stony soil with a chalky sub-soil; this retains water, thus making the region better for wines than La Mancha. There are two grape varieties producing high alcoholic wines, the Airén and the Tempranillo, known here as Cencibel. White wines are from the Airén, rosés and light reds from a mixture of the two, and reds from the Cencibel. The whites and rosés should be drunk young, when they are fresh and fruity. Mostly red wines are produced, classified either as light reds or reds. The light reds are high in alcohol (11.5–14.5% abv) and are best when young, light, fresh and fruity. The *reserva* and *gran reserva* reds must be 100 per cent Cencibel and are 12.5–15% abv). The regional parliament law referred to under La Mancha (p. 84) also applies

to Valdepeñas. The light reds accompany light meat dishes such as veal and poultry; the reds are good with lamb cutlets particularly, and other red meats.

Cava

This is a delimited region, where good-quality sparkling wine is made by the *método tradicional*. This DO was created when Spain joined the EU. Until this time it was an appellation referring to the production method rather than to the origin. The majority of Cava wine is produced in and around Penedés, with San Sadurní d'Anoia being the main centre. The Cava wines produced in the Penedés are generally made from a blend of Macabeo, Xarel.lo and Parellada, and very often Chardonnay. Outside Penedés the Macabeo is the principal varietal used. Cordonníu and Freixenet are the two largest producers of high-quality Cavas. Of the smaller producers, 'Juvé y Camps Reserva dela Familia' is exceptional.

Vinos Espumosos

This is a national DOC (Denominación de Origen Controlada) for sparkling wines (see Chapter Five).

PORTUGAL

Although Portugal is best known for its port wine, this accounts for perhaps 2 per cent of the wine production of the country. The improved quality and control of Portuguese wines, together with their excellent value for money, is making them better known and more acceptable to table wine drinkers. Until recently the wine industry, with the exception of one or two private companies, has lacked organization and direction, and the very low prices for their grapes received by the farmers was insufficient to allow them to invest in new, modern equipment. Entry into the EU has caused large amounts of money to be invested through the Common Agricultural Policy. The quality of the wines has risen considerably since the late 1980s and is continuing to do so. The predicted change in

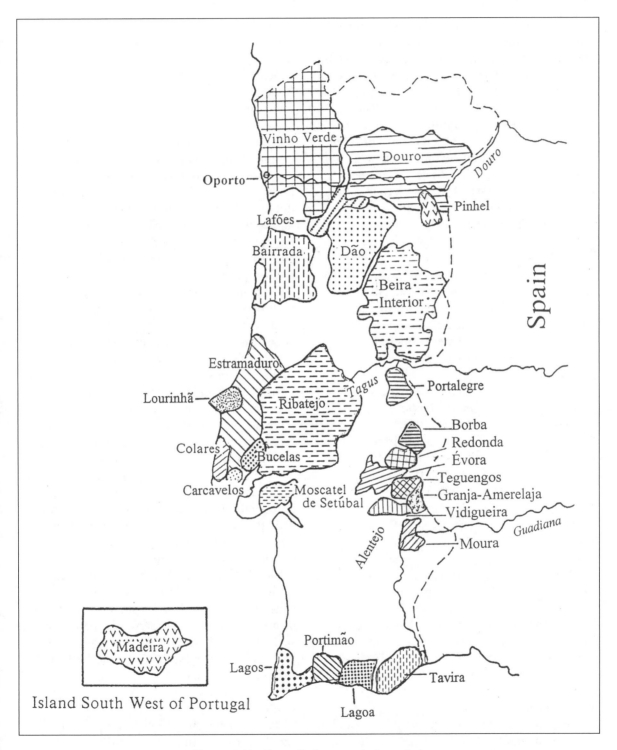

Figure 4.11 *Portugal's demarcated wine regions*

the outdated barrel-ageing regulations will further assist this improvement. The refreshing factor in this transformation is that the indigenous varietals have been retained with just 500 ha of Cabernet Sauvignon having been planted, representing 0.2 per cent of the vineyard area. Portuguese wines therefore offer the wine consumer an interesting range of flavours and styles. At the time of writing there are 42 DOCs similar to the French AOCs (see Figure 4.11), 9 IPRs (Indicação de Proveniencia Regulamentada) close to the French VDQSs, and 8 VRs (Vinhos Regionais) regional wines similar to the French VdP. The DOCs are:

Vinho Verde	Ribatejo
	Ribatejo Toma
Porto	Ribatejo Santarém
Douro	Ribatejo Cartaxo
Beira Interior	Ribatejo Chamusca
Dão	Ribatejo Almeirim
Bairrada	Ribatejo Coruche
Lafões	Alentejo
Távora/Varosa	Alentejo Portalegre
Colares	Alentejo Borba
Carcavelos	Alentejo Redondo
Bucelas	Alentejo Reguengos
Arruda	Alentejo Vidigueira
	Alentejo Évora
	Alentejo Moura
Alenquer	Alentejo Granja-Amareleja
Lourinhã	Lagos
Torres Vedras	Portimão
Óbidos	Lagoa
Setúbal	Tavira
Palmela	Madeira

Other than Madeira (see Chapter Five) from the island of that name, whose wines are sold under the name of the grape, most of Portugal's wines are sold under the name of the region.

Vinho Verde
This region is mainly in the Minho province and is in the extreme north-west of Portugal. There are six areas:

Monção
Lima
Braga
Penefiel
Basto
Amarante

Monção, Basto and Amarante are the best areas.

Vinho Verde derives its name from the fact that the grapes used are 'green', meaning slightly under-ripe. Red, white and rosé wines are produced. Although the white wines are better known in this country, red wines account for over half the Vinho Verde production. The white wines are fairly popular in the UK, the red wines are rarely exported.

The grapes are trained high off the ground on trellises or even on the branches of trees. This method of cultivation is called *enforcado* and allows the ground underneath to be used for crops while being shaded from the sun. Growing so high off the ground, the grapes do not benefit from reflected and radiated heat from the ground as do those grown in the normal way. They are therefore under-ripe at harvest time and contain a very high proportion of malic acid. This produces a strong malolactic fermentation which traditionally (although not always now) takes place in the bottle, others have a little carbon dioxide added, both methods giving a slight sparkle. This applies to all the Vinho Verde wines, and they should both be drunk when very young and fresh. They should both be served chilled.

The white wines are highly acidic, dry and low in alcohol, although some less dry and softer wines are being produced to suit the British palate. They are excellent served as aperitifs in hot weather. The white and rosé wines will accompany fish dishes or even Chinese meals; the reds will accompany stews.

Minho VR
As stated previously, Vinho Verde has been and still is the predominant wine produced in the Minho province and is sold under its own DOC.

The region has recently been divided into 11 sub-regions and the Minho DOC has been created for table wines with characteristics other than those of Vinho Verde. Possibly the most important wines in the future will be made from the Alvarinho grape which is producing good-quality wines in the north-east of the region. This is the same varietal as the albariño which is producing such good wines across the border in north-west Spain.

Porto (see pp. 126–8)

Douro

Famous for its Port wines (now a separate DOC), the Douro is also responsible for producing red, white and rosé (*vinho rosado*) still and sparkling wines. Barca Velha was the first red wine of real quality produced in the Douro by Fernando Nicolau de Almeida at Ferriera and this was in the 1950s. It has taken a long time for table wines to be taken seriously by the growers in the Douro, and it is only since the 1990s that they have been planting vineyards for the specific purpose of producing table wines. Touriga Nacional, Tinta Roriz (Tempranilla) and Tinto Cão are three of the Port grapes which are producing quality red table wines. These wines benefit from some oak and bottle ageing. The white wines are generally dry and are suitable with hors-d'oeuvres and chicken dishes; the reds have a deep colour and will accompany stews and offals, for example liver and bacon.

Dão

Just south of the Douro, Dão (pronounced 'down') is situated in the centre of Portugal. The twelve approved grape varieties are grown on terraced slopes of granite hills, producing 80 per cent red and 20 per cent white wines. As in the Douro, Touriga Nacional, Tinta Roriz and Tinto Cão are producing good red table wines.

The red wines, which may be of a very high quality, mature in cask for a minimum of eighteen months, but usually a lot longer. They are then matured in bottle, often for many more years.

The white wines are dry and light and should be drunk young, as they become flabby quite quickly. The white wines are suitable as aperitifs or served with light fish dishes, quiches, Chinese meals and chicken dishes. They should be served well chilled.

The reds may be strong powerful wines, which are hard and full of tannin when young, but which mature into soft full-flavoured wines. They will accompany all roast meats and cheese.

Bairrada

Bairrada is situated between the southern half of the Dão region and the western coast. This region became a regulated area only in 1979. Its name originates from the local name for the clay soil, *barro*. This is the best soil for the *Baga* grape. It has been producing high-quality wines for a very long time.

Red wines accounting for close to 80 per cent of the production are usually blended, *Baga* being the principal variety. They are strong in colour, flavour and alcohol and currently must be matured for one and a half years in cask plus a further six months in bottle before sale, but this is set to change in the near future. Many are matured in cask much longer, and the best Bairrada wines will mature in bottle for many years. They are suitable for service with strong meat dishes and will accompany game, roasts and strongly flavoured cheeses.

The most widely planted white grape is the *Maria Gomes*. The white varietals are planted on a sandy soil. The wines are either light and fruity, and ready for drinking a year after the harvest, or more structured full-bodied wines which may have undergone some wood fermentation and will mature in bottle. A large quantity of sparkling wine is produced by the traditional method (second fermentation in the bottle), which has a controlled appellation. Rosé wines and brandies are also produced in Bairrada

Estramaduro VR

This is the largest wine-producing region in

Portugal with 63,302 ha of vines. Although the cooperativess produce the majority of the wine due to the very high number of growers (56,167), small producers are being recognized helped by the upgrading of seven areas to DOC. These are Lourinhã, Tores Vedras, Arruda, Alenquer, Òbidas, Encostas de Aire and Alcobaça. Lourinhã produces only brandy (*aguardente*) which is 35% abv, and aged a minimum of two years before bottling.

Colares

This small region situated on the west coast, north-west of Lisbon, is famous for its ungrafted Ramisco vines. These appear to be immune to the ravages of phylloxera owing to the depth of the sand 'soil', which reaches down 8–10 metres.

Red and white wines are produced, the majority being red. They are very dark in colour, best when aged in bottle for a few years, and suitable for service with the same dishes as the red Bairrada wines. The white wines are produced from the Malvasia grape.

The vines are planted in trenches to protect them from the strong salty winds. The vineyard workers wear peculiar hats to prevent them from suffocating if the sand should collapse and bury them.

Carcavelos

This is a very small region on the coast just west of Lisbon, where sweet white fortified wines with an almond/nutty bouquet and flavour are produced. These wines are little known in the UK.

Bucelas

Just north of Lisbon, this is a small region where the soil is mainly clay, producing a dry white wine from the Arinto grape which often ages well and will accompany fish, chicken and veal dishes.

Setúbal

This region is a little further south and produces a famous fortified dessert wine (16–20% abv)

which ages well in cask. The younger wines (five years old) are dark straw-coloured and have a strong honeyed nose and flavour. The older wines (25 years old and upwards) are almost brown in colour and have a caramel taste. When produced from a minimum of 85 per cent Muscat grapes with the variety stated on the label, it may be called *Moscatel de Setúbal*. These wines are suitable to serve with strong cheese, on their own or at the end of a meal.

Alentejo

Covering 30 per cent of Portugal, this region produces mainly red wines. Eight of its districts have been upgraded to DOC. They are Portalegre, Borba, Redondo, Reguengos, Vidigueira, Évora, Moura and Granja-Amereleja. The granite and clay soil and climatic conditions create an excellent environment for winemaking. All other wines are sold under the Alentejano regional appellation (VR).

Ribatejo

White wines predominate in this large region north of Lisbon, but it is the stronger and fuller red wines from the limestone hills which are the best wines. The best-quality and most popular red grape is the periquita. This region is where most 'international' varietals were planted in the 1980s, but the wines produced under the seven DOCs (see p. 90) must be produced from native grape varieties. All other wines are sold under the Ribatejano regional appellation (VR).

Algarve VR

The Algarve is better known as a holiday resort than a wine-producing area, and the red and white wines are of average quality. There are four DOCs: Lagos, Portimão (better known for its sardines), Lagoa and Tavira.

Madeira

See Chapter Five.

OTHER COUNTRIES

USA

The USA is the world's fourth-largest wine producer, with 48 of the 50 American states producing wine; there are 1,500 wineries in North America. The major areas are found in California and New York State, and other regions have been developed in Oregon, Washington, Idaho, Texas and Virginia, but California produces 90 per cent of American wine. It is usually the cooler areas, the temperature often regulated by sea mists coming in from the Pacific, which produce the best wines. Napa and Sonoma are the best-known regions and they produce the finest wines in America. Mendocino is a producer of quality wines and Monterey County is coming to the fore with some excellent Chardonnays and Pinot Noirs in particular.

A wide range of grape varietals are grown in California but it is the Cabernet Sauvignon, Merlot, Pinot Noir, Zinfandel, Chardonnay and Sauvignon Blanc which predominate and top-quality table and sparkling wines are produced here. Although these coastal areas produce the majority of the fine wines it is the vast Central Valley region which produces 85 per cent of all Californian wine. The Central Valley output is predominantly of ordinary quality, but there are one or two fine wines being produced.

In 1980 five general wine-growing areas were defined in California: North Coast, Central Valley, Sierra Foothills, Central Coast and South Coast. Within these large areas there are smaller areas taking their names from their county. The AVA (Approved Viticultural Area, now called American Viticultural Area) classification system commenced in 1978 but the first AVA, which was in Augusta, Missouri, was not designated until 1980. This system is controlled by the Tax and Trace Bureau (TTB) of the Treasury Department. There are currently around 128 designated AVAs, but to complicate things there are AVAs for the general wine-growing areas, for some of the counties such as Napa and Monterey as well as the smaller districts such as Chalone and Livermore, which are both in the Central Coast area. Besides this system there is a labelling law.

Wines carrying a region, state or county appellation must contain a minimum of 75 per cent of grapes from that state or county. All AVAs (which include Napa, Sonoma Valley, Monterey and Mendocino) must contain a minimum of 85 per cent of the named varietal. If two or three grapes are to be named the percentage of each must be stated. If the year of the vintage is to be stated, the wine must contain 95 per cent of grapes from that year. 'Estate bottled', means 100 per cent of the grapes have come from a single AVA, from an estate's own vineyards, or from vineyards owned or controlled by the estate.

Many of the top red wines of California are made from the classic Bordeaux blends of grapes and in 1998 the name Meritage was introduced to provide a recognizable high-quality name. Red Meritage wines are made from a blend of two or more of the following varieties: Cabernet Sauvignon, Merlot, Cabernet Franc, Malbec, Petit Verdot, St Macaire, Gros Verdot and Carmenère. White Meritage wines are made from a blend of two or more of the following varieties: Sauvignon Blanc, Semillon and Sauvignon Vert. No single variety may make up more than 90 per cent of either blend (Meritage Association). A licence to use the name must be obtained from the Meritage Association.

California

North Coast   This is probably the best-known area, made up from the following counties: Lake, Mendocino, Sonoma, Napa, Solano, Contra Costa and Alameda.

Napa is California's top wine region and with Sonoma produces much of America's best wines. It stretches from south of the town of Napa, in a north-north-west direction, to beyond Calistoga, a distance of approximately 35 miles. It is perhaps thirteen miles wide at its widest point, but considerably less in parts. It is cooler in the south due to the proximity of the Ocean and there are marked

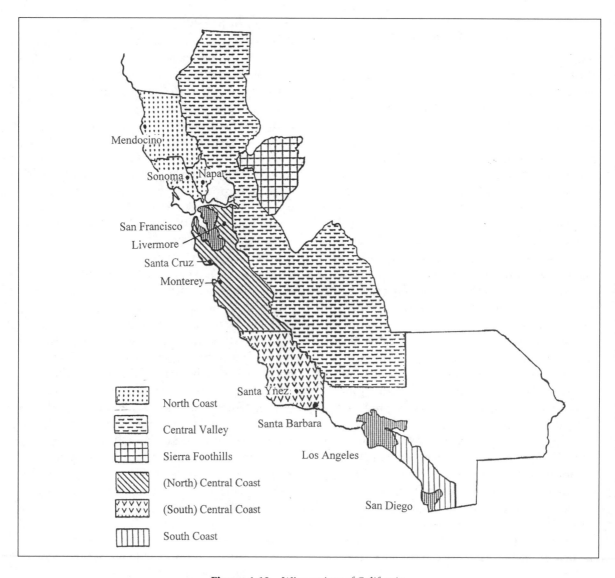

Figure 4.12 *Wine regions of California*

differences between the hillside vineyards and those on the valley floor. There are currently (2002) thirteen sub-appellation AVAs within the Napa County AVA. They are Howell Mountain, Chiles Valley District, Diamond Mountain District, Spring Mountain District, St Helena, Rutherford, Oakville, Atlas Peak, Stags Leap District, Yountville, Mount Veeder, Wild Horse Valley, Pope Valley and Los Carneros. A fourteenth, Oak Knoll, has been applied for.

Sonoma shares Napa's western border and runs in the same direction, a distance of approximately 58 miles, and is 24 miles wide at its widest point. Although considerably larger, it has a similar amount of land under vines.

Napa and Sonoma also share one of the very best AVAs, that of Carneros in the extreme south of both counties, which is their coolest area, kept cooler due to the proximity of the Ocean and San Francisco Bay. These cause cool breezes and sea mists which prolong the growing season. Some of the best Pinot Noir and Chardonnay wines are produced from grapes from this AVA. Within the Sonoma AVA there are two regional AVAs, Northern Sonoma and Sonoma Coast. The sub-appellations are Rockpile, Alexander Valley, Knight's Valley, Dry Creek Valley, Russian River Valley, Chalk Hill, Sonoma County Green Valley, Sonoma Valley, Sonoma Mountain, Sonoma Coast and Carneros.

Mendocino   The wine-producing AVAs are in the southern part of the county. Mendocino AVA is the general AVA for the area. The sub-appellations are Anderson Valley, McDowell Valley, Mendocino Ridge, Cole Ranch, Yorkville Highlands, Potter Valley and Redwood Valley. These are smaller and more specific AVAs.

Fetzer Vineyards, McDowell Valley Vineyards and Parducci Wine Cellars are well-known and well-respected large producers. Roederer is making traditional method sparkling wine.

Lake   Lake County is on the eastern border of Mendocino and has three sub-appellations: Clear Lake, Guenoc Valley and Benmore Valley. Clear Lake, which surrounds this large lake, is the largest and most important of the three with the majority of the vines planted on the south-west side.

Central Valley   This area produces 85 per cent of all Californian wine, but it is not recognized for its quality wines.The main wine area is situated between Yolo, just north-west of Sacramento and Fresno in the south, although grapes are grown further south. Perhaps the Central Valley's biggest claim to fame in the wine business is that E&J Gallo, the largest winery and producer in the world (40 per cent of California's total wine production) is located at Modesto, halfway between Sacramento in the north and Fresno in the south.

Sierra Foothills   The following counties make up this area: Yuba, Sierra Nevada, Placer, El Dorado, Amador, Calaveras, Tuolumne and Mariposa

which are situated on the border with Nevada and the middle section of the Central Valley.

Central Coast   This regional AVA runs down the coast from Oakland and San Francisco in the north through Contra Costa, Santa Clara, San Benito, Monterey, San Luis Obispo and Santa Barbara in the south, just north of Los Angeles. The recently approved (1999) San Francisco Bay area AVA has created a northerly sub-region comprising the counties surrounding San Francisco to the south of the Golden Gate Bridge, and includes the Santa Cruz Mountain area, the Santa Clara Valleys and Livermore.

South Coast   This area, which is to the south of Los Angeles, is in San Bernardino and Riverside counties.

European vines are grown extensively, producing wines sold under the name of the vineyard coupled with the grape variety (varietal) or varieties used to produce the wine. Occasionally a mark is used, for example 'Trilogy', which is a blend of Merlot, Cabernet Sauvignon and Cabernet Franc. This is produced by the Flora Springs Wine Company in Napa. For many years European names such as Chablis and Burgundy were used to market the wines, but this has all but died out.

Throughout the Californian wine regions, excellent Chardonnay, Sauvignon Blanc, Pinot Blanc, Cabernet Sauvignon, Merlot, Pinot Noir and Zinfandel wines are produced. The local grape varietal of Zinfandel produces a large amount of white (blush-coloured) wine as well as the high-quality full-bodied reds. Many of these wines have a very strong fruity bouquet and are high in alcohol.

Quality *méthode traditionnelle* sparkling wines are also produced, particularly in Sonoma county and the Napa valley. The terms *Champagne* and *méthode champenoise* are permitted to be used in America.

There are about 800 wineries in California. Some of the best are: Chalone, Saintsbury's, Beaulieu and

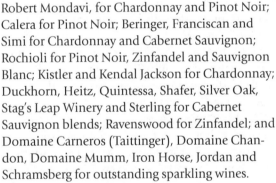

Robert Mondavi, for Chardonnay and Pinot Noir; Calera for Pinot Noir; Beringer, Franciscan and Simi for Chardonnay and Cabernet Sauvignon; Rochioli for Pinot Noir, Zinfandel and Sauvignon Blanc; Kistler and Kendal Jackson for Chardonnay; Duckhorn, Heitz, Quintessa, Shafer, Silver Oak, Stag's Leap Winery and Sterling for Cabernet Sauvignon blends; Ravenswood for Zinfandel; and Domaine Carneros (Taittinger), Domaine Chandon, Domaine Mumm, Iron Horse, Jordan and Schramsberg for outstanding sparkling wines.

Pacific Northwest
Three states make up the Pacific Northwest: Oregon, Washington State and Idaho.

Oregon, situated between California in the south and Washington State in the north, has six wine regions. The main one is the Willamette Valley AVA which is in the west of the state, stretching from Eugene in the south to Portland at the border with Washington. It is best known for its high-quality Pinot Noir wines, but Pinot Blanc, Pinot Gris and Riesling are well rated. Eyrie vineyards are also producing some good-quality Chardonnays. To the south is the Umpqua Valley AVA and further south reaching to the Californian

border, the Rogue Valley and Applegate Valley AVAs. Here Cabernet, Merlot and Gewürztraminer are of main importance. Small parts of the Columbia Valley and Walla Walla Valley AVAs are shared with Washington State. AVA wines which carry a grape varietal on the label must contain a minimum of 90 per cent of that varietal except for Cabernet Sauvignon for which 75 per cent (EU 85 per cent) is the minimum. If the origin is stated, it must be 100 per cent from the designated area.

Washington State relies on irrigation from the Columbia River to make up for the lack of rain. The shared AVAs noted above are mainly in Washington State, with the Columbia Valley by far the largest, encircling Red Mountain, Yakima Valley and Walla Walla AVAs. Puget Sound AVA is in the far west of the state and includes the islands in the Sound. Washington is known for its Merlots and Chardonnays, with Cabernet Sauvignon being the second-most-planted red grape. Sauvignon Blanc and Semillon grow well and there is a large quantity of off-dry Rieslings being produced.

Idaho has a very small wine region but produces some good Chardonnay, Chenin Blanc and Riesling wines.

New York State

Although known for its indigenous vines and crosses such as Concord, Catawba and Delaware, which produce wines with an unusual so-called *foxy* flavour, European vines are gradually taking over from them. The Finger Lakes, Lake Erie, Hudson River, Long Island with its sub-districts, The Hamptons and North Fork of Long Island; these are the AVAs, and are the districts which produce the quality wines.

Canada

Although wine production in Canada dates back to the middle of the nineteenth century, it is really only during the last 25 years that it has developed into a serious industry. Lead by the Inniskillin winery the introduction of vinifera vines was probably the turning point, since when non-vinifera vines have been steadily replaced with vinifera varietals. The other great influence was the success of the Icewines which were originally and still are produced from the hybrid Vidal, and later also from the Riesling. A number of European vines are being planted with a bias towards Alsace and German varietals, although Chardonnay and Merlot are producing quality wines. A federal appellation control system has been introduced called the Vintners Quality Alliance VQA which both Ontario and British Columbia have joined. There are controlled appellations (VAs) and all wines bearing the VQA seal must have been passed by both an analysis and a tasting panel. Wines displaying a designated VA must contain 85 per cent from that area. Wines displaying a varietal on the label must contain 85 per cent of that varietal with the other 15 per cent coming from their respective province.

The four provinces which produce wine are Ontario, British Columbia, Nova Scotia and Quebec, with Ontario and British Columbia being by far the most important. All the vineyards are located in the extreme south of the country. In Ontario, which has the largest Canadian wine-growing region, the vines are grown close to Lake Erie, Lake Ontario and into the Niagara peninsula.

The VAs are Niagara Peninsula, Lake Erie North Shore and Pelee Island, which is in Lake Erie. In British Columbia, the wine-growing region is in the extreme south-east of the province, on the border with Washington State. The VAs are Frazer Valley, The Islands, Similkameen and the Okanagan Valley, which is the largest and most important. Mission Hill is an important winery in British Columbia accounting for 20 per cent of the province's wines.

Argentina

Argentina is the fifth-largest producer in the world, producing wines of increasing quality. It has little rainfall and depends on irrigation for its viticulture. Mendoza is the largest region, producing over two-thirds of all Argentinian wine. Important sub-districts within Mendoza are Maipú, Lujon de Cujo and Tupugato. The Rio Negro is the most southerly wine region well south of Mendoza, and is therefore cooler, which suggests that Sauvignon Blanc may produce some good-quality wines here. The Salta area to the north of Mendoza is producing some of the best Argentinian Cabernet wines.

Good-quality wines as well as large quantities of ordinary reds and whites are produced from Cabernet Sauvignon, Malbec, Merlot, Chardonnay, Chenin Blanc, Johannisberg Riesling, Muscat and some local varietals, in particular Torrontez (white) and Bernardo (red). Malbec produces some of the best wines, and Cabernet Sauvignon and Merlot wines are developing well. Some Italian and Spanish red varieties have been introduced with marked success, as has a small amount of Syrah. There are some producers who are using stainless steel vats and maturing in oak, and some of these wines show very good potential.

Australia

Since 1960 Australian wines have undergone considerable change and have risen in popularity at a meteoric rate. From producing high alcoholic, heavily fortified and syrupy wines, Australia has

Figure 4.13 *Wine regions of Australia*

developed production of good-quality varietal wines. These wines are still reasonably high in alcohol, with strong characteristic grape flavours and intense fruit. Like many Californian wines they are ready for drinking earlier than some of the better-known European wines made from the same grape varieties. The red wines have less astringent tannins than their European counterparts, and the modern cool fermentation techniques coupled with enlightened blending have produced high-quality table wines at competitive prices. In 1997 the industry had expanded to 900 wineries.

Many of Australia's wines have an oaky bouquet and flavour, which are obtained during cask maturation and sometimes fermentation. This balances well with the strong fruit and grape flavours and the high alcohol content, but some of the wines are over-oaked, over-powering the fruit in the wine.

Wine is sold under the names of the grape varietals and the name of the producer. The most popular red grapes used are the Shiraz (Syrah) and the Cabernet Sauvignon, often being blended together. The Rhine Riesling had been the most popular for the white wines, but Chardonnay and Semillon have now overtaken it. In 1997 Chardonnay accounted for 57 per cent of the vintage of premium white wine grapes, Semillon nearly 23 per cent, and Riesling 15 per cent. Other varieties widely planted are the Sauvignon Blanc, Pinot Noir and the Merlot. There is currently slightly more white than red produced. All Australian states produce wine, but it is only in the southern parts of the country where there are real commercial producers. There are over 1,400 miles between the Swan Valley region in Western Australia and the Hunter Valley in New South Wales, so it is inevitable that there should be marked differences in the wines and the most suitable grape varieties. However, the Australian 'approachable' style seems to run through most of the wines which are exported.

Australian wine regions or Geographical Indications (GIs) are in the process of being redefined, therefore the regions and sub-regions identified on the map (Figure 4.13) and in the text are as at 2002. The regions or sub-regions marked with an asterisk were not finalized at time of going to print. The larger wine zones of Australia have been listed under Appendix 7.

South Australia

This is by far the largest wine-producing State, accounting for 55 per cent of all Australian wine. The Barossa Valley, Coonawarra Valley*, Padthaway, McLaren Vale, Eden Valley, Clare Valley, Langhorne Creek, Adelaide Hills, Adelaide Plains and Riverlands are the most important regions for winemaking. Riverlands produces 60 per cent of the state's wine but it is mainly of jug and box wine quality. The Barossa Valley is the best-known region, and produces some of Australia's best Shiraz, Cabernet Sauvignon and Riesling wines with an abundance of Chardonnay and surprisingly Grenache and Mourvèdre wines. Coonawara, without doubt the leading Australian Cabernet Sauvignon region, owes this to the famous 'terra rossa' soil found here coupled with the extensive

cloud which moderates the ripening period. Shiraz and Chardonnay followed by Riesling are the next most important varietals. Clare Valley, another important region, produces Australian top-of-the-range Riesling wines with Cabernet Sauvignon and Shiraz following close behind.

South Australia's most famous wine is Penfold's Grange made from a blend of predominantly Shiraz grapes.

New South Wales

This is the next largest producer, accounting for 27 per cent of Australian wine. The Hunter River Valley is the centre of the state's quality wine production. More white than red is produced. Other lesser regions are Riverina, which is wholly irrigated, Hastings River, Mudgee, Orange, Cowra and Canberra District. The lower part of the Hunter Valley produces outstanding Semillon and Shiraz wines which require bottle age, the Semillon up to ten years, the Shiraz twenty years and more. The upper part of the Hunter Valley is predominantly for white grapes, with Chardonnay and Semillon producing early maturing full-bodied fruity wines of high quality. The Riverina area is producing outstanding dessert wines.

Victoria

This State produces just half the quantity of NSW. It is known for its sweet Muscat dessert wines as well as for table wines. All the popular premium grapes are grown here, but the regions round Melbourne such as Geelong, Yarra Valley and Mornington Peninsula are producing some interesting Pinot Noir wines from young vineyards which have great potential. The Yara Valley is already established as the top Pinot Noir area in Australia. North East Victoria is famous for its Muscat and Tokay fortified wines. Rutherglen and Glenrowan are the most important regions for these, although even here good Chardonnay and Semillon wines are produced. Goulburn Valley, King Valley* and Grampians are other top regions. It is also developing a sparkling wine industry.

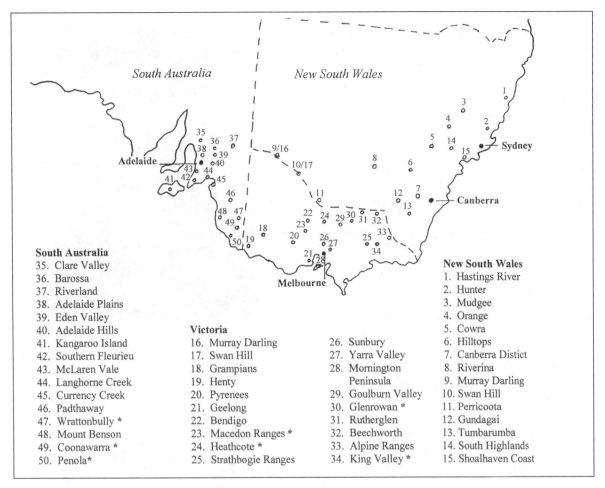

South Australia
35. Clare Valley
36. Barossa
37. Riverland
38. Adelaide Plains
39. Eden Valley
40. Adelaide Hills
41. Kangaroo Island
42. Southern Fleurieu
43. McLaren Vale
44. Langhorne Creek
45. Currency Creek
46. Padthaway
47. Wrattonbully *
48. Mount Benson
49. Coonawarra *
50. Penola*

Victoria
16. Murray Darling
17. Swan Hill
18. Grampians
19. Henty
20. Pyrenees
21. Geelong
22. Bendigo
23. Macedon Ranges *
24. Heathcote *
25. Strathbogie Ranges

26. Sunbury
27. Yarra Valley
28. Mornington
    Peninsula
29. Goulburn Valley
30. Glenrowan *
31. Rutherglen
32. Beechworth
33. Alpine Ranges
34. King Valley *

New South Wales
1. Hastings River
2. Hunter
3. Mudgee
4. Orange
5. Cowra
6. Hilltops
7. Canberra Distict
8. Riverina
9. Murray Darling
10. Swan Hill
11. Perricoota
12. Gundagai
13. Tumbarumba
14. South Highlands
15. Shoalhaven Coast

Figure 4.14 *South Eastern Australia*

Tasmania
This island to the south of Victoria is a very small producer concentrating on Chardonnay, Rhine Riesling, Pinot Noir and sparkling wines. The wine-growing regions are situated round Launceston in the north and Hobart in the south. Pipers River, with the excellent Pipers Brook vineyards, and Tamar Valley sub-regions are in the north, the Coal River, Derwent Valley, Huon Valley and East Coast sub-regions are in the south. The Pipers River region concentrates on producing fine Chardonnays, Rhine Rieslings and sparkling wines, the Tamar Valley on Cabernet Sauvignons, complex Chardonnays and powerful Pinot Noirs.

Fifty per cent of the southern region's grapes are Pinot Noir which is the major grape, except for the Coal River where Cabernet Sauvignon produces the best wines. Chardonnay is again the main white varietal.

South Eastern Australia
This is a region created to allow blending across states (see Figure 4.14) without breaking the label integrity scheme. It comprises New South Wales, Victoria, the south-east quarter of South Australia and the south-east quarter of Queensland, and Tasmania. Chardonnay is once again the main white varietal.

Western Australia
Although producing less quantity than Victoria, these wines are considered by many to be the very best from Australia. The Great Southern Region, Margaret River, Pemberton*, Perth Hills, Geographe and Swan Valley are the main regions. Chardonnay and Cabernet Sauvingnon account for 21 per cent and 17 per cent of the grapes in the Great Southern Region, followed by Riesing, Shiraz and Pinot Noir. The Margaret River specializes in Semillon, Cabernet Sauvingnon and Chardonnay, and Pemberton specializes in Chardonnay, Cabernet Sauvignon and Pinot Noir. Other varietals such as Sauvignon Blanc are being introduced.

In 1987 Australia introduced a Label Integrity Programme which since the 1990 vintage has been enforced by the Wine and Brandy Corporation. It means that:

- if a varietal is stated, there must be a minimum of 85 per cent of that varietal in the wine.
- if the origin is stated, it must contain a minimum of 85 per cent from the stated region;
- if the vintage is stated, it must contain a minimum of 95 per cent from the stated year.

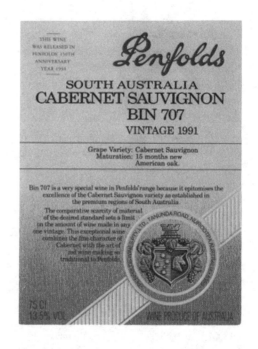

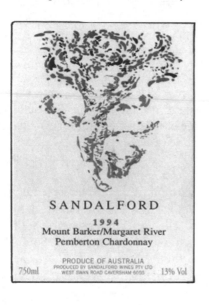

Austria

Following the 1985 scandal, Austria has developed an important wine industry, which produces more wine than Germany. It produces still red, white and rosé wines, sparkling wines (*shaumwein*) plus a small quantity of *strohwien*, a term for wine made from grapes of Beerenauslese (sugar content) level which have been dried on straw mats or reeds for a minimum of three months.

There are four principal wine regions: Niederösterreich (Lower Austria), Burgenland, Steiermark (Styria) and Wien (Vienna). These four regions comprise a number of sub-regions.

Niederösterreich

This is the most northerly and completely surrounds Wien. The north of Wien is Weinviertel which is by far the largest sub-district of Austria. While there are a few producers making high-quality red as well as white wines the majority is white of a table wine quality. To the south of Weinviertel is Donauland, with Traisental, Kremstal and Kamptal on the west side, the latter two producing good-quality Grüner Veltliners and Rieslings. Immediately west of Kremstal is Wachau which is justly respected for its excellent Grüner Veltliners and Rieslings which are known for their ability to age well. South of Wien are Thermenregion and Carnuntum, two regions which produce interesting wines from local varietals.

Wien

Wien is by far the smallest of the four regions with just over 700 ha of vines in and around Vienna. The wines are made from a number of indigenous and international varietals and are of ordinary to good quality.

Burgenland

This region is to the south of the Niederösterreich and runs south along the western border of Hungary. The sub-district Neusiedlersee borders Hungary in the extreme north and is renowned for its outstanding botrytised wines which are made from a number of varietals. The grapes for these wines are grown along the banks of Lake Neusiedl which is the cause of *botrytis*. In other parts of this sub-district good-quality red wines from Zweigelt, Blaufränkisch and Cabernet Sauvignon are produced, along with very good Chardonnays. Neusiedlersee-Hügelland, on the west side of the lake also produces botrytised wines from its lakeside vineyards. Besides the *Beerenauslese* (BA) and *Trockenbeerenauslese* (TBA) wines, it is known for its outstanding *Ausbruch* wines. *Ausbruch* wines were traditionally made in the town of Rust, by adding fresh grapes to botrytised grapes of TBA quality. This assisted the fermentation and produced a wine more akin to Sauterne and Barsac than the TBAs of Germany. The minimum oechsle level for *Ausbruch* is 138° which is between the BA and TBA levels. Away from the lake, quality red and white wines are also produced. Both Neusiedlersee and Neusiedlersee-Hügelland produce *Eiswein*, particularly in years when *botrytis* does not form. Mittelburgenland and Südburgenland to the south have a reputation for spicy red wines made from Bläufränkisch grapes.

Steiermark

Steiermark, to the south of Südburgenland, borders Slovenia. It has three sub-districts: Südosteiermark, Süsteiermark and Weststeiermark. Südosteiermark and Süsteiermark produce high-quality white wines from Chardonnay and Sauvignon Blanc, while Weststeiermark produces rosé wines.

Bulgaria

Since the industry was re-established between 1950 and 1960, Bulgaria has become a major force in wine production. Ninety per cent of its wine is exported. The most common exports are Cabernet Sauvignon, Merlot and Chardonnay, but there are some local grape varieties which also do well, such as the red Mavrud, Kadarka and Melnik, and the white Rkatziteli. The 1978 wine regulations introduced delimited areas within five regions and instituted three quality levels.

Controliran is the highest classification which is similar to the French *appellation controlée* system, designating areas and permitted varietals within these areas. There are two lower-quality levels similar to French VDQS and Vin de Pays wines: Special Reserve and Reserve. The requirements for these categories are that the red wine has been matured in oak for a minimum of three years, and white wine two years. Only the very best wines are permitted to be labelled Special Reserve. The five regions are: Northern, Southern, Eastern, South-western and Sub-Balkan, the central area, which is situated in the Balkan mountains.

Figure 4.15 *Wine regions of Bulgaria*

Chile

Chile stretches 2,650 miles north to south, and averages just 110 miles wide. The wine area is halfway down, between 33° and 36° south. It is bounded by the Andes in the west and the Pacific Ocean in the east, with a coastal range of hills running north to south between the plain and the ocean. It is thought the isolation caused by the Andes and Pacific Ocean is the reason why Chile has never been attacked by *Phylloxera* or *Oidium* (powdery mildew). Irrigation is a simple matter as

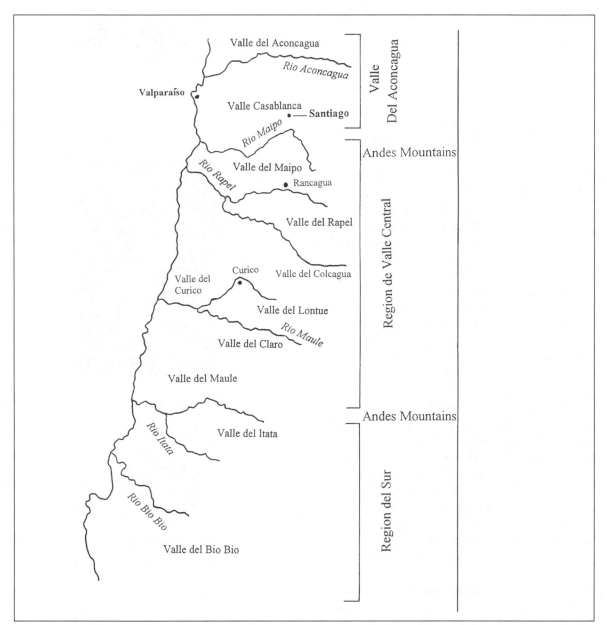

Figure 4.16 *Wine regions of Chile*

in Argentina, with the melting snows running down from the Andes in a number of rivers.

There are five viticultural regions. From north to south these are:

1   Atacama
2   Coquimbo
3   Aconcagua
4   Valle Central
5   Sur

Atacama and *Coquimbo* are of little consequence, producing mainly table grapes and very little wine. *Sur*, divided into two sub-zones: Valle del Itata and Valle del Bio Bio, produces wine for local consumption.

Region de Aconcagua is named after the river and is north and west of Santiago. It is divided into two sub-regions: Valle del Aconcagua and Valle Casablanca. The Valle del Aconcagua is to the north of Santiago and is producing some of the best Cabernet Sauvignon wines of Chile. Near to the west coast, and south of Valparaiso, is the Valle Casablanca. This sub-region is open to the Pacific and has a similar situation to the Carneros and Monterey regions of California in that sea mists roll in from the ocean, dropping the temperature considerably and thus prolonging the growing season. The vintage may be a month later than in the nearby Maipo Valley. A relatively new sub-region, it produces the best Sauvignon Blanc and Chardonnay wines of Chile and some excellent Carmenères, but is prone to late frosts, which in 1991 reduced the vintage by 50 per cent. The wines are concentrated, of high quality and more expensive than other Chilean whites. Good examples are Vermonte and Caliterra.

Region de Valle Central is divided into four sub-regions: Maipo, Rapel, Curico and Maule.

The Maipo Valley is the classic area for Cabernet Sauvignon, Caliterra, Cousino Macul, Concha Y Toro and Santa Rita being some of the best producers. There are also some outstanding Cabernet Sauvignon wines produced by Errazuriz in Aconcagua.

The Rapel Valley has two zones, Valle del Cachapoal and Valle del Colchagua. Los Vascos is a top producer of Cabernet Sauvignon, and there are some good Chardonnays being made. Valle del Curico and Valle del Maule generally produce quantities of table wine quality, but with one or two vineyards producing high-quality wines.

The wine law of 1995 defined the above regions and sub-regions and introduced labelling laws. Wine sold under the name of a grape must contain a minimum of 75 per cent of the stated varietal. Wine sold under the name of a region or sub-region of origin must contain a minimum of 75 per cent from the stated varietal. Wine sold under a vintage must contain a minimum of 75 per cent of the stated year's harvest. However, for the EU market these percentages are raised to 85 per cent.

Confederation of Independent States (CIS)

Although very little wine from what was previously the Soviet Union is seen in the Western world, these states are the third-largest producer of wine in the world. Red, white, rosé, sweet, dry, still, sparkling and fortified wines, are all produced here, from a variety of Western European varietals and some local ones. *Ratziteli* is popular for white wines and *Saperavi* for red wines.

Large quantities of semi-sweet and sweet sparkling wines are produced: some by the traditional method of secondary fermentation in the bottle (bottle fermented), some by the Charmat process (bulk method), but the majority by the Russian Continuous Method, which involves passing the wine through a number of continuous pressurized tanks while it is fermenting.

Cyprus

In 1996 the EU banned the use of the word 'sherry', so Cyprus sherry and British sherry made from Cypriot grape must, which until then was the main outlet, was no longer permitted. With the introduction of this regulation, the wine industry was updated and revolutionized and now produces a range of red, white and sparkling crisp light wines, although many of these suffer from non-temperature controlled storage and transport. The best-known wine from Cyprus is still the red sweet dessert wine Commandarie St John. It is made from sun-dried grapes, fortified with grape spirit up to a maximum of 20% abv and is often *solera* matured. It is now the first wine of Cyprus to have a delimited area and protected name.

England and Wales

In the variable and unpredictable climate of England and Wales, 430 vineyards produce wines of from poor to good quality. Nearly all the wines (and certainly the better ones) are white but there is an expanding sparkling wine industry. They are often similar in style to the German wines, which after all are produced in similar latitudes, although some quality dry white wines are becoming available. Latitude 50.5°N passes through the vineyards of the Ahr and also through Torquay in the south-west of England. The majority of the vineyards are in the southern and south-eastern counties of England. The largest vineyard by far (100 ha) is Denbies in Surrey, but the average size is two hectares.

Müller-Thurgau, Seyval Blanc, Reichensteiner, Huxelrebe and Madeline Angevine are all popular grape varieties, and there are many others, such as Pinot Noir, which are being experimented with. English wines are usually rather highly priced in comparison with wines of similar quality from Germany due to the unreasonable UK taxation system. The excise duty alone is £1.12 plus 17.5 per cent VAT compared with French wine, which carries an equivalent of 2.5 pence on quality wines!

The excellent weather conditions in 1989 and 1990 produced a great improvement in both the quality and quantity made. The 1992 harvest exceeded 25,000 hl which meant that according to EU regulations an appellation system had to be brought in. Although the EU regulations do not permit hybrids such as Seyval Blanc to be considered for quality wine status, in 1992 the terms 'Welsh Vineyard Quality Wine' and 'English Vineyard Quality Wine' were introduced. In 1997 a third category, 'English Counties Regional Wine', was introduced which permits hybrid vines; but this does not permit VQPRD or QWPSR to be put on the labels of wines containing the juice from hybrid vines. UK wines do not as yet have any defined regional characteristics; they are best judged on the grapes used, and the winemaker.

Greece

Greek lettering and words do not come easily to most Britons and Americans. It is therefore difficult for the wines to become accepted in these countries, added to which the spectre of Retsina is still present and puts the majority of people off Greek wine.

Most Greek wine is produced for blending and local consumption. Less than 8 per cent is of controlled appellation, for which there are 29

designated regions. The best of these are for red wines and sweet muscat wines.

Retsina TA (Traditional Appellation)   The best-known wine from Greece is Retsina. This wine has had resin from Aleppo pine (best) added to it so that it is really an aromatized wine. Originally, when wine was stored in *amphorae*, these vessels were sealed with resin to prevent oxidation of the wine. It was thought that as the wine was better than unsealed wine, the resin must contain some preservative qualities. Soon pine resin was added to the wine itself, and then to the must prior to fermentation. The Greeks became accustomed to this flavour and grew to like it. However, the flavour of Retsina has very little appeal to Western European palates. There are three controlled appellations for Retsina, for which 20 per cent of the Retsina made qualifies. Most Retsina is white, 10 per cent is rosé and a little is red.

Côtes de Meliton AO is from the north of Greece, producing some good wines including the wines from Domaine Carras.

Château Carras is a high-quality Greek wine. The operation is modelled on a Bordeaux château. This wine is a blend of Cabernet Sauvignon, Cabernet Franc, and the Greek varietal Limnio, producing an excellent red wine.

Mavrodaphne of Patras AO (15% abv)   This is an AC wine produced in Patras. It is a slightly fortified sweet red dessert wine made from the grape of the same name. It is one of the better-known Greek wines in the UK.

Naoussa AO   This is a small area in the north of Greece producing sound red wines from the Xynomavro grape, which can age well. Boutari, a good reliable producer, makes excellent Naoussa wines: the Naoussa Grande Reserve is outstanding.

Nemea AO is another sound wine-producing area but from the southern part of Greece, producing good-quality red wine from the native grape Agiorgitiko. Boutari again produces high-quality wine here. The vineyards of both Naoussa and Nemea are planted high up, thus experiencing a cooler climate.

Samos AO (15% abv)   This sweet white dessert wine is made from the Muscat grape on the island of Samos. Other Muscats include Muscat of Patras, Muscat of Rhodes AO and Muscat of Lemnos AO.

Santorini AO   Once again a Boutari product proves to be exceptional – the Kallisti white wine which is made from the local Assyrtiko grape. There are also isolated good-quality blends with no AO. An example is the excellent Cava Tsantalis, which is a blend of Xynomavro and Cabernet Sauvignon, which has been aged in small oak casks. Much Greek wine is made from interesting local varietals, making a change from the usual run of Chardonnays, Cabernets and Merlots, although these grapes are being experimented with.

Hungary

Hungary produces red and white wines, the whites ranging from dry to very sweet. Egri Bikavér (Bull's Blood of Eger), probably the best-known red wine, is made from the Kékfrankos, Nagyburgundi (Blaufränkisch), Zweigelt and Merlot, although an increasing amount of Cabernet is being produced. The native white grapes such as Furmint, Hárslevelü, Olaszrizling and Ezerjó produce the majority of Hungarian wine, although Chardonnay, Sauvignon Blanc and other international varietals are being planted.

Some of the best Hungarian wines are produced along the northern shores of Lake Balaton, the largest lake in Europe. Balatoni Riesling is a medium sweet, full-bodied white wine, which is at its best when young. Balatoni Furmint is made from the Furmint grape and is a full-bodied sweet and luscious wine.

Tokaji (Tokay)   Tokay (Tokaj) is a town in the northeast of Hungary close to the Russian border. The wines come in various styles, but they are all made from the Furmint, Hárslevelü and Muskotály grapes. Wines made from non-aszú grapes are sold as *Tokaji Furmint*, *Tokaji Hárslevelü* and *Tokaji Muscat*. *Tokaji Szamorodni* is a full-bodied white wine, which may be either dry or sweet. This will be stated on the label.

Tokaji Aszú   This wine is made from grapes from the same vineyards as Tokaji Szamorodni. However, some grapes are left on the vine to be attacked by *Botrytis cinerea* (giving noble rot); the grapes are picked separately and lightly pressed. The remainder of these grapes is pressed into a paste; this is added to the must in measures of 20–25 kg, the capacity of a *putton* (a wooden bucket or tub). Three *puttony* on the label of a Tokaji Aszú means that 60–75 kg of this concentrated mixture has been added to a *gönc*, a cask which holds 136 litres of must. *Aszú* wines in the UK and USA are sold as three, four, five or six puttonyos; the more puttonyos, the richer and sweeter the wine will be. This very rich, sweet dessert wine is also slightly maderized (bitter, like Madeira). *Tokaji Aszú* wines are matured in oak barrels. The barrels for the high *puttony* wines must be a minimum of twelve years old.

Tokaji Eszencia   This is even sweeter and made from free-run Aszú grapes. It is extremely difficult to ferment and is rarely produced.

In 1997 new wine laws were introduced to replace the previous state-controlled system. These are more in line with the EU regulations. Quality wine is indicated on the label by the words *minosegu bor*, but the new system is still being consolidated.

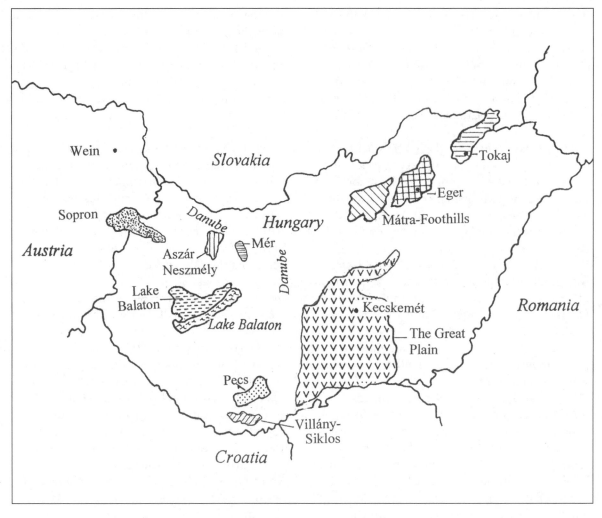

Figure 4.17 *Wine regions of Hungary*

Luxembourg

The vineyards of Luxembourg are situated on the River Moselle and produce similar wines to the country's northern neighbour, Germany. The appellation is Moselle Luxembourgeoise and the majority still white wine, although some Pinot Noir light reds and rosés are produced. The appellation for white and rosé sparkling wines produced by the méthode traditionnelle is *Crémant de Luxembourg*. Most of the production is drunk in Luxembourg but a little is now being exported.

New Zealand

Vines were introduced to New Zealand in 1819. European émigrés to New Zealand pioneered the wine industry, but it was not until the late 1970s that it really got on its feet. Today the majority of vineyards are on North Island, but an increasing number are appearing in the northern part of South Island, particularly in the Marlborough region.

New Zealand comprises two islands, North Island and South Island, North Island being on the same latitude as Tasmania. Its vines are the most easterly and southerly in the world. It has a

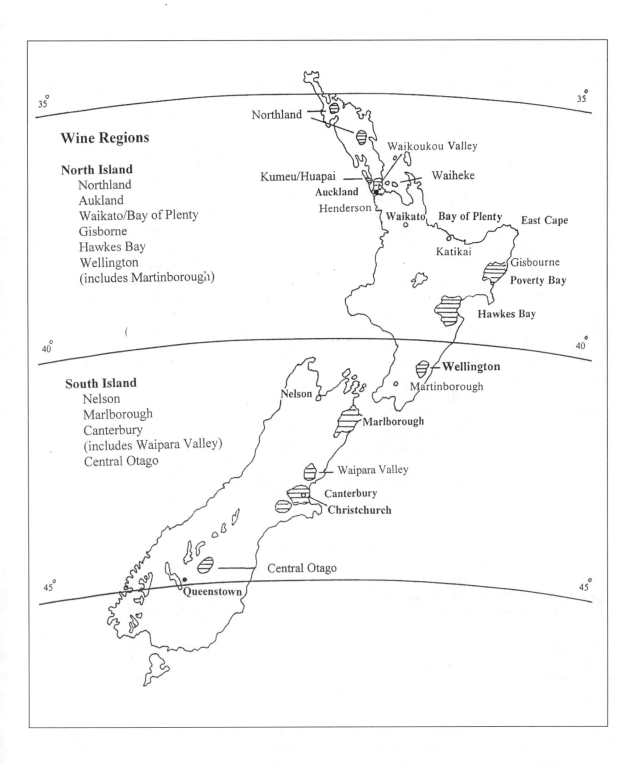

Figure 4.18 *Wine regions of New Zealand*

cooler and longer ripening period than Australia and is best known for its white wines. Wine production started around Auckland in North Island but has spread north to Northland and Kumeu, east to Bay of Plenty, Gisborne and Hawkes Bay, and south to Martinborough. In South Island the vineyards are sited in Marlborough, Nelson, Canterbury and Central Otago. Since 1973 Marlborough has been developed and is now New Zealand's largest exporter of wine, being justly famous for its powerful, pungent Sauvignon Blancs. The Chardonnay wines are of a high standard and the Pinot Noir red wines are beginning to establish themselves.

Chardonnay is now the most widely planted varietal in New Zealand, followed by Sauvignon Blanc and Müller Thurgau. Riesling, Chenin Blanc, Sémillon and Gewürztraminer are also grown. For the reds, Cabernet Sauvignon produces the best wines, often blended with some Merlot. Pinot Noir is tipped to develop well in the Wellington region round Martinborough, and a small amount of Pinotage is being developed; but it is Merlot that may prove to be the most suitable red grape for New Zealand. Like Australian wines, these wines are sold by the name of the grape variety or varieties used with name of the producer.

Slovenia
Established as a country in its own right in 1991, Slovenia produces a large amount of red and white table wine, the best known being the Lutomer Riesling. It is situated in the north-west part of what used to be Yugoslavia, close to the Austrian and Hungarian borders.

South Africa
The vineyards are situated in the south-western Cape and along the Orange River further to the north. The overwhelming majority, and the ones which produce the exported wines are in the south-west. South Africa produces a complete range of wines from 65 approved cultivars although only 30 of these are planted in any quantity. Of these the majority are from French and German vines plus the Pinotage, which was propagated in South Africa. It is a cross between the Cinsault and the Pinot Noir and was created by Professor Abraham Perold of the KWV (Ko-operatieve Wijnbouwers Vereniging or Co-operative Wine Growers' Association) in 1925. The first bottling of Pinotage was in 1961.

Both red and white still and sparkling table wines have reached a high standard. The South African sherry-style wines are still of high quality but the market for these is now small.

The Wine of Origin Scheme (WO) was introduced in 1973 and is administered by the South African Wine and Spirit Board. The WO seal on a bottle stating an origin guarantees that 100 per cent of the grapes have originated from the specified production unit which, from the smallest to the largest, can be an estate, ward, district or region. A ward is a demarcated viticultural area of which there are 46 (see Appendix 8). These comprise a small number of farms or estates which enjoy similar natural characteristics. A district (13) is a larger area such as Paarl, and a region (5) is a number of districts, e.g. Coastal Region. These larger delimited units allow for cross-district blending while still marketing the wine under a single origin.

All WO with a grape cultivar and or vintage stated, must contain 75 per cent (EU 85 per cent) of that varietal and or vintage. All WO wines must pass Wine and Spirit Board tasting and laboratory panels. The tasting panel will refuse certification if the wine is untypical of the grape variety, vintage or other characteristics, and surprisingly if the flavour is dominated by wood.

In 1993 an amendment to the Wine of Origin legislation introduced two geographical units – Western Cape and Northern Cape. The Western Cape comprises twelve of the thirteen delimited districts, the exception being Douglas (Northern Cape) which is well to the north on the Orange River. Wines sold under one of these geographical units may not claim WO status. Estate Brandy certification was also introduced for Potstill Brandy, brandy and Vintage Brandy.

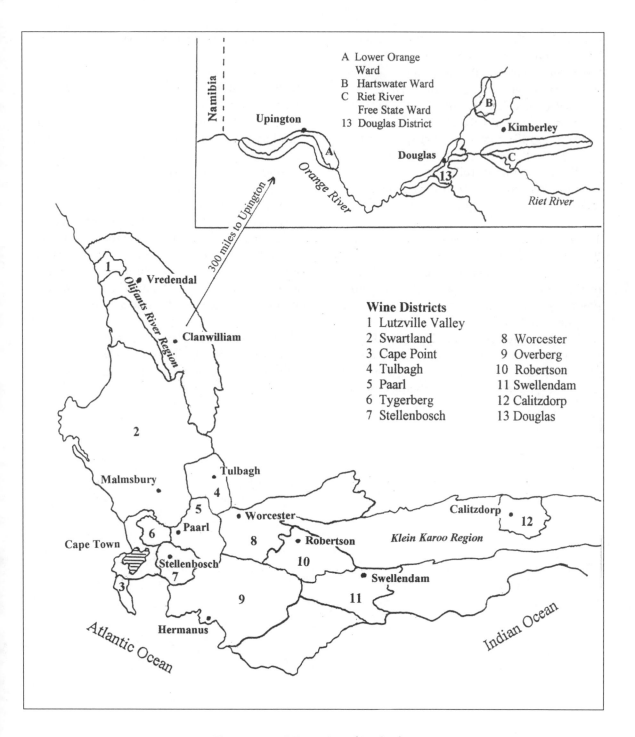

Figure 4.19 *Wine regions of South Africa*

Coastal Region is a common WO designation and comprises the districts of Stellenbosch, Paarl, Swartland, Tygerberg, Tulbagh, Cape Point, plus the wards of Constantia and Durbanville.
Boberg Region, which is for fortified wines only, comprises Paarl and Tulbagh.
Breede River Valley includes Robertson, Swellendam, the south-west section of Worcester and a small part of southern Tulbagh.
Olifants River and *Klein Karoo* are the other regions.

The most widely planted white grape is Chenin Blanc (also known as Steen), followed by Colombard, much of the latter being used for brandy distillation. Chardonnay is currently next and plantings are increasing at a rapid pace. Cabernet Sauvignon is the most
widely planted red grape closely followed by Pinotage, Merlot, Cinsault and Shiraz. Surprisingly the ratio of white to red is 73 per cent to 27 per cent (1999) but red cultivars are being more widely planted and this gap is set to reduce considerably.

Switzerland

Switzerland may be divided into three parts by language – French, German and Italian. The wine production of each part is influenced by the styles of these three countries. Little Swiss wine is imported into the UK or USA, mainly because of its high price. The best-known wine is Dôle, a red wine made from a blend of Pinot Noir (minimum 50 per cent) and Gamay grapes. Merlot, a red wine from the grape of that name, is produced mainly in the Ticino or Italian section; Johannisberg is a white wine made from the Silvaner; and Fendant, a white from the Chasselas grape produced in Valais. In nearby Vaud it is sold as Dorin.

The Czech Republic, Croatia, Slovakia, Algeria, Lebanon, Romania, Turkey, India and many other countries all produce wine in greater or lesser quantities.

CHAPTER FIVE

Sparkling and Fortified/Liqueur Wines

SPARKLING WINE

There are four main methods of producing sparkling wine. The aim of all the methods is to produce a clear wine containing bubbles of carbon dioxide, but each has different characteristics.

The first and most complex process is that used in the Champagne region – *la méthode champenoise*.

Champagne and la méthode champenoise

The Champagne region
The Champagne region is 145 km north-east of Paris, and is the most northerly vineyard of France (Figure 5.1). It is situated on a base of belemnite chalk, which has a very small layer of soil on top; the chalk gives good drainage while still retaining sufficient moisture for the vines. This chalk base is the main reason why the region is so suitable for the production of Champagne. There are 30,000 hectares under vines.

There are 301 crus (villages) in the Champagne region, which is divided into five areas: Montagne de Reims, Vallée de la Marne, Côte des Blancs, Côte de Sézanne and the Côte des Bars (Aube). The main producers or houses of Champagne are in Reims, Epernay and Aÿ. The Marne flows through the middle of the area and was the route by which Champagne reached the outside world in its early days, when Aÿ was the port of Champagne.

The Comité Interprofessionel du Vin de Champagne (CIVC) is the governing body for Champagne and enforces all the AC regulations. It was formed in 1941, and comprises growers and producers with government representatives. All stocks of Champagne and movements of Champagne are kept on records by the CIVC. This body also promotes the wines of this area, and regulates the size of the harvest each year; and until 1990 it fixed the price for the grapes. Since 1991 all press houses in Champagne have had to be registered with the CIVC. Champagne is probably the most controlled appellation in the world ensuring that high-quality levels are maintained.

The grapes used for the production of Champagne must come from the delimited area of Champagne. There are three permitted grape varieties: Pinot Noir (black), Pinot Meunier (black) and Chardonnay (white). Most of the black grapes are grown in the Montagne de Reims and the Vallée de la Marne, while most of the Chardonnay is grown in the Côte des Blancs and the Côte de Sézanne. The grapes must not be damaged during the harvesting and must be pressed as soon as possible, to ensure that the skins of the black grapes are not able to colour the wine.

The vineyards are graded from 100 per cent (Grand Cru) down to 80 per cent. This grading system is called *l'echelle*. For a vineyard graded 100 per cent the grower used to sell his grapes for 100 per cent of the price fixed by the CIVC, and so on. In 1990 they were permitted to fix their own prices, but this was not a success. A CIVC committee of six growers and six négociants now set a recommended price for the grapes, which still reflects the classification of the vineyards. Only three methods of pruning are permitted. These are Guyot simple, Guyot double, Chablis and Cordon de Royat. This is to ensure that the quantity is restricted and the quality of the grapes is kept to a high standard.

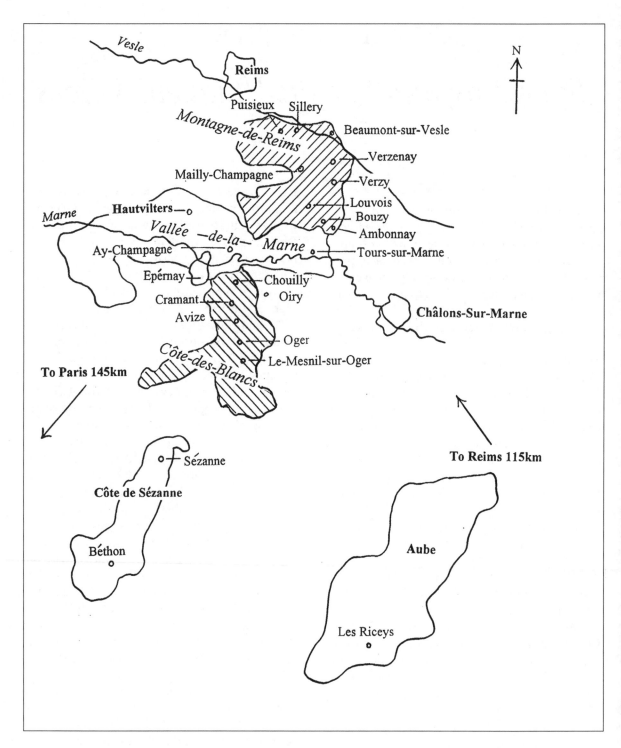

Figure 5.1 *Champagne*

The 17 villages graded 100 per cent are Grand Cru (see Figure 5.1), the 40 villages graded 90–99 per cent are Premier Cru and the 244 graded 80–89 per cent are Cru. The Grand Cru and Premier Crus villages are listed under Appendix 6.

The following letter codes found on champagne bottles are some of the professional registration codes of the CIVC.

CM   stands for Co-operative de Manipulant, which means it is a co-operative making champagne.

NM   stands for Négociant-Manipulant, which means the wine is sold under the name of the House which made it.

RM   stands for Récoltant-Manipulant, which means the champagne is produced by a grower from his/her own grapes.

RC   stands for Récoltant-Coopérateur, which means the grower is selling champagne produced by a co-operative.

MA   stands for Marque d'Acheteur, which means the champagne has been bought from a producer and sold under another name. An example would be one sold under the name of a supermarket. It is also referred to as a BOB, buyer's own brand.

La méthode champenoise

This terminology is only permitted to be applied to Champagne production. It is the method of producing a sparkling wine by inducing a secondary fermentation to take place in the bottle (see Figure 5.2). It is used to produce Champagne and other sparkling wines, but is the only method permitted by the CIVC for the production of half-bottles, bottles, magnums and Jeroboams of Champagne. Since 1994 sparkling wines other than Champagne produced by this method have not been permitted to carry the words *la méthode champenoise* on the label. After 1994 most of these wines have been labelled *la méthode traditionelle*, *traditional méthode classique* or *classic method*.

Countries outside the EU such as the USA are not restricted by this legislation and are able to, and do, call some of their sparkling wines Champagne, or put Champagne Method on the label. These would not be permitted to be imported into EU countries.

The quantity of must permitted to be extracted from the grapes is limited to 2,550 litres from 4,000 kg of grapes, or 100 litres from 157 kg of grapes. The standard size press in Champagne holds 4,000 kg. The first fermentation takes place in large glass-lined or stainless steel tanks, with the exception of Champagne produced by the houses of Krug, Bollinger, Alfred Gratien and one or two others, who complete the first fermentation in oak casks in the traditional manner.

Four or five months later, in late February or early March, the cuvée is prepared. This is the blend, and is the hallmark of each Champagne house. Non-vintage Champagne blends contain on average 40–50 wines from as many as ten different years, whereas vintage Champagne is made almost totally from a blend of just one year. A small quantity of wine from other years is permitted in vintage Champagne to ensure that the correct balance is achieved.

The wine is now mixed with carefully measured quantities of liquid sugar, yeast, a little tannin and finings. This addition is called the *liqueur de tirage* and it produces a second fermentation in the bottle. If too much sugar is contained in this preparation, the bottles would explode owing to too much carbon dioxide being produced. The bottles are then sealed with a stainless steel crown top with a small plastic cup fitted into the top of the neck. The bottles are stored on their sides in underground cellars where, during the first three to four weeks, the second fermentation takes place, producing carbon dioxide and sediment. The wine is left to mature on the sediment for a minimum of fifteen months for non-vintage and three years for vintage. These periods begin from the date of bottling prior to the second fermentation. The better-quality Champagnes are matured longer than this, averaging three years for non-vintage; Krug Grand Cuvée is matured six years. During this maturation period the carbon dioxide

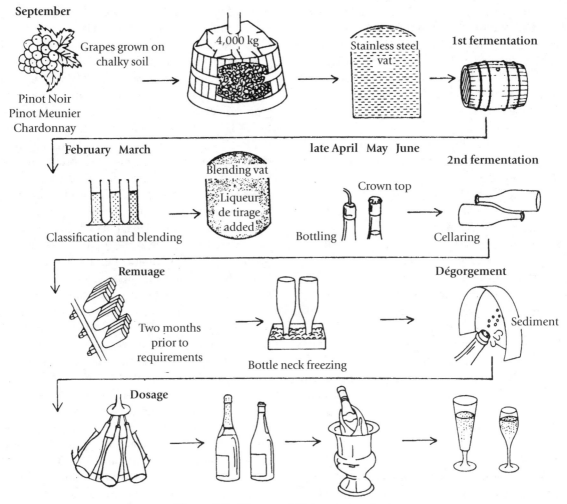

Figure 5.2 *The story of Champagne production*

is absorbed into the wine, and the bubbles become an integral part of the Champagne.

The wine is now ready to undergo the *remuage*. This is the movement of all sediment of dead yeast cells caused by the second fermentation on to the crown top ready for removal. The traditional method of *remuage* is to shake the bottle thoroughly to loosen the sediment and then to place the bottles into *pupitres* (Figure 5.3) where, over a period of twelve to twenty weeks, the bottles are very lightly shaken and twisted to bring them to an almost inverted position. The sediment is now in the small plastic cup next to the crown top. A mechanical system of *remuage* called the gyro pallet is used by many of the producers. The bottles are now upside down and can remain *mise en masse* this way for years.

Next, the bottles are placed into a shallow trough containing freezing mixture, which will freeze a small pellet of wine below the sediment. The house of Bollinger produce a marque called Bollinger RD (*récemment dégorgé*, or late degorged) which is often kept ten years before *dégorgement* takes place. The bottles are removed

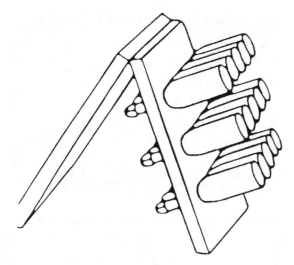

Figure 5.3 *Pupitres*

and the crown top is released, allowing the gas to force the ice pellet and sediment out of the bottle (*dégorgement*). The wine which is lost is replaced by a measured amount of sweetened wine (*dosage*). At *dégorgement* the Champagne is completely dry, because all the sugar will have been used up during the second fermentation. The percentage of sugar syrup in the *dosage* determines the style of the wine, as follows:

Style		Approximate amount of syrup in dosage
Brut naturelle (bone dry)	None	0–6 gm/litre
Brut (very dry)	1%	Less than 15 gm/litre
Extra sec (dry to medium dry)	3%	12–20 gm/litre
Sec (medium sweet)	5%	17–35 gm/litre
Demi-sec (sweet)	8%	33–50 gm/litre
Demi-doux (sweeter)	10%	
Doux, rich (very sweet)	10%	50 gm/litre upwards

The *dosage* is sometimes referred to as *liqueur d'expédition*.

The traditional Champagne cork is inserted and it is wired and dressed ready for sale. The wine is now kept for up to six months before shipment.

Champagne bottle sizes are as follows:

Quarter-bottle	185 ml	
Half-bottle	375 ml	
Bottle	750 ml	
Magnum	1.5 lt	2 bottles
Jeroboam	3 lt	4 bottles
Rehoboam	4.5 lt	6 bottles (discontinued)
Methuselah	6 lt	8 bottles
Salmanazar	9 lt	12 bottles
Balthazar	12 lt	16 bottles
Nebuchadnezzar	15 lt	20 bottles

The Rehoboam and Imperial pint sizes were discontinued in 1989 to comply with EU law, which states that all oversized bottles above magnum size must be multiples of one litre.

Quarter-bottles and the larger sizes of Champagne bottles are produced by the secondary fermentation taking place in magnums, followed by *remuage* and *dégorgement*. The wine is then transferred in a clear state to the larger or smaller bottles under pressure.

Non-vintage Champagne accounts for the vast majority of Champagne produced and reflects the style of the house more definitely than vintage Champagne, as this will vary according to the year. Good advice to all new students of Champagne is to drink a lot of non-vintage Champagne before splashing out on vintage.

Dom Pérignon, cellar-master at the Abbey at Hautvillers from 1670 to 1715, is credited with inventing *la méthode champenoise* and the production of a sparkling white wine from black grapes from a large number of vineyards. This abbey is presently owned by the Champagne house of Moët et Chandon, who have named their de luxe marque after Dom Pérignon. It was M. Nicole-Barbe Clicquot-Ponsardin who invented and developed the *remuage* part of the operation.

Blanc de Blancs
Blanc de Blanc Champagne is made entirely from the Chardonnay grape, which is white. This Champagne has a strong Chardonnay bouquet, is of a lighter style than the normal blends, and comes from the Côte des Blancs.

Blanc de Noirs
Blanc de Noirs Champagne is made entirely from black grapes. These wines are strong flavoured and darker straw coloured than the Blanc de Blancs.

Rosé Champagne
Rosé Champagne (or Pink Champagne as it used to be known) is still regarded by many as something of a novelty. Although this is undoubtedly what it was when it was first produced, it has increasingly been taken seriously by the producers and is now an excellent product, with a strong strawberry nose.

The House of Gosset has been producing rosé Champagne in clear glass bottles for decades. Perrier Jouet and Laurent Perrier Rosé Champagnes are two of the better-known brands in the UK. Gatinois from Aÿ and Paul Déthune from Ambonnay are smaller but high-quality rosé Champagne producers. Their wines are made exclusively from Grand Cru grapes.

Rosé Champagne is generally made by blending red wine with white wine prior to bottling, but in isolated cases it is made by leaving the must in skin contact for a short period during fermentation. It is the only AC wine for which the method of producing a rosé wine by blending red and white wines is permitted. The best red wine for making rosé Champagne is reputed to come from Bouzy.

Coteaux Champenois
This is the AC for the still wines of Champagne. Each year the *rendement* – the amount of grapes permitted to be used from one hectare of vines for the year – is set for the Champagne district by the CIVC. For example, this may be set at 9,500 kg per hectare for AC Coteaux Champenois and 8,500 kg per hectare for Champagne. This means that a maximum of 8,500 kg per hectare can be used for Champagne, leaving 1,000 kg per hectare for AC Coteaux Champenois. Some of the 8,500 kg could be used for Coteaux Champenois, with a corresponding amount less for Champagne.

Ratafia de Champagne (see p. 130) and *Marc de Champagne* (see p. 139) are other products of the region.

Crémant
Crémant wines are *appellation contrôlée*, dry sparkling wines produced in areas of France other than Champagne, which are made by *la méthode traditionnelle*. They are restricted to the pre-1994 yield limit of Champagne – 2,666 lt from 4,000 kg of grapes or 100 lt from 150 kg.

Some examples of these are:

Aude	Crémant de Limoux, from Carcassonne.
Loire	Crémant de Loire from Anjou and Touraine.
Alsace	Crémant d'Alsace
Rhône	Crémant de Die.
Burgundy	Crémant de Bourgogne

Méthode traditionelle wines from other countries

California   Many regions produce these wines, in particular Napa and Sonoma.

Spain   Spanish sparkling wines produced in the Cave delimited areas made by this method are called *cava* wines. If they are made by the *cuve close*, carbonation or transfer methods (see below) they are known as *vinos espumosos*.

Cuve close or Charmat process

These are the names, which appear on labels of sparkling wine, which have been produced by the bulk or tank method. The still wine is pumped into large tanks together with a measured quantity of sugar and yeast. The temperature is controlled to aid the secondary fermentation and the wine is circulated in the closed tanks by propellers. The fermentation is completed in a matter of days. Then the wine is drawn off through filters, still under pressure, and bottled.

   This method is much quicker and cheaper than the Champagne method, but is not permitted to be used for *Appellation Contrôlée* wines. It is permitted for *Qualitätswein* from Germany and *Denominazione di Origine Controllata* wines from Italy. The bubbles are generally a little larger in these wines than in those made by the Champagne method and usually do not last as long in the glass. However, this method has been improved and developed to such a degree that it is sometimes difficult to distinguish between the wines made by the two methods on appearance. Examples of sparkling wines made by this method are Henkell Trocken Sekt from Germany and Asti from Italy.

Transversage method

In this method the second fermentation and dégorgement is carried out in the bottle as for Champagne, but the wine is then chilled and placed in a tank. The dosage is then added and it is filtered and rebottled under pressure in clean bottles. This method is used for quarter bottles and large-sized bottles.

Carbonation

This is the quickest and cheapest method of producing a sparkling wine. It is also the poorest in terms of quality. The wine is chilled in large tanks and carbon dioxide is pumped into it. The wine is then bottled under pressure. The resulting wine resembles a fizzy drink in the glass with large flabby bubbles which don't last long, rather than an exciting sparkling wine fit for celebrating.

Other sparkling wine terms

Vin mousseux	French term for sparkling wine but in the case of Vouvray it refers to a particular AC (see Chapter Four).
Pétillant	French term, but used universally, meaning slightly sparkling; in Vouvray it also refers to a particular AC (see Chapter Four).
Perlant	French term meaning very lightly sparkling.
Spritzig	German term meaning slightly sparkling.
Schaumwein	German term for sparkling wine usually of lesser quality than Sekt.
Perlwein	German term referring to wine which has been deliberately made to be slightly sparkling.
Sekt	German term for sparkling.
Spumante	Italian term for sparkling.
Espumante	Portuguese term for sparkling.
Espumosos	Spanish term for sparkling.

FORTIFIED/LIQUEUR WINES

Fortified wines are defined as wines produced by having grape spirit added during their production in order to:

- Increase the alcoholic strength
- Halt the fermentation process to preserve sugar content
- Stabilize the wine after fermentation, particularly if it is to be sweetened

Sherry

The name 'sherry' originates from the Spanish town of Jerez de la Frontera, which is situated in the heart of the sherry district (Figure 5.4). This district is in Andalucia in the south-western corner of Spain, immediately around Cádiz. It covers an area of about 50 km square.

Since 1996 the name sherry must not be used by other wines of a similar style even with the name of the country of origin; e.g. sherry-style wines from Cyprus and Britain are now 'Cypriot fortified

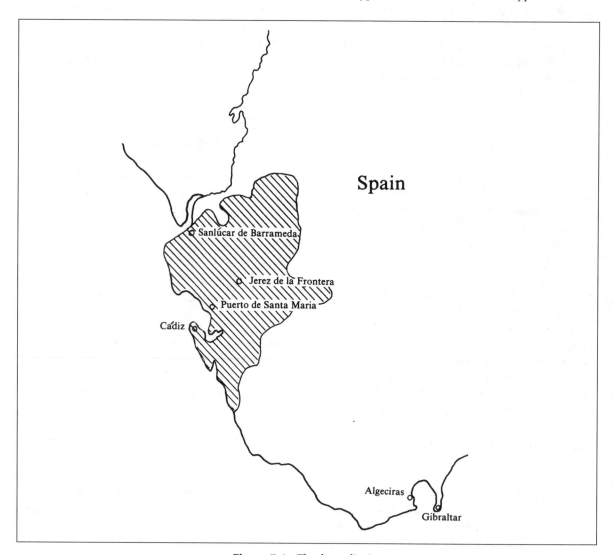

Figure 5.4 *The sherry district*

wine' and 'British fortified wine'.

Sherry is a fortified wine and a blend. Although single vintage sherry is not produced commercially, one or two very small lots have been and are made (Jeffs J. *Decanter* March 1996). The special characteristics of sherry are governed by the climate, soil and the process of vinification. The wine is produced by the shippers rather than by individual growers, although the shippers now own large vineyards themselves. The smaller growers are therefore only interested in the wine up to the pressing of the grapes. From then on the shipper takes over.

There are three types of soil in the district. The best is called *Albariza*, which is 60–80 per cent chalk and is very white. This chalky soil absorbs and holds moisture and reflects the sun, preventing the sub-soil from drying up too much. *Albariza* areas are classified as Jerez Superior and divided into *pagos* or individual vineyards. There are approximately 150 *pagos* registered with the Consejo Regulador, the largest is Macharnudo and two others are Miraflores and Añina. This soil is planted with the white Palomino grape, which is the principal grape for sherry, accounting for 94 per cent of the total. The other two grapes used are the Pedro Ximénez (PX) and the Moscatel, both of which are white. These two grapes are grown for blending purposes and for sweetening and colouring the sherry. *Arenas* soil is sandy and *Barros* soil has more clay in it; both contain about 10 per cent chalk and are inferior to the *Albariza* soil. They are planted with Pedro Ximénez and Moscatel.

Vinification of sherry
The steps in the vinification are as follows:

Harvest
Pressing
Fermentation
Fortification
Classifications
Blending (by the *Solera* system)

The Final Blend is made to a set formula (*cabeceo*). This is often a blend of wine from the *Solera* (bottom scale) with some wines from other levels (*criaderas*) plus some sweetening or colouring wine and some more fortification:

Fining
Chilling to remove tartrates
Bottling

The harvest takes place in mid-September. The Palomino grapes are picked and taken to the press houses. Before pressing, the Pedro Ximénez and Moscatel grapes are dried out by the sun on esparto grass mats in clear plastic tunnels, making these grapes very high in sugar. This process is called the *soleo* and takes from two to three weeks. The grapes are destalked and sieved. Free-run must is produced and what is left is pressed. The free-run must is the best quality; it accounts for 70 per cent of the total and is vinified separately. Traditionally, *yeso* (gypsum) was added to the pressing, which makes the wine drier and more acidic and assists in clarification. Nowadays tartaric acid is usually used in its place.

After the first three days of fermentation, when most of the sugar is converted into alcohol, the wine is drawn off into casks to complete its fermentation. The casks are not filled right up to the top, as it is an important part of the sherry vinification method to allow air to come into contact with the new wine. These casks are taken to the *bodegas* and kept in these casks while the fermentation is completed. In the January following the vintage the wine is classified, then fortified with grape spirit, but the quantity used varies according to the wine. Some will have turned to vinegar and will have to be distilled; some will have oxidized, taking on a toffee or nutty smell and flavour; and some will have been attacked by *flor*. The best wines will be raised to 14.5% abv, the poorer ones to 16.5% abv. At this higher level no *flor* will grow. The wines on which *flor* is allowed to grow will make the best finos (dry sherries). This *velo flor* comprises four yeasts: sacchromyces beticus, sacchromyces montuliensis, sacchromyces cheresiensis and sacchromyces rouxii.

This *flor* forms a covering on the wine like froth, preventing air from getting to the wine and oxidizing it; it lives on the wine, imparting a characteristic smell and flavour to it. The wines with *flor* are fortified up to 15.5% abv, while the other wines will be fortified up to 17.5% abv to prevent further *flor* growth. These wines are made into olorosos, which will become the sweeter sherries. The wines are known as wines of the year (*añadas*). They are racked and left at least until the following spring when, at eighteen months old, they have their final classification. They are classified into five basic types:

Palma
Palo Cortado
Raya
Dos Raya
Pata de Gallina

Palma is the best and is used for finos and amontillados. *Palo Cortados* are used for palo cortado sherries, *Raya* for medium-quality olorosos, *Dos Raya* for lesser-quality olorosos, and *Pata de Gallina* for the very best olorosos.

Solera system

This is the system of blending sherry whereby old wine is constantly refreshed by the addition of younger wine of the same type (Figure 5.5). This procedure is followed because the wines vary so much from year to year and cask to cask. The wines are blended to form a palatable sherry and also to form a standard product to market. Sometimes a date, for example 1872, is found on the label of a sherry or on a wine list. This means that the *solera* was laid down in the year stated, not that the bottle was made in that year.

The number of *criaderas* or scales in a *solera* system will vary from shipper to shipper and from style to style. The example in Figure 5.5 shows four tiers or stages (scales) before the sherry enters the bottom level, which is called the *solera*. When sherry is drawn off from the *solera*, this cask is topped up from the no. 1, *criadera*, which is the next cask back in the system. This in turn is topped up from *criadera* no. 2, which is topped up from *criadera* no. 3, and so on up to the top scale. This is topped up with new wine. The new wine, *vino d'añada* (single-year wine), usually about two years old – is added to a suitable *solera*.

Although the casks are stacked up high in the *bodegas*, the *criaderas* do not have to be stacked above each other as shown. It is the order of replenishing that matters, not the height. Extra care must be taken with those wines which have *flor*, when transferring wine from one stage to another. When wine is sold from the bottom level of the *solera*, no more than one-third is taken, by law.

To make the sherry darker, *vino de color* may be added. This is made by boiling *mosto* (unfermented grape juice) from Pedro Ximénez and Moscatel grapes down to one-fifth or one-third of its original volume. To make the sherry sweeter, *vino dulce* (known as PX) may be added. This is made by fermenting Pedro Ximénez or Moscatel juice to 5% abv then arresting the fermentation by the addition of grape brandy leaving a lot of sugar in this wine. *Dulce Pasa* is made by adding grape brandy to current pressings of Palomino grape-juice and is also used to sweeten the sherry. Pedro Ximénez grapes may be dried out in the sun until very little moisture is left in them, but they are very sweet and brown. These grapes are then pressed and the resultant juice known as PX is used to sweeten and

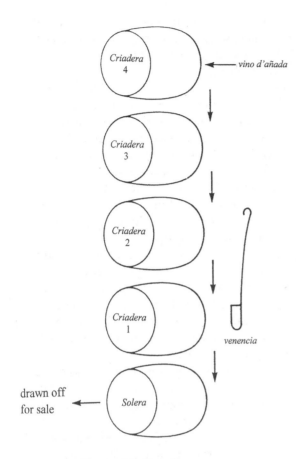

Criadera
4

vino d'añada

Criadera
3

Criadera
2

Criadera
1

venencia

drawn off
for sale

Solera

Figure 5.5 *The solera system*

darken sherry, particularly brown sherries. Caramel is used by some shippers to colour their sherries. Wines must spend a minimum of three years plus one day in the *solera* system, but for the better-quality sherries five to eight years is the norm.

Before sale, the sherry is fined with egg whites and white Spanish earth.

The *venencia* is a special cup used to take a taste of wine from a sherry butt through the bung hole. It was originally made from whalebone with a silver cup fixed to the bottom. The *copita* is the ideal sherry glass (see Figure 8.1).

In EU countries the word 'sherry' means that the wine is of Spanish origin from the Jerez DO.

Types of sherry
From dry to sweet, the types are as follows:

Manzanilla This sherry is very dry, it must fulfil the same requirements as for *Finos* and must be entirely matured in Sanlúcar de Barrameda, which is on the west coast. The wines are matured in cask, and it is said that the sea air imparts a slight salty tang to the wine, but this unusual character is most likely caused by the *flor* being able to grow throughout the year due to the mild temperature.

Fino Very dry, delicate wine on which *flor* must have grown and which must be between 15.6% and 17% abv. It is slightly less dry than *manzanilla* and the better ones are matured for many years.

Amontillado Dry wine but older. There are two types of *amontillado*. The commercial *amontillado*, which is medium dry, has added colour and sweetening and is of medium quality. The traditional *amontillado* is a matured *fino*, of high quality and more expensive. All *amontillados* must be between 16% and 18%.

Palo Cortado These are quite rare and much sought after. They are made from wine which attracted *flor* originally but which died off early. Instead of becoming a *fino* it becomes dry *oloroso*. These wines are very expensive.

Olorosos are 18–20%, less dry, more medium in style, but fuller. Some cream sherries are made from this by the addition of sweetening. Some dry *oloroso* wine is now also being produced, but this is less common.

Raya is a lower-quality wine and is used to produce some of the cheaper brands. These, and some *oloroso* sherries, are often sold as cream sherries. They are made by adding, sweetening or colouring wine. Although, like brown sherry, they are not an official type of sherry, they are used to describe styles of wine in the UK.

Almacenista means storekeeper. Investors in sherry buy butts of *añada* sherry and sell it back to the sherry houses when it is mature. Some of these are now being bottled and sold as *almacenistas*. These are old original-style dry unblended sherries. They are not available in large quantities: they are more for the connoisseur than the average market. A similar system of maturation is being carried out with Scottish malt whiskies.

Port

The name of port is protected in the UK. In 1703 the Treaty of Methuen gave preferential treatment to port over French wines, aiding its popularity. At this time it was not fortified. The quality of port is controlled by the Instituto Do Vinho Do Porto.

Port is a fortified wine produced from approximately forty grape varieties, but there are eight or ten which account for the majority of wine produced. The most important of these are the Touriga Nacional, Tinta Roriz, Tinta Barroca, Touriga Francesa and Tinta Amarela. The vineyards are situated in the Douro *região demarcada* on the upper reaches of the River Douro, in northeast Portugal, between Régua and the Spanish border. Of the three sub-districts, the Cima Corgo around the small town of Pinhão is the best, west of this sub-region is the Baixo Corgo which is the next-best. It stretches from the confluence of the Rivers Corgo and Douro, to the west of Régua.

Douro Superior between the Cima Corgo and the Spanish border is the third sub-district. The best vineyards are around Pinhão, 32 km up-river from Régua. The grapes are grown on terraces, which have been blasted out of the slate and granite. The vineyards are graded from A (the best) to F, according to the soil (schist is the best, granite the worst), location, aspect, grapes used, the concentration of the vines, yield (lowest is best), and maintenance of the vineyard. The climatic conditions are severe, with temperatures ranging from well over 38°C in summer to below freezing in winter. In spring there is heavy rain; precipitation is up to 130 cm per annum.

The best port seems to be produced from vines with the smallest harvest. The grapes are picked in September and carried by hand to the press houses, which are situated in the vineyards. The grapes are crushed and put into auto-vinificators, where the short fermentation (approximately 36 hours) takes place and the colour of the grape

skins is extracted. The auto-vinificator is a sealed container with an upper trough and a water valve. The fermenting must gives off carbon dioxide which forces the must up a central tube into the upper trough. When the water valve releases itself the gas is allowed to escape and the must from the upper trough pours down onto the cap of the fermenting wine thus assisting the rapid extraction of colour. The water valve returns to its original position and the process repeats itself every 10 to 20 minutes. The short-fermented must, low in alcohol (6–8% abv) but high in sugar content, is strained off into vats containing grape spirit, known as *aguadente*, in the ratio of 10 parts brandy to 40 parts must. The brandy is in sufficient quantity to prevent further fermentation, thus ensuring that the wine remains sweet. The brandy, which must be bought from the government-controlled Casa do Douro (vinegrowers' co-operative), was traditionally made from distilled Portuguese wine.

In the spring the wine is put into casks called pipes which hold 550 litres and most of it is transported down to the port lodges at Vila Nova de Gaia, which is situated on the opposite side of the Douro estuary to Oporto. The port lodges are shippers' warehouses similar to the sherry *bodegas*. The port is further fortified, classified and blended. Since 1986 port producers have been allowed to blend port away from Vila Nova de Gaia. This has enabled some small producers to market port under their own label. Some port producers are now maturing small quantities of their port at their Quintas and marketing it with the words 'Douro Bake' on the label. Confusingly the capacity of a pipe of port, when it is sold, is 534.24 litres.

Ruby port

This is the youngest and cheapest of the red ports. It is a blend of wines from more than one year, and is usually bottled and sold after approximately four years. It is an everyday port and is the one which should be used for such drinks as port and lemon. It is perfectly suitable to be drunk on its own, but it is not of the same quality and smoothness as the other ports. It is, as its name suggests, ruby red in colour. It is sweet and may be a little fiery, and is ready for drinking as soon as it is bottled.

Tawny port

As with Amontillado sherry, there is a commercial tawny port and a traditional tawny port. The commercial tawnies are made by blending white port with ruby ports to produce a tawny colour. It is young and inexpensive – similar in price and quality to ruby port.

Fine old tawny or aged tawny ports

These are made by blending ports from several years and maturing them in cask for seven or eight years. Some tawnies are matured in wood for ten, twenty, thirty or over forty years, and this is stated on the bottle. This wood maturation causes the wine to become tawny in colour and to lose some of its sweetness. Fine old tawny ports are smooth, mellow and ready for drinking as soon as they are bottled. They are at their best slightly cool rather than at room temperature, and are very suitable to be served at the end of the meal.

Colheita ports

These are tawny ports made from a single vintage which are matured in cask for a minimum of seven years by law, but often for many more years. The date of the vintage and date of bottling will be stated on the label and they are ready for drinking when bottled.

Vintage port

A vintage year is declared by the individual shippers, when they believe that their wine is of sufficient quality. Therefore in some years some shippers may declare a vintage, producing vintage port, while others may not.

Vintage ports are only made in these years from a blend of wines of this one year. The wine is matured in cask for two years and is then bottled. A white splash of paint is often put on the bottle to show which way up it has been stored so that the bottles may be put into racks in the same position. This ensures that the crust (sediment) which forms in vintage port is not disturbed. The corks are branded with the name of the shipper and the date of the vintage, and these are then often sealed in the bottle with wax to protect them. Labels are not usually put on the bottles until a later date, as they would probably rot or fall off over the long bottle maturation time. Vintage port will mature in bottle for ten to fifteen years and may continue to improve up to forty years or more, depending on the vintage and quality of storage.

Vintage port is deep purple in colour, sweet, and full-bodied, with an alcoholic content of 20–22% abv. It throws a crust (sediment) in the bottle, which may be very heavy, and it must be handled carefully so that this is not disturbed. All vintage ports must be decanted before service (see Chapter Seven). They are very suitable for service with cheese or at the end of a meal, and they are very expensive. Less than half the production of a vintage year is made into vintage port. Recent vintage years are 1966, 1967 (only declared by four houses), 1970, 1975, 1977, 1980, 1982, 1983, 1985, 1991, 1992 (only declared by four houses but very good), 1994, 1997.

Single quinta (or off vintage)

Many port companies are now producing vintage ports in years when they have not declared a vintage. These wines are made in the same way as vintage ports, but they are sold under names of their quintas, for example Graham's Malvedos 1979, Fonseca Guimaraens 1990, Taylor's Vargellas 1987. Other names are Warre's Quinta do Cavadinha, Dow's Quinta do Bomfim, Croft's Roeda, and Calem's Quinta da Foz, and Quinta do Noval's Quinta do Silval. They should be matured in bottle and treated in the same way as vintage port. They are sometimes as good as vintage port, and have even been known to be better on occasions. They are less expensive than vintage ports.

Late-bottled vintage (LBV)

This is port from a single year, usually other than a

declared vintage, which has been matured in wood for four to six years before being bottled. This allows the maturation process to be speeded up and the sediment to drop out of the wine. This port is ready for drinking when bottled and does not require decanting; thus it is very useful to the catering industry. If it is kept for a few years before use it may well throw a small sediment. It is a dark garnet colour. It has slightly less body, depth of flavour and bouquet than vintage port but is excellent value for money, being much less expensive. It carries the date of the vintage and the year of bottling on the label.

Crusted or crusting port
A blend of good wines from more than one year, it is bottled young and unfiltered, then matured in bottle for a minimum of two years, throwing a crust (sediment). It is like a combination of vintage port and LBV. Like vintage and single quinta port it requires careful handling and decanting before service.

Vintage character
This is a blend of good-quality ruby ports of more than one year, is matured in wood, and is less expensive than vintage or late-bottled port. It is intended to be similar in style to vintage port, but it is a long way from being its equal.

White port
White port is made from white grapes, some of the best being Donzelinho, Malvasia, Rabigato and Esgana-cão. It is blended and matured in a similar fashion to ruby port and is a similar price. It varies between dry and sweet, and from a light straw to a golden colour. It is best served chilled, and the dry style is excellent as an apéritif.

Since 1975 vintage ports, including those of an 'off' year, LBV and fine old tawny ports, must all be bottled in Portugal.

Other fortified wines

Madeira
In Madeira the vines are grown in the south part of the island in small plots called *poios* on terraced hillsides. Some of the vines are grown on trellises similar to those for *vinho verde*, allowing other crops to be grown below them; there is a shortage of cultivated land on this volcanic island. The topsoil was enriched in the fifteenth century by a seven-year fire, which burned all the forests, making the soil excellent for viticulture.

There are four main styles of Madeira wines drunk in the UK; each of them takes its name from the grape variety (see below) and are fortified. There are vintage Madeiras, but these are rare.

The grapes are harvested and the *mosto* (grape juice) is fermented. The sweeter wines are fortified and then placed in their casks in an *estufa* (heating room); the drier wines are fortified after this process. The wine is warmed up gradually in the estufa to 45–50°C and then gradually cooled again. The process takes about six months and makes the wine able to withstand extremes of temperature and to resist oxidation. It imparts a caramel flavour to the wine which is characteristic of Madeiras. The wine is then blended. Lower-quality Madeiras undergo heat treatment in a vat fitted with heating pipes. The wine is treated for a minimum of 90 days. The very highest-quality Madeiras are matured in casks and exposed to the sun by being placed by glass window walls for many years. This process is called *Estufa do Sol*.

Until recently Madeiras, other than vintage Madeiras, were often blended by the *solera system* with the date of the laying down of the *solera* marked on the bottle, but this has now been discontinued.

The four main styles of Madeira are:

Sercial   This is a pale dry white wine, excellent as an aperitif or with consommé.
Verdelho   A darker, more golden, medium dry wine which is ideal as an apéritif or served with consommé and other soups. Rainwater is a lighter

style of Verdelho, and not the name of a grape. It is not one of the four main styles of Madeira, but is exported to the UK and USA.

Bual   Slightly darker in colour but sweeter than Verdelho. It is suitable to be drunk at the end of a meal or on its own.

Malmsey takes its name from the Malvazia grape. It is sweet and luscious, and best suited to after-dinner drinking. It was in a butt of Malmsey wine that the Duke of Clarence drowned himself while imprisoned in the Bloody Tower in 1478.

If the Madeira is sold under the name of the grape it must contain 85 per cent of the named varietal. The remainder may be made up with Tinta Negra Mole or other grape varietals. The age of the wine is taken from the date it completes the *estufagem* process.

Vintage Madeira must be made from 100 per cent of the varietal stated and must have spent a minimum of 20 years in wood and a further two years in bottle.

Other qualities of Madeira are:

Extra Reserve:	15 years in wood
Special or Old Reserve:	10 years in wood
Reserve:	5 years in wood
Finest:	3 years old aged in tank not wood

Commercial Madeiras are made mainly from the Tinta Negra Mole grape, sweetened and coloured with caramel and sold simply as 'Madeira'.

Marsala

This is a DOC white fortified wine produced in Sicily, and it may be dry or sweet. Some slowly heated unfermented grape juice (*cotto*), or a mixture of sweet wine and grape alcohol (*sifone*), may be added to the natural wine to sweeten it. Dry Madeira is suitable as an apéritif, the sweet is used more in cookery than as a dessert wine. *Marsala Superiore* is dry or sweet, is of a high quality and is aged for two years, while *Marsala Superiore Riserva* is aged four years in wood. *Marsala Vergine* or

Soleras is dry or very dry and aged for five years; the *Stravecchio* or *Riserva* versions are aged ten years in wood.

Malaga

This is a sweet brown wine from the demarcated region of Malaga on the Mediterranean coast of Spain, 160 km from Gibraltar. The main grape used is the Pedro Ximénez. Although extremely popular in the past, only a small amount is now made. Many of these are blended using the *solera* system.

Vermouth

Vermouth is an aromatized wine and takes its name from one of its ingredients – wormwood (*Wermut* in German). It is made from a base of dry white wine (except for the rosé variety) with the addition of extracts of herbs, spices and other flavourings, plus a fortification of grape brandy.

Dry vermouths are called 'French' and sweet vermouths are referred to as 'Italian', although the two styles are made in both Italy and France. The Italian red (*rosso*) vermouth is coloured with caramel. The Noilly Prat brand of dry vermouth gets its golden colour from maturing in casks for two years in the open air. Chambéry, a small city in Savoie, produces an excellent pale and light dry vermouth. Lillet, which is white and rosé, is produced in Bordeaux. There are four types of vermouth:

Dry   This is light yellow to gold in colour and is dry.
Sweet   Reddish-brown in colour, sweet and full.
Bianco   Straw-coloured, sweet with a touch of vanilla in the flavour.
Rosé   A blend of rosé wines forms its base; it is medium dry and light.

Barolo Chinato DOCG
See p. 77.

Saint Raphaël
An aromatized fortified red wine from France, Saint Raphaël has a predominant flavour of quinine. Its sweetness is counteracted by the bitterness of the quinine. It is served as an apéritif.

Vin doux Naturel (VDN)
VDNs are produced by adding neutral grape spirit to fermenting must to arrest the fermentation. This raises the alcohol level to 15–18% abv and ensures that much of the sugar content of the must is retained in the wine. VDNs are always sweet and should be served well chilled.

Muscats
Muscats and Muscatels are produced from the Muscat grape, which is found all over the wine-growing world. Apart from Muscat d'Alsace, and dry Muscats from Australia, Muscat wines are all sweet and raisin-like with a strong Muscatel bouquet.

The most famous is AC Muscat de Beaumes-de-Venise. It is produced in Vaucluse in the Côtes du Rhône and takes its name from the village of Beaumes-de-Venise. As mentioned in Chapter Four, it is fortified before the fermentation is complete, thus leaving some of the unfermented sugar in the wine. This is classified as a natural sweet wine – *vin doux naturel* (VDN), as although it is very sweet, no sugar has been added. It is rarely sold under a vintage, and is at its best when young; it is not for keeping. The white wine is a pale gold colour and there is some rosé wine produced. They are ready for drinking young, up to three years old.

Muscat de Rivesaltes
Muscat de Rivesaltes and Rivesaltes are two large AOCs in Roussillon. Muscat de Rivesaltes is made from muscat grapes and is either white or rosé. The white is a light golden colour. Rivesaltes AC is made red, white and rosé. This wine needs to be matured for at least ten years. This AC accounts for half of the VDN produced in France.

Banyuls (see p. 69) Rasteau (see p. 66) and Muscat de Setúbal (see p. 92) are other examples of VDNs.

Maury AOC is from a small district in Roussillon, the wines are fortified red, white and rosé.

Muscat de Frontignan is an AOC from Languedoc. It is white and either a VDN or a vin de liqueur (VDL).

Vin de Liqueur (VDL)
VDLs are made by adding grape spirit to the must before any fermentation has taken place. For red VDLs the grape spirit is added to the red grapes. Another name for these wines is *mistelle*. They are very sweet with an alcohol level of 16–17% abv and should be served well chilled or on ice.

Pineau des Charentes AOC/Pineau Charente
This is either a pale gold or rosé sweet aperitif wine. It is produced by adding Cognac (minimum one year old) to unfermented grape juice from grapes from the Cognac region in the ratio of 25 per cent Cognac to 75 per cent must.

Vieux Pineau
This wine is matured in oak casks for five years.

Floc de Gascogne AOC
The Armagnac equivalent to *Pineau des Charentes*. Year-old Armagnac is added to unfermented grape juice from the Armagnac region.

Ratafia de Champagne AOC
This is made by adding Marc de Champagne to unfermented Champagne grape must.

The Australian Liqueur Muscats and Liqueur Tokays (see p. 100) are also examples of *VDLs*.

CHAPTER SIX

Spirits, Beers and Other Drinks

SPIRITS

A spirit is the distillate of a fermented liquor (wash). The most common base ingredients of potable spirits are fruit, cereals, molasses and vegetables. Distillation concentrates the strength and flavours of the liquor by removing most of the water.

Distillation of spirits

There are two types of still used to produce spirits – the pot still and the continuous still. The continuous still is also called the patent still or Coffey

still (it was invented by Aeneas Coffey in 1832). Although there are two types of still, the process is basically the same.

Pot still

A fermented liquor (wash) is put into a closed vessel and boiled (Figure 6.1). The first vapours, which come off are called the 'heads' or 'foreshots' and are not used. Alcohol boils at 78°C and will vaporize before water. The vapours are passed along a closed pipe through a cold-water tank where they are cooled; they condense into a liquid, which is the spirit. This spirit will contain a

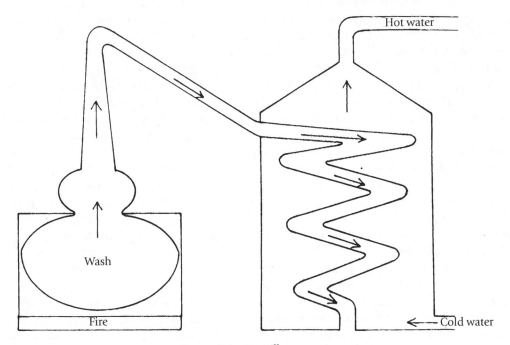

Figure 6.1 *Pot still*

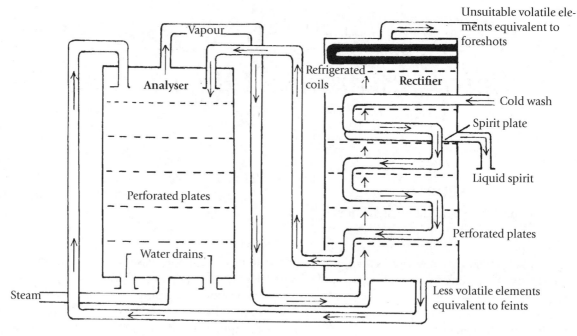

Figure 6.2 *Continuous still*

high proportion of alcohol, with some water, certain gases and flavouring oils, which have been carried in the vapour. The gases and oils impart particular characteristics and flavours to the spirit. The residue left in the still is called the 'tails' or 'feints' and is not used.

Although a very pure spirit can be obtained by modern distillation methods, it would have no character or flavour. For this reason the pot still is used to produce the 'fine' spirits. Some whiskys, rums and brandies are produced in pot stills, and these are double distilled.

Continuous still

As its name suggests this is a continuous process, unlike the pot still. It produces a purer spirit containing fewer impurities.

The still comprises two tall columns (Figure 6.2). One column is the analyser, where the wash is vaporized, and the other is called the rectifier, where the vapours are condensed. The wash is heated in the analyser by superheated steam, whereas the pot still uses direct heat.

Continuous stills are designed specifically for the individual spirit required. For example, a grain whisky still will allow more flavouring to remain in the spirit than a vodka still.

Alcoholic strength

The alcoholic strengths of drinks are stated as the percentage of alcohol by volume (abv) in the drink at 20°C: this scale is standardized by the Organisation Internationale de Métrologie Légale (OIML).

Table wines are usually between 9% and 13% abv, and fortified wines are usually 16% to 26% abv. Spirits are normally sold at 40% abv (80% American proof, AP) with vodka at 37.5% abv (75% AP). There are higher strengths for some spirits.

Gin

Gin is a spirit produced by distilling a wash made from fermented grain, malted barley, maize or rye. This gin is flavoured with botanicals either by passing the vapours from the distillate through the flavourings, or by steeping them in spirit and distilling them in a separate run. The distillate is then used to flavour the spirit. Sometimes the flavourings are added to the grain mash, and distilled in one process. The flavourings used are juniper berries (genièvre), coriander, angelica root, orange and lemon peel, liquorice, orris root, cassia bark, cardamom seeds, calamus root, fennel and almonds. The most important flavouring is juniper berries. Gin is flavoured and coloured at will and is brought to the required strength by the addition of distilled water. It does not require maturing, as do whiskys and brandies.

London dry gin is the standard gin and is dry.

Plymouth gin is wholly unsweetened and is the correct gin to use for a Pink Gin, which is a mixture of a little Angostura bitters and gin, served with iced water. Plymouth gin is made by Coates and Co., Plymouth UK.

Old Tom gin is a sweetened gin, but is rarely seen now.

Dutch gin or *Genever gin*, takes its name from genièvre. It is sold under the names of Genever, Hollands and Schiedam. Oude (old) Genever is made from malted barley and is aged before sale; Jonge (young) Genever is made mainly from grain and is best drunk neat.

Sloe gin is made by steeping sloes in gin. This is a West-country drink and is classified as a liqueur.

Vodka

Vodka originally came from Russia and Poland. It is distilled in a continuous still, is colourless, and is filtered through charcoal filters to purify the flavour. The best is made from rye, molasses, a mixture of these or from other grain. Genuine Russian vodka is distilled from wheat. It is odourless and flavourless and thus is ideal for mixed drinks and cocktails. Vodka is now made by British companies and in other Western countries. The majority of Vodkas are neutral spirits, but flavoured vodkas are available from Russia and Poland. Vodka is diluted and sold between 35% and 45% abv (70%–90% AP).

Whisky

Whisky and its relatives – Whiskey, Rye and Bourbon – are made by distilling the fermented wash (wort) made from unmalted barley, malted barley, maize or rye and water.

Scotch whisky

This is whisky which is made in Scotland. Its flavour and quality are governed by the type of cereal used, the malting process, the peat used, the water, the distilling equipment, and the skills of the distiller and the blender. In this it is very much akin to quality wine.

There are two distinct types of Scotch. One is made from malted barley and double distilled in a pot still; this is called *malt whisky*. The other is made from barley and maize, is usually unmalted, and distilled in a continuous still; this is called *grain whisky*. The Scotch on the market is either straight malt or a blend of grain and malt whisky. The cheaper blends contain up to 70 per cent grain and the best as little as 30 per cent grain. There is one straight-grain Scotch whisky made and sold as Old Cameron Brig.

Malt whisky may come from four regions:

The Highland   Eighty per cent of all Scotch whisky distilleries are in this region and it produces Glenlivet, Glenfiddich, Glen Grant and many other famous whiskys. It is divided into four sub-regions – *Perthshire, Speyside, Northern Highland* and *Island*.

The whiskies from the Highlands are considered to be light and refined, slightly smoky with a touch of spice, and full flavoured. Towards the west of the region the whiskies are more peaty. The Island region includes Jura and Skye; these whiskies have a stronger peat flavour.

Campeltown is the smallest region and is situated on the Kintyre peninsula, close to Ireland. Glen Scotia and Springbank are the only two distilleries left. The whiskies have a light peatiness and saltiness obtained during their maturation close to the sea.

Islay   These whiskies such as Laphroaig and Lagavulin have a strong peat and smoky aroma.

They are the most pungent and biggest whiskies with a salty seaweed flavour.

Lowland   Auchentoshan and Rosebank sell a small amount of straight malt, while the rest is used for blending. They are lighter and softer than the other malt whiskies and have a slight sweetish taste. Both of these distilleries use a triple pot still distillation process.

Malt whisky is made as follows. Barley is malted by steeping it in water and then spreading it out on a concrete floor in a warm atmosphere. The grains germinate, converting the starch to sugar. The germination is stopped by heating the grains over a peat fire. The peat smoke adds to the flavour of the Scotch. The malt is cracked and added to boiling water in a mash tun, and the sugars and flavours are extracted. The liquid (wort) is drawn off and fermented with the addition of yeast. This wash is then twice distilled in a pot still.

Scotch must be matured in Scotland in cask for a minimum of three years by law. Ten years is a good age for high-quality malt, but in that ten years as much as 25 per cent may be lost by evaporation. The best casks for maturing Scotch are old sherry or bourbon casks. Malts are now being matured in old casks from Madeira, Port, Cognac, Bordeaux and other wine regions. They have very distinctive characteristics which are dependent on the district, ingredients and the skill and style of the producer. Malts from Spey are considered the best, while those from Islay the most distinctive.

Irish whiskey

Irish whiskey is made in Ireland from a wash of malted and unmalted barley with some grain. The germination of the grains during the malting process is stopped by heating the grains in a closed kiln, rather than over a peat fire as for Scotch whisky.

When made by the pot still method, it is distilled three times, but the majority is now made by the continuous still method. It is normally not sold until seven years old. 'Whiskey' is the Irish spelling, which is also used for American whiskeys.

Rye whiskey

This whiskey is distilled mainly from a wash containing a minimum of 51 per cent rye, is distilled in a continuous still and aged for a minimum of two years (but usually four years) in new, charred oak barrels. The majority of rye whiskey is produced in Maryland and Pennsylvania but it is also produced in other parts of North America.

Bourbon whiskey

Bourbon is an American whiskey, which is made from maize, rye and malted barley. Bourbon takes its name from Bourbon County, Kentucky. It must contain at least 51 per cent maize spirit, plus rye, wheat or malted barley. It is distilled in a continuous still and is matured in charred oak casks for a minimum of four years. Kentucky Bourbon must be distilled and matured in Kentucky for a minimum of one of these years.

Corn whiskey

This American whiskey is made from 80 per cent corn mash.

Sour mash

This is made by using some of the spent mash from one fermentation to start the next fermentation. This will continue the flavour and style. Makers Mark is an example of a sour mash whiskey.

Tennessee whiskey

This is a sour mash whiskey which is charcoal filtered before being matured in barrels.

Japanese whisky

Japanese whisky is made from millet, corn and rice. Both the pot still and continuous still methods of distillation are used. Sometimes genuine Scotch whisky is added.

Rum

This is a spirit distilled from fermented molasses. Molasses is a syrup by-product of the sugar industry from which crystalline sugar cannot easily be obtained by further refining. The type of yeast used in the fermentation has a great bearing on the resultant rum. Other factors are the method of distillation, the type and amount of caramel used for colouring, and the maturation. Rum can be matured in uncharred or charred oak casks. As with whisky, rum must be three years old before being sold in the UK.

White or Silver Rum was originally from Cuba, but now it is also produced in Puerto Rico and Jamaica. It is distilled in the continuous still and matures for just one year in glass or stainless steel, or traditionally in uncharred oak casks. This rum is light in body, flavour and smell.

Dark rum is rich and full-bodied. It is produced in Jamaica and is known as Jamaican rum. The fermentation is started with Dunder, which is the lees from the previous year's fermentation. It is matured in wood for five to seven years and adjusted with caramel.

Light rum This refers to the more aromatic rums which are produced in Martinique, Puerto Rico, Trinidad, Barbados, Haiti and Guyana. Demerara rum comes from Guyana, and takes its name from the River Demerara. They are matured in wood for three years and adjusted with caramel.

Brandy

Brandy is the distillation of the fermented juice of fresh grapes without the addition of any other spirits. EU law states that eau-de-vie de vin, which is grape spirit, must not be distilled above 86 per cent of alcohol; a product labelled brandy must not be distilled above 94.8 per cent of alcohol and must be matured at least six months in oak casks.

Cognac

Cognac is produced in the delimited (1909) region of Cognac (see Figure 6.3). The Grand Champagne soil has the highest calcium content

and is the best sub-region, followed by Petite Champagne and Borderies.

The quality of the brandy finally produced depends on the soil where the grapes are grown as well as on the distillation, maturing and blending processes. The more chalky soils are the best for Cognac. Although the AC regulations permit eight varieties of vine in Cognac, 90 per cent of any Cognac must come from three of these varietals. These are St Emilion (Ugni Blanc), Folle Blanche and Colombard. St Emilion accounts for 90 per cent of the vines.

The names of the districts in order of merit are:

Grande Champagne
Petite Champagne
Borderies
Fins Bois
Bons Bois
Bois Ordinaires, Bois à Terroir

The vineyards are picked in one go. The grapes are pressed and the must is fermented for seven to ten days. The wine produced is acidic and harsh and is between 8% and 10% abv. The more unpalatable wine seems to produce the best Cognac.

Only Charentais stills, which are copper pot stills are used for the distillation, which by law must be completed by 31st March of the year following the harvest. The distillation is done under French Excise supervision. The wine is heated slowly for two hours in the stills by open flames fuelled by coal or gas. At 172°F (78°C) the alcohol vaporizes and travels through the coiled pipes in the cooling tank where it condenses into *brouillis*. This contains all the alcohol and some water plus other flavourings and trace elements. The brouillis is at about 30% abv and is approximately one-third of the quantity of wine which was put into the still. The vast majority of what is left behind in the still is water. The still is cleaned out and the process is repeated with more wine.

When there are three lots of *brouillis*, they are put together in a clean pot still, and re-distilled. This second distillation may take as long as ten

135

hours. Only the middle portion of this distillation, which is called the *bonne chauffe*, is used. The foreshots or *tête* which is the earliest part of the distillate, and the aftershots or *queue* which is the end part of the distillate, are not used for Cognac; they are put in with another batch of wine for re-distilling.

The *bonne chauffe* is run off into Limousin or Tronçais oak casks to mature. At this point the raw spirit is colourless and at 72% abv – a strength which must not be exceeded if it is to be made into Cognac. It has taken approximately nine casks of wine to produce one cask of *bonne chauffe*.

During the maturation period (minimum three years by law) the Cognac absorbs tannin and some colour from the French (Limousin and Tronçais) oak casks and loses some of its harsh and fiery taste. This is a most important phase of the production and is responsible for many of the differences in the characteristics of the various producers. If the Cognac is matured in new oak, there will be more tannins and vanillins, resulting in a heavier-style Cognac; if old casks are used, a lighter style will be the result. Cognac evaporates at about 2–3 per cent per year, and this is called 'the angels' share'. The brandies are blended by the cellar master to produce house styles and qualities. Before they are sold the Cognacs are brought down to 40–45% abv with the addition of distilled water, and the colour is usually adjusted with a little caramel. Cognac will only mature while it is in cask; it will not improve after bottling.

The finest Cognacs are:

Grande Champagne, Grande Fine Champagne
These are made entirely from brandies produced from grapes grown in the Grande Champagne region.

Petite Champagne, Petite Fine Champagne   These are made entirely from brandies produced from grapes grown in the Petite Champagne region.

Fine Champagne   This is made entirely from brandies produced from grapes grown in the Grande and Petite Champagne regions, with a minimum of 50 per cent coming from the Grande Champagne region.

The age of cognac refers to age in cask before bottling. Cognac does not improve with age in the bottle. The terms used are:

Three Star (***) and *VS Cognacs*   This blend must be a minimum age of three years, but in practice they are usually an average age of five years. These Cognacs may be drunk on their own, with mixers, or used in cocktails.

VSOP, VO and *Réserve Cognacs*   VSOP stands for very special (or superior) old pale. The Cognac law states that all Cognacs used in these blends must be a minimum of four and a half years old, but in practice the average wood age is much older.

XO, Cordon Bleu, Centeur, Antique   Terms used to denote very old brandies with an average age of twenty years upwards but legally they must be a minimum of six and a half years old. VSOP and older Cognacs are termed 'liqueur brandies' and should be drunk on their own with nothing added.

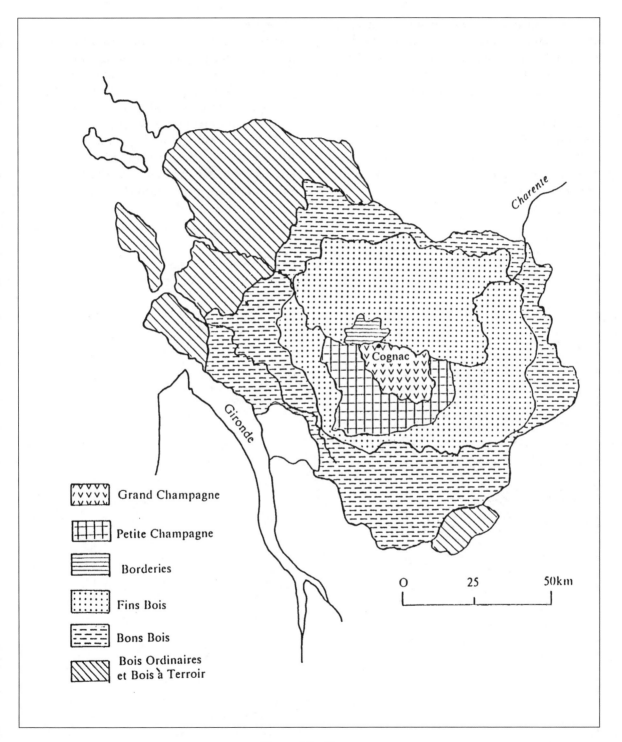

Figure 6.3 *Cognac*

The word 'Champagne' used in the regional classi-fication has no connection with the sparkling wine of that name. It is the old French word for field or country, and was originally used because the ground or soil is similar to that found in the Champagne region.

After French law outlawed Vintage Cognacs in 1963 and in the UK in 1973, they were reinstated following the 1989 vintage so that Vintage Dated Cognacs are once again permitted, but these are still the exception.

Armagnac

This brandy is produced in the delimited (1909) region of Armagnac, the majority of which is in the département of Gers in the south-west of France. It is situated 150 km south of the Charente area where Cognac is produced. There are three regions: Haut-Armagnac, Bas-Armagnac (the best) and Ténarèze. Most of the grapes for Armagnac come from Bas-Armagnac and Ténarèze.

There are four ACs: Armagnac, Armagnac-Ténarèze, Bas-Armagnac and Haut-Armagnac.

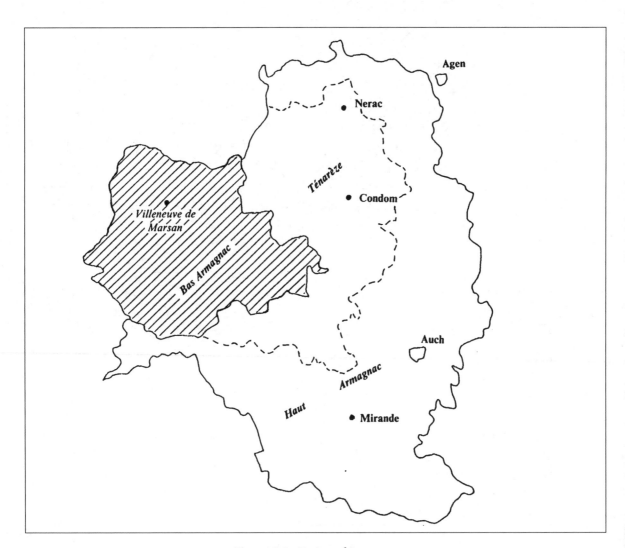

Figure 6.4 *Regions of Armagnac*

The main grapes used are the same as for Cognac – St Emilion (Ugni Blanc), Folle Blanche (Picpoul) and Colombard. The Baco Blanc (a hybrid) is currently permitted but no new planting of this variety is allowed. The grapes are picked, many by mechanical means, and made into a very dry and acidic wine. The distillation must then be completed (by law) before the end of April following the year of the harvest.

The traditional method of producing Armagnac is by using the travelling continuous or rectifying still rather than the pot still. However, it is a different type of continuous still from that used to produce other spirits. It has a much shorter rectifying column with fewer plates or levels in it. Because the rectifying part is smaller, the spirit is nothing like as pure as gin, vodka or grain whisky spirit. The spirit comes over the still at only 53% abv compared with Cognac which averages 72% abv, so there is more flavour left in it. The two largest producers of Armagnac, Janneau and Samalens, distil all their own Armagnac, but the area is made up of many smaller producers whose base wine is distilled by specialist distillers.

Since 1973 the Cognac pot still, which is manufactured in Cognac, has been used in Armagnac, as well as the old continuous still. The same method as for Cognac production, a double distillation, is used. The resultant distillate (*bonne chauffe*) is approximately 70% abv. Some of the larger producers use a combination of spirits from both types of still. After distillation the spirit is placed in black oak casks – so called because the leaves of the oak trees used for the wood are black in summer. This oak (Monlezun) is very sappy and causes the Armagnac to mature more quickly than Cognac. The casks are not kept completely filled as a small amount of oxidation is necessary to produce a true Armagnac. After eight to ten years in wood the Armagnac will have developed its characteristic taste. After twenty years Armagnac is well matured, but in some cases can improve further. No caramel or sugar is added to Armagnac as is practised with most Cognacs. It obtains all its flavourings and colour from the dis-tillation and maturing process.

Similar designations to Cognac are used to denote age, but with slightly different age thresholds: Three Star (minimum one year old – but it is illegal in the UK to sell it under three years old), VO and VSOP (minimum four years old), and XO, Vieille Relique, Très Vieille Réserve and Napoléon (minimum five years old). Vintage Armagnac is made and is more common than vintage Cognac.

Other grape brandies
Grape brandies are produced wherever wine is made. Some countries (such as Germany) also import wine to make brandy.

The qualities of these brandies vary considerably, but with a few exceptions they are considerably lower in quality and in price than Cognac and Armagnac. One such exception is Asbach, which is produced in Germany from wine imported from France.

Californian brandy   This brandy must be made from 100 per cent Californian grapes, must not be distilled above 85% abv and must have a minimum of two years in oak.

Marc   Marc brandy is made by distilling the fermented liquor obtained from steeping the grape pips and skins left after the grapes have been pressed for the production of wine. These brandies usually have a slightly perfumed bouquet and are less smooth than Cognac and Armagnac. Marc de Bourgogne is produced in Burgundy. A small percentage of it is sold at the Hospice de Beaune wine auction, and this is stated on the label. Marc de Champagne is distilled by one company, is then oak matured and sold by most of the top Champagne houses. EU regulations state that Marc may only be produced from the distillate of grape pomace with or without water, and must not be distilled above 86 abv. *Grappa* is Italian Marc, and under EU law may only be produced in Italy. The best Grappas are made from single grape varieties and held in glass rather than oak. *Invecchiata* means aged and

Stravecchia means extra maturation, both these terms refer to oak ageing.

Fruit spirits (Eau-de-vie)

Brandy is the best-known fruit spirit, but there are many others.

Calvados is produced in the département of Calvados in northern France. It is made by distilling fermented apple juice. It is dry, apple flavoured and brown in colour. Two delimited areas have their own *appellation contrôlée* – Calvados Pays d'Auge (best) and Calvados Domfrontais. Calvados Pays d'Auge must be made by a double pot still distillation, must age a minimum of two years in wood and be sold between 40% and 45% abv. Other regions producing Calvados may use the AC Calvados.

Framboise is made from the distillation of fermented raspberries and is colourless. It is usually French, German or Swiss.

Kirsch is made from the distillation of fermented cherries and is colourless. It is used extensively in cooking, and in particular with fresh fruit. It is usually French, German or Swiss.

Mirabelle is made from the distillation of fermented mirabelles, which are small yellow plums. This spirit is again colourless.

Poire William   This fruit spirit is made from the distillation of fermented pears and is colourless. It is usually French, German or Swiss.

Slivovitz is made from the distillation of fermented plums and is colourless. It is produced in Hungary, Yugoslavia and Romania.

Quetsch is similar to Slivovitz but is made from red plums and produced in Alsace.

All these fruit spirits except Calvados are aged in glass, not wood; that is why they are colourless, and referred to as *alcools blancs*. *Alcools blancs* are at their best when served slightly chilled in cold glasses.

Other spirits

Aniseed-based spirits

Pernod is a spirit flavoured with aniseed.

Pastis and *Ricard* are spirits flavoured with aniseed and liquorice. These and Pernod are yellow in colour.

Ouzo is a Greek spirit flavoured with aniseed, and is colourless.

All these aniseed apéritifs are usually served with iced water. They all turn cloudy with the addition of water, except ouzo, which becomes milky.

Bitters

Bitters are spirits which have been infused with strongly flavoured plants, roots, bark, etc. They are served as apéritifs, digestifs, as a cocktail ingredient, or used to flavour other drinks.

Angostura bitters   Produced in Trinidad from rum, gentian, vegetable spices and vegetable colouring matter, brownish-red in colour and used for the 'pink' in Pink Gin. It is 44.7% abv.

Amer Picon   This French bitters is orange flavoured and light red in colour. It is usually served as an apéritif.

Campari is a well-known Italian bitters, flavoured with herbs and spices and red in colour. It is served as an apéritif either neat on ice with a slice of orange, or as a long drink with the addition of a mixer, usually soda.

Fernet Branca   Produced in Italy and France, it is particularly strongly flavoured and is dark brown in colour. It is served as a digestif or pick-me-up.

Orange bitters   Produced from spirit flavoured with Seville orange peel, it is used in cocktails and other mixed drinks.

Peach bitters   Produced from spirit flavoured with peaches, it is used in mixed drinks and cocktails.

Underberg   Produced in Germany and made from spirit flavoured with natural herb bitters from 43 countries. It is served as a digestif.

Saké
This is produced in Japan from fermented rice. It is more like a wine than a spirit and has an alcoholic content of approximately 17% abv. Traditionally it was served hot in a small porcelain pot with small cups but is now commonly served in wine glasses.

Schnapps
Schnapps is a Dutch, Danish or German spirit, made from the distillation of fermented grain.

Aquavit is a Danish schnapps, is 51% abv, and is the national drink of Scandinavia. It is flavoured with caraway, and should be served ice-cold in chilled glasses.

Mezcal
Mezcals are produced from seven varieties of maguey in Mexico. The state of Oaxaca in the south of Mexico produces some of the very best by the traditional method. The hearts of the maguey are baked in rock pits under very hot stones and covered with earth, for two to three days. The baked maguey hearts are ground to a mash, mixed with water, and fermented slowly in wooden vats before being twice distilled producing Mezcal.

Tequila
All Tequilas are Mezcals, but all Mezcals are not Tequilas. Tequilas are only produced from one species of the Agave, within the state of Jalisco, Mexico. Agave Tequilana which is known locally as the Maguey Azul or Blue Maguey is the only variety permitted. These grow well around the towns of Tequila and Tepatitlan. The Blue Maguey matures over six to eight years. The spikes are hacked off and the heart called *piña* (pineapple) weighing 80–175 lb is chopped up and steamed. When cooked the *piña* is shredded and pressed for its juice. Sugars and yeasts are added. Mexican federal law permits a maximum of 49 per cent of other sugars to be added, while allowing the product to be called 100 per cent Blue Agave Tequila. Fermentation takes place in stainless steel vats

over a few days before being double distilled in stainless steel pot stills to 104–106% American proof (AP). It is then filtered through charcoal and aged in wooden casks for between eight months and seven years. The longer the Tequila remains in the cask, the more golden it becomes. The traditional way to drink Tequila is to hold a shot glass of Tequila in one hand, and have salt sprinkled on the back of the other hand holding a slice of lime. The salt is licked, the Tequila drunk down in one, and then the slice of lime is bitten into. It is now commonly served with lime with the rim of the glass coated with salt.

Liqueurs
Liqueurs are sweetened flavoured spirits. The flavourings are extracted from fruits, seeds, plants, herbs and spices by three methods: infusion, percolation and distillation.

Advocaat is a low-strength liqueur, yellow in colour, made from egg yolks and brandy. The best is produced in Holland.
Amaretto is a brown-coloured Italian liqueur flavoured with apricot kernels, tasting almost of marzipan.
Apricot brandy   A golden-coloured liqueur usually made from apricots and brandy, the best being flavoured with apricot kernels.
Bénédictine   French golden-coloured liqueur produced at the Monastery at Fécamp in Normandy. It is made from a secret recipe made up from a mixture of brandy and 27 other ingredients, made up of herbs, seeds and spices. Bénédictine is matured in wood for a minimum of four years. The letters DOM on the label stand for Deo Optimo Maximo (to God most good most great).
Chartreuse   A high-quality French liqueur also made from a secret recipe flavoured with herbs and produced by Carthusian monks at Grenoble in France and Tarragona in Spain. There are two strengths: green Chartreuse at 55% abv and yellow Chartreuse at 43% abv.
Cherry brandy is a reddish-brown cherry-flavoured liqueur produced in many countries. Cherry

Heering is the most traditional of these and is produced from cherry kernels.

Cointreau is distilled from oranges, and is a colourless liqueur made in Angers, in France. It is named after the family that produced it.

Curaçao is similar to Cointreau. It is a Dutch liqueur made from spirit and the peel of green Curaçao oranges. It is made in various colours – brown, red, blue and green.

Triple Sec is the clear variety of Curaçao.

Van der Hume   An amber-coloured South African liqueur flavoured with Naartjie tangerines.

Chocolate liqueurs   *Crème de cacao* is a brown or colourless chocolate-flavoured liqueur produced in many countries. *Royal Mint chocolate liqueur* is a pale green mint- and chocolate-flavoured liqueur.

Coffee liqueurs   *Tia Maria* is a Jamaican dark brown liqueur made from rum, coffee and spices. *Kahlúa* is a Mexican brown liqueur made from rum and coffee. It is produced in Denmark under licence. There are many other coffee-flavoured liqueurs made in various countries, for example Crème de Café.

Cordial Médoc is made from a blend of Crème de Cacao, Brandy and Curaçao.

Cream liqueurs   *Baileys Original cream liqueur* is a blend of Irish cream and Irish whiskey. *Devonshire Royal cream liqueur* is a blend of whisky, brandy and Devonshire cream. *Sheridans* is an Irish liqueur comprising two separate spirits in a divided bottle, one white, one dark brown. The brown liquor is coffee and chocolate flavoured, the white liquor is a mixture of cream and spirit. These are just three of the many cream liqueurs now on the market.

Crème de menthe is a mint-flavoured liqueur, either green or colourless. Freezomint is the name given to Crème de Menthe made by Cusenier.

Frangelico is an Italian liqueur, light lemon in colour and flavoured with hazelnuts, berries and flowers.

Galliano   Italian herb-flavoured yellow liqueur, owing its popularity to the cocktail Harvey Wallbanger in which it is a major ingredient.

Grand Marnier is a French liqueur. It is an orange-flavoured liqueur using Cognac as its base. There are two varieties, cordon rouge and cordon jaune, the former being of the higher strength. Both are golden-brown in colour.

Kümmel   Originating in Holland, it is a colourless caraway-flavoured liqueur.

Licor 43 (Cuarenta y Tres) is produced in Spain, is yellow in colour and flavoured with vanilla and citrus fruits.

Malibu is a colourless low-strength coconut-flavoured liqueur, with a base of Jamaican light rum.

Maraschino   A colourless cherry-flavoured liqueur produced in Italy. It is made from the distillate of fermented maraschino cherries.

Midori is a melon-flavoured liqueur, originally from Japan.

Sambuca   An Italian colourless liqueur with a flavour of liquorice and elderberry. This drink is served flaming with a coffee bean floating in it.

Strega   A sweet yellow-coloured liqueur from Italy, flavoured with herbs and bark.

Whisky/ey-based liqueurs   *Drambuie, Glayva* and *Glen Mist* are all golden-coloured liqueurs produced in Scotland from a base of Scotch whisky sweetened and flavoured with herbs and heather honey.

Irish Mist is made from a base of Irish whiskey and is sweetened and flavoured with heather honey and herbs.

Southern Comfort is another golden-coloured whisky liqueur made from a base of Bourbon whiskey, peaches and oranges. These whisky liqueurs must not be confused with liqueur whiskies, which are old mature whiskies.

BEERS: ALES, STOUTS AND LAGERS

All beers are brewed as shown in Figure 6.5. The various colours and flavours are obtained by the use of various types and colours of malt, hops and yeasts.

Malt is made by steeping barley in water for 48 to 72 hours, until it begins to germinate. When this occurs the starches in the grain are converted

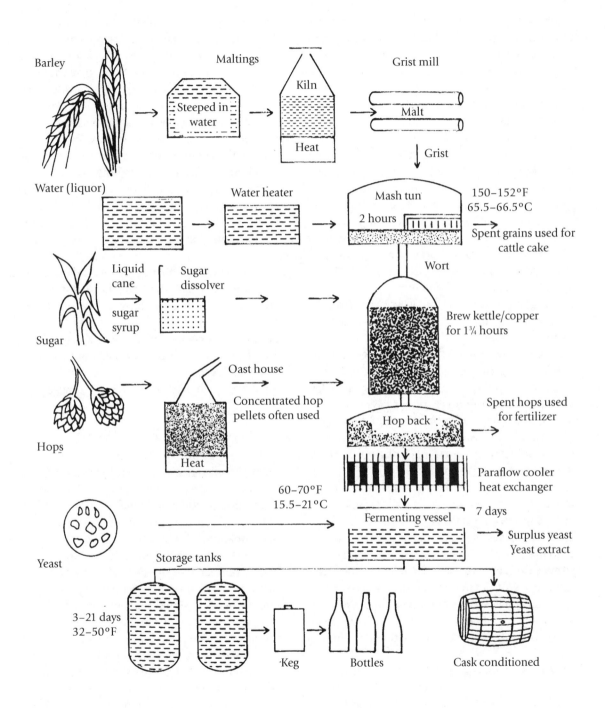

Figure 6.5 *The brewing process*

to sugars. The grains are then dried by hot air in a kiln, which stops any further growth. The grain is then 'cooked' to the required colour and flavour. Light malt and crystal malts are used for light ales, bitters and lagers. Chocolate malt and black malts are used for mild ales and stouts.

Next the malt is 'cracked' in a mill, producing grist. This is mixed with hot liquor (water) at 149–151°F (65–66°C) for two hours. The flavour and colour has now been drawn out of the malt, and the wort (as the liquid is now called) is run off into a brew kettle/copper. Here it is boiled for thirteen hours with sugar syrup and hops. The wort is then run off into the hop-back where it settles before being strained off into a paraflow (heat exchange) system, which cools it to 59–61°F (15–16°C). The wort is then moved on to the fermenting vessel. Yeast (*Saccharomyces cerevisae*) is added, and fermentation starts and continues for about seven days.

The beer now either goes into a storage tank for 3–21 days (lagering is longer) to await pasteurization, bottling or kegging, or after two or three days is put into casks for unpasteurized cask-conditioned beer which will be sold as draught beer. During this time hops are often added (dry hopping) to add flavour and to make the clarification of cask-conditioned beers easier.

For lager production the yeast *Saccharomyces carlsbergensis* is used. This is a bottom fermentation yeast, working at the bottom of the fermentation vessel rather than at the top. The fermentation takes longer than for other beers because the temperature is much lower. The lager beer is then run off into storage tanks called layering vessels for 10–24 weeks, where the beer is conditioned at a temperature of 1–3°C. The lager will withstand low temperatures after this without turning cloudy.

The majority of bottled beers are pasteurized and are therefore free of sediment. White Shield Worthington, Red Label (triangle) Bass and Guinness are the traditional bottle-conditioned beers which contain sediment, caused by yeast being left in the bottle to ferment, but there are many more being produced by the microbreweries. These beers must therefore be stored and served with more care. The variety of hops used affects the flavour of the beer and this is increasingly being stated on the label by the microbreweries.

The average strength of beer is approximately 4% abv, but there may be as much as 10% abv in the strongest beers, often called Barley Wine or Strong Ale. These very strong beers are normally sold in small bottle sizes of about 180 ml.

There has been a big increase in the number of microbreweries and brewpubs (pubs with their own small brewery attached), which is increasing the types and flavours of beers.

Ice Beer is now established in the market and is an alternative to pasteurization. The beer undergoes cold sterile filtering, resulting in a slightly higher alcoholic content.
Lite Beer means that it is low in calories.
Malt Liquor is a high alcohol, 7.5% and above abv, American beer.
Most American beers such as Bud are lagers.

CIDER AND PERRY

Cider is the alcoholic beverage obtained from fermented apple juice, or a mixture of apple and a maximum of 25 per cent pear juice. Perry is the alcoholic beverage obtained from fermented pear juice, or a mixture of pear and a maximum of 25 per cent apple juice.

After the cider apples are harvested in October/November, they are sliced or grated (the old method was to pound them) before pressing. The juice is then fermented at a temperature of 18–24°C for from four to six weeks. Sometimes the cider has carbon dioxide pumped into it, or is given a secondary fermentation by adding yeast and sugar to it. Perries are usually either carbonated or subjected to a second fermentation.

Cider has a strength of between 4% and 8% abv, but 7% is a good average. The legal limits for cider alcoholic strengths are 1.14%–8.5% abv.

Cider has a lower excise duty than beer in the

Some well-known mineral waters:

Name	Origin	Mineral content	Style
Appollinaris	Ahr valley, Germany	High	Sparkling
Badoit	Saint-Galmier, France	Low	Sparkling
Contrexéville	Contrexéville, France	High	Still
Evian	Evian, France	Low	Still
Perrier	France	Low	Sparkling
San Pellegrino	Italy	Medium	Sparkling
Vichy Célestine	France	High	Sparkling
Vittel	France	Medium	Still
Spar Reine	Belgium	Low	Still
Spar Marie-Henriette	Belgium	Medium	Sparkling
Vichy Catalán	Spain	High	Sparkling
Henniez	Switzerland	Medium	Still and sparkling
Buxton Spring water	Buxton, England	Low	Still and sparkling
Malvern	Malvern, England	Low	Still and sparkling
Ashbourne	Ashbourne, England	Low	Still and sparkling
Highland Spring	Blackford, Scotland	Low	Still and sparkling
Calistoga	Calistoga, California	Low	Still and sparkling
Mountain Valley	Arkansas, USA	Low	Still

UK, as it is classed as an agricultural product and is therefore cheaper than beer. Sparkling cider is also produced by the bottle fermentation method and is marketed in Champagne-style bottles. The English West country and Northern France are the top producers of Cider.

MINERALS

Natural mineral waters

Natural mineral waters must originate in a ground water body or deposit. All natural mineral waters which are intended for human consumption, must be extracted from the ground through a spring, well or bore-hole.

Bottled natural mineral waters may be either still or sparkling. Sparkling mineral waters are labelled as carbonated natural mineral water, naturally carbonated natural mineral water, or natural mineral water fortified with gas from the spring.

All natural mineral waters must be bottled at the place of origin, without any additions or treatment other than filtration to remove iron or sulphur, and the addition of carbon dioxide. Natural mineral waters contain mineral salts and have been proved to be beneficial to health. Fruit-flavoured still and sparkling mineral waters are also available.

Some of the better-known mineral waters are given below.

Aerated waters and mixers

Manufactured aerated waters (often termed minerals) contain flavourings, for example, lemonade, orangeade, cherryade, ginger beer and cola. All these are best served chilled. They are drunk on their own or mixed with other drinks, for example Cinzano and lemonade.

Mixers are the same as manufactured aerated waters but are considered more as mixing drinks, although they are also very popular drunk on their own. They are in styles and flavours which mix very well with spirits, for example gin and tonic. The most common mixers are:

Bitter lemon, which contains lemons and quinine.
Ginger ale (original dry ginger ale, American and Canadian)   Ginger flavoured, golden-brown coloured.
Ruschian   Peach flavoured, rosé coloured.
Soda water   Colourless.
Tonic water   Contains quinine and is colourless.

ALCOPOPS

These are 'soft-drink' flavoured drinks, with an alcoholic content.

JUICES, SYRUPS AND CORDIALS

Fruit juices

Fresh fruit juices may be extracted from fresh fruit in the bar with the juice extractor, but the most common bar fruit juice is bottled in 113 ml (4 fl oz) bottles.

Many bars use bottled lemon juice in their cocktails, but this often produces a different flavour from the original recipe.

The most common juices available are orange, lemon, grapefruit, pineapple, passion fruit, apple, mixed fruits, blackcurrant and cranberry.

If freshly extracted juice is served, castor sugar should be offered with it, together with ice and straws.

Syrups

Syrups may be diluted to make a long drink or used in the preparation of mixed drinks and cocktails. Some of the more common ones are:

Name	Flavour	Colour
Cassis	Blackcurrant	Purple
Citron	Lemon	Yellow
Framboise	Raspberry	Red
Gomme	Sugar	Colourless
Grenadine	Pomegranate	Red
Orgeat	Almond	Colourless

Cordials

Cordials may be alcoholic or non-alcoholic. Lime juice cordial is the best-known non-alcoholic cordial.

Alcoholic cordials are usually drunk in a combination with one or more other drinks. They are often added to spirits, for example rum and peppermint, or used in cocktail recipes. They have a long history in England; they were very popular in country districts and in particular in the West Country. Phillips of Bristol are one of the oldest and finest producers of cordials, and their range is listed below:

Green peppermint, white peppermint (5% abv)
Mint grown at Mitcham in Surrey (known as Mitcham mint) is used to flavour these cordials. They can be drunk neat and are thought to be good for stomach upsets. The most common mixed drink is rum and peppermint.
Lovage (8% abv)   This cordial is flavoured with celery, herbs and spices and is considered to be a good pick-me-up. Its recipe originated in Devon and it is still popular there. The most common mixed drink is brandy and lovage.
Shrub (6% abv)   Shrub is flavoured with a blend of herbs and spices. Its recipe originated in Cornwall, and it is very popular in the West Country. The most common mixed drink is rum and shrub.
Aniseed (5% abv)   The aniseed flavouring comes from the seeds of the anise plant. It is most commonly drunk mixed with spirits.
Pink cloves (7.5% abv)   This is made from pink cloves produced in Zanzibar, and is used in any drink where the recipe calls for cloves, for example punches and cups. If added to vodka or gin it will not only flavour them but will impart a pink flush.
Grenadine (8% abv) This red-coloured cordial, like the syrup of the same name, has a pomegranate flavour. It is used in many cocktail recipes.

CHAPTER SEVEN

Serving Beverages and Tobacco

MISE-EN-PLACE

Good mise-en-place is the basis of quality service. It is the complete preparation required before service commences, and in the case of top-quality wine service it comprises the following:

Selection and preparation of all glassware and equipment necessary for the service operation. All the selected glassware must be polished and checked for clean odour and damage, that is chips and cracks. The bases of glasses, the handles and lips of water jugs and the lips of decanters are often missed but these must all be polished and checked for soundness.

All wine lists must be checked for cleanliness and a list of unavailable wines (if any) prepared for each sommelier.

All dining tables are accurately glassed-up with the house standard lay-up.

Equipment will cover such items as wine lists, bottle opener, cork extractor, champagne tweezers, wine coolers, decanting funnel if used, candle, coasters if used, matches, cedar spills if used, ashtrays and cigar cutter if there is a smoking area, a good stack of side-plates, serviettes, service cloths and cotton cloths for polishing glassware.

CHOICE OF GLASSES/STEMWARE

Glasses have evolved to enable the particular characteristics of different drinks to be appreciated to the full. One glass manufacturer (Reidel) has developed specific glasses for each of the main types of wine and quality spirits.

Whatever the shape or size of glass, it must be sound (with no chips) and highly polished when placed on a table or used for the service of a drink. The best-quality glasses are made of thin glass. If a major part of the enjoyment of a drink is the appreciation of its appearance and bouquet, then a glass with a full bowl should be used. For a drink such as gin and tonic or vodka and lime, the correct size of the glass is a more important factor.

The shapes and sizes of glasses have changed over the years as more people have come to understand the best way to enjoy the various drinks. Glasses with coloured bowls should be reserved for ornaments; glasses for drinking should always have a clear glass bowl. When choosing a suite of glasses for an establishment, a degree of standardization should be practised to prevent too many glass sizes, making purchasing, storing and service more difficult.

| Elgin | Copita | Sherry |

Figure 7.1 *Sherry glasses*

Sherries

The classic glass for the service of a sherry is the *copita*. The shape of this glass (Figure 7.1) concentrates the bouquet of the wine at the top of the glass. However, it is difficult to wash and polish and is liable to have a high breakage rate. The next-best glass for sherry is one which is large enough to be filled about one-third full by 2 fl oz (USA) or 50 ml (UK), which is the normal pour or measure for sherry (Figure 7.1).

Various other glasses are used, and many of these are measures in themselves when filled to the top. These do not allow the bouquet of sherry to be appreciated fully.

The commonest commercial sherry glass in the UK is the Elgin. This is not very suitable for the enjoyment of sherry, but is very economical and robust (Figure 7.1).

Another acceptable sherry glass is a stemmed glass with a small bowl, which is the type often found in private homes (Figure 7.1).

Port

Port is often served in a glass just large enough to take 2 fl oz (USA) or 50 ml (UK) when filled nearly to the top. When a wine such as vintage port has been maturing for ten years upwards it is deserving of better treatment. A similar glass to

Figure 7.2 *Commercial glasses*

the second glass suggested for sherry, or a 4–5 fl oz (12–15 cl) Paris goblet would be most suitable, once again allowing the bouquet to be fully appreciated. Fortunately for those who enjoy port, the present trend is towards this larger glass. Other fortified wines can be served in the same type of glass.

Still wines

Many shapes and styles of glass are suitable for the service of still wines. Once again the glass should be large enough for the appearance and bouquet of the wine to be appreciated.

It is becoming the practice to use a suite of glasses of different sizes for red, white, sparkling and dessert wines (Figure 7.2). The red and white wine glasses should be of a minimum capacity of 7 fl oz (20 cl). If different sizes are used for red and white wines, then the red wine glass is now normally the larger glass; for example, use a 10 fl oz (28 cl) or larger for red wine, and 7 fl oz (20 cl) for white. Dessert wines are often served in smaller glasses, as smaller measures of these wines are normally served when they are offered towards the end of a meal. A 5 fl oz (14 cl) glass would be the minimum satisfactory size.

German wines were traditionally served in tall green or amber-stemmed glasses (Figure 7.3). Green stems were used for Mosel wines and amber stems for Hocks or Rhine wines. The light which is refracted through these stems and into the wine tended to accentuate the natural colouring of the wine. The highest-priced Hocks (Rhine wines) are sweet and amber in colour, whereas Mosel wines are a very light colour with just a hint of greenness. The traditional German glass is the *Römer*, which is also either green- or amber-stemmed. This glass has a hollow stem and base which causes more coloured light to be refracted into the wine. Almost universally now the green- and amber-, tall-stemmed glasses have been replaced by tall clear-stemmed glasses, or standard white wine glasses.

Wine served by the glass in the UK may be served only in 125 ml (4.4 fl oz), 175 ml (6.2 fl

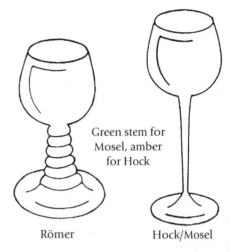

Green stem for Mosel, amber for Hock

Römer   Hock/Mosel

Figure 7.3 *Traditional German wine glasses*

oz) and 250 ml (8.8 fl oz) measures. The measure or measures of wine served must be advertised in a prominent position or on the wine list and the glass should have a line on it showing the level to which it should be filled. Alternatively a separate measure may be used to measure the wine before pouring it into an unlined glass. 125 ml is a useful size as this gives exactly eight glasses of wine from a litre bottle and six glasses from a 75 cl bottle.

Sparkling wines

Much time and effort and not a little expertise go into the production of a quality sparkling wine, therefore the glass used for its service must be one which offers the customer the maximum pleasure and enjoyment. The most suitable style of glass will be one which enables the customer to enjoy the wine's bouquet to the full, and allows the wine to show off its elegance and effervescence without losing its sparkle too quickly.

The best glass for these wines will have an elongated bowl of minimum size 7 fl oz (20 cl), narrowing towards the top, with a medium stem (Figure 7.4). Other glasses may be better suited to commercial establishments because of their ease of cleaning and polishing. If there are no champagne flutes, tulip-shaped or tall glasses available, a white wine glass is the next best. Never use a

| Champagne | Saucer | Cocktail | Brandy |

Figure 7.4 *Cocktail, Champagne and brandy glasses*

saucer-shaped glass for the service of sparkling wine. The bowl is too shallow and too wide, and this causes the bouquet and effervescence to dissipate quickly.

Liqueurs

Liqueurs are often served in glasses of a normal 1 fl oz (USA), 25 ml (UK) measure, which is very useful when serving large numbers quickly such as for a banquet. It also prevents loss of the liqueur through some of it adhering to the inside of a separate measure (which would also need to be washed after the service of each liqueur). Liqueurs are usually quite thick and sticky, so again small glasses have an advantage over large ones in that less of the liqueur will get left in the glass sticking to its inside.

The Elgin shape is again very popular, the glass being the measure, and it does show off the appearance of the liqueur. Other glasses (for example a small brandy glass) are not measures in themselves but allow the bouquet of the liqueur to be fully appreciated, and they are excellent for serving frappes. Liqueurs may be served in any quantity; there is no legal requirement to serve a specific measure.

Cocktails

Cocktail glasses vary considerably like the drinks they hold, and are chosen for their shape and size to suit the cocktails being offered. Cocktails usually fill the glass, whereas wine should never do so; therefore a variety of sizes may be used in one bar (Figure 7.5). Many of the original cocktails were small quantities, usually about 2 fl oz (5–6 cl), but the modern trend is for larger cocktails, and consequently the glasses are now larger.

Beers

Draught beer glasses in the UK are regulated in size. By law, draught beer in the UK must be served in ⅓ pint, ½ pint or 1 pint measures. They must be government stamped and must be filled up to the brim or up to a line marked on the glass showing the correct level. The ⅓ pint measure is rarely used. Bottled beers may be served in unstamped Worthington, Wellington, Paris or Slim Jim glasses, usually of 12 fl oz (35 cl), which allows for a head on the beer. Bottled nip beers are served in smaller glasses, for example 7 fl oz (20 cl) Paris goblets or the same size Wellington glasses (see Figure 7.5).

Brandies

Three-star brandy served with soda or ginger ale

| Thistle | Saucer | Martini | Old-Fashioned |

| High Ball | Sleever | Nonic | Slim Jim |

| Dimple | Worthington | Wellington | Pilsner |

Figure 7.5 *Cocktail, beer and other glasses*

should be served in 7 fl oz (20 cl) Paris goblets. Brandy on its own should be served in a brandy balloon. These vary in size, but the most practical size for everyday use is 7–9 fl oz (20–25 cl). Some brandy balloons are as large as 20 fl oz (55 cl), but these are very expensive, take up a lot of shelf space and are liable to get broken more easily than the smaller ones. The brandy will cling to the inside of the glass and therefore more will be left behind in the larger glasses and wasted by the customer. A good brandy balloon is made from thin glass to enable the drinker to warm the brandy in the glass in the palm of the hand quite quickly. Brandy balloons should not be warmed over a flame.

Other spirits

When whisky is served straight or with water it may be served in a 5–7 fl oz (14–20 cl) Paris goblet, club goblet, small tumbler, Old-Fashioned glass or a highball glass. If it is to be served with a mixer such as dry ginger it should be served in one of these types, of minimum size 7 fl oz (20 cl). Gin, rum and vodka are served in similar glasses.

Minerals

Mineral waters should be served cool, chilled or with ice in Paris goblets, Slim Jims, tumblers or highball glasses.

TEMPERATURES

Temperature ranges for the service of wine are open to much discussion and individual choice, but there are general rules of thumb, which should be followed.

Red wines

Light-bodied red wines, which are young, often benefit from being served very slightly cooler than full-bodied reds – at about 55°F (13°C), which is slightly above a perfect cellar temperature. Some light red wines such as Beaujolais Nouveau are at their best served slightly cooler – at 50–55°F (10–13°C).

Full-bodied red wines should always be served

chambré, which means at 59–64°F (15–18°C). To ensure that red wines are at the correct temperature for service, many establishments keep a stock of wines in a dispense area or in the restaurant itself. One problem of keeping the wine in the restaurant is that there is usually a great fluctuation of temperature over each day, which is bad for the wine and will cause it to deteriorate.

White wines

White wine should be served cool or chilled. Many wines are served too cold, thus preventing the full flavour of the wine to be enjoyed to the full. If a white wine is of a poor quality, it is best to chill it well, then its poor flavour will be masked by the cold temperature and not tasted.

The lighter and more delicate white wines should be served cool or, as the French say, *frais*. This is at 45–50°F (7–10°C). Heavier white wines at 50–55°F (10–13°C) and heavier sweet white wines, such as Sauternes and Muscat-de-Beaumes-de-Venise are at their best served cooler at 43–47°F (6–8°C). Sweet white wines should be served cooler than dry white wines.

Other beverages

Rosé wines are at their best when served cool – *frais* 45–50°F (7–10°C).

Sparkling wines contain carbon dioxide gas which expands when warmed and contracts when chilled. These wines are at their best when served slightly chilled at 45–50°F (6–10°C). If the wine is too cold, the flavours will be masked.

Dry sherries and the drier Madeiras are best served cool or slightly chilled at 50–55°F (10–13°C). A modern trend is to drink all sherries at this temperature. Sweet Madeiras, ruby and vintage ports should be served at 64–68°F (18–20°C); the better quality tawny ports are best served slightly cooler at 54–61°F (12–16°C).

Mineral waters should be served chilled at 43–47°F (6–8°C), as for sparkling wines. Lemon and ice should be offered but should not be added automatically because the ice is made from tap water, and the drink would not be pure mineral water any longer.

For service in a restaurant, the bottle should be opened at the table to prove its authenticity and is generally chilled in advance, although it can be served in a wine cooler.

Beers Draught bitter beers and bottled light ales are best served at 54–57°F (12–14°C) or cellar temperature. Draught and bottled lager is best served cooler at 48–52°F (9–11°C). Bottled brown ales and stouts are served at room temperature. Some people prefer bottled beers to be cooler than room temperature, so it is normal practice to keep some of each on a cooling shelf and to ask the customer which he or she prefers.

SERVING WINE

Identification of the host or hostess

The host or hostess should be identified when a party arrives in the establishment. He or she is usually the person who checks the reservation of the party (if previously booked) with the restaurant manager on arrival, or requests a table if they are chance customers. The host or hostess also usually handles the ordering of the meal. Chapter Nine further covers identification of the host and welcoming of customers.

Carafes

Carafes are open glass containers into which wine is poured for service by the carafe. This is a method of serving 'house' wines, which are often in 1-litre or 1.5-litre bottles. The legally permitted quantities for service in carafes in the UK are 25, 50, 75 and 100cl, and 10 and 20 fl oz; and the quantities which are being served must be clearly stated on the wine list by law. The amount served must have an exact measure of one of the above quantities, so carafes now have a line marked on them showing how full to fill them. Unlined carafes may be used, but in this case the wine must be measured exactly before it is poured into the carafe. The shape of the carafe must be such that the carafe will empty of all its contents when tilted at an angle of 30° with the horizontal or 120° with the vertical (Figure 7.6). Carafes which are used as decanters for complete bottles or half bottles, are not governed by this regulation.

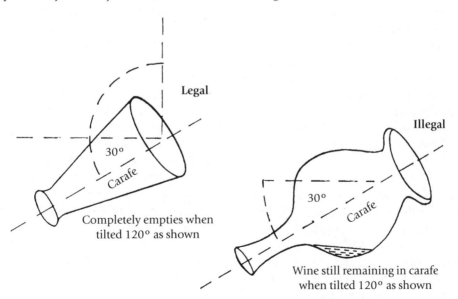

Legal

Completely empties when tilted 120° as shown

Illegal

Wine still remaining in carafe when tilted 120° as shown

Figure 7.6 *Carafe design*

Figure 7.7 *Ice cooler and bucket*

Coolers and ice buckets

Coolers are open-topped double-walled plastic cylinders which keep pre-chilled bottles of wine cool at the table (see Figure 7.7). Most coolers do not cool the wine; they merely maintain its temperature, and then only for a short period. However, a variety of cooler is available, which has two small freezer packs to insert to keep the wine cooler for longer.

Ice buckets (also called coolers) are filled with ice and water and are used to cool white, rosé and sparkling wine to the required temperature for service (see Figure 7.7). As much as possible of the bottle should be submerged in the ice and water to chill the wine effectively. Cold water remains below warm water, so that if only the lower part of the bottle is in the ice and water, the upper part of the wine will not cool down very quickly. It is

therefore a wise precaution to slightly tilt the bottle when removing it from an ice bucket so that the wine in the top of the bottle will mix with the rest. Then when the customer is offered a taste, he or she will be given wine which is at the temperature of the whole bottle.

If the wine bucket is to be taken to the restaurant table it should be placed either in a wine cooler stand on the floor to the right of the host, or on a plate or silver flat on the restaurant table. A crisp, clean napkin should be draped over the top of the bucket in either case, which will enable the customer to serve himself if the sommelier is not available. It also improves the presentation.

When the wine has reached the required coolness it is sometimes advisable to remove the bottle (or part-bottle if some has been poured from it) from the ice and to wipe the water off it. It should then be placed on either a coaster or a side plate on the restaurant table in front of the host. This will prevent the wine from becoming over-chilled.

Placing glasses on the table

If wine has been ordered in advance (which is often the case with functions) and where wine orders are taken in the bar before the customers enter the restaurant, the required glasses should be placed on the table before the customer arrives at the table (Figure 7.8).

The glasses should be arranged in a neat and tidy manner. They should be highly polished and placed upside down on the table until just prior to service. The glasses should be lined up with each other right along the table's length; this particularly applies when laying up tables for functions and private parties. Ensure that the bases of the glasses are highly polished as well as the bowls. Always carry glasses to and from tables on a salver. Handle them by the stem or base, *never* by the bowl.

If the wines are not ordered in advance, then it is usual to lay up two glasses, one for water and one for wine. If the wine order is taken at the table then the correct glasses for this wine should be placed on the table before the wine is presented

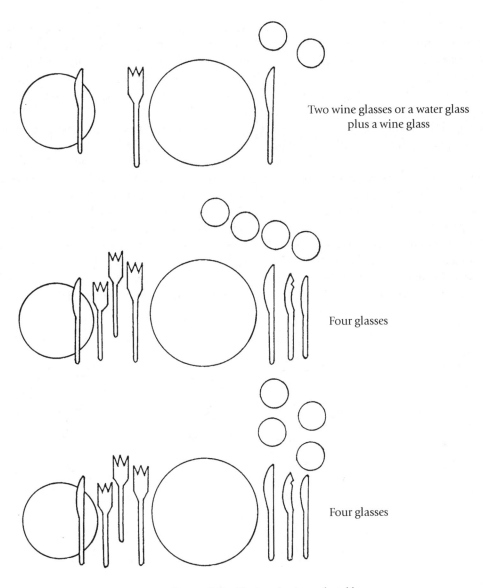

Two wine glasses or a water glass
plus a wine glass

Four glasses

Four glasses

Figure 7.8 *Placing glasses on the table*

for service. Glasses must be placed in exactly the same positions for each cover on the table.

Presenting and opening the bottle
The method of opening a bottle of wine is often affected by the policy of the house but the bottle should never touch the table or table cloth, and it should always be opened in full view of the customer unless there has been a request that it

should be opened or decanted in advance of the customer's arrival.

There are *twelve* basic stages to follow after checking the label to ensure the bottle is the one which was ordered.

1   Present the bottle to the host with label uppermost, stating the name of the wine, and vintage and producer where appropriate.

2 Cut the capsule.

3 Wipe the neck of the bottle.

4 Insert the corkscrew.

5 Lever the cork out.

6 Remove the cork from the screw and present on a side plate or small tray.

7 Wipe the top of the bottle.

8 Pour a small quantity from the right for the host to taste.

9 When accepted by the host, serve the other guests in a clockwise direction.

10 Top up the host's glass, to the same level as the other glasses.

11 Return the bottle to the cooler or place it on the table on a coaster or side plate in front of the host, with the label facing him/her.

12 Top up the glasses as required.

When a bottle of wine has been ordered, the sommelier should always present the bottle to the host on his right-hand side, with the label uppermost. State the name of the wine, and vintage and producer where appropriate. This is to ensure that it is the wine which the host has ordered. This is a sensible precaution as sometimes the customer is not fully concentrating on checking the wine, and many labels are similar in appearance. There should be a cloth under the bottle; one hand is under the cloth, the other steadies the bottle (Figure 7.9a). It is then prepared as necessary.

If it is a white wine and has been placed in a wine cooler/ice bucket, it should be taken out and wiped dry with a clean service cloth or clean napkin before presentation. The best method is to open the bottle on a cart or guéridon to the right

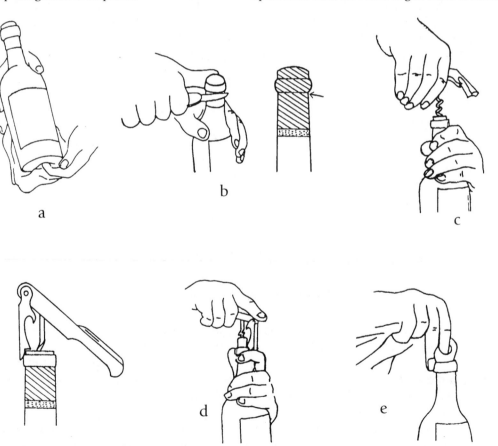

Figure 7.9 *Presenting and opening a bottle of wine*

156

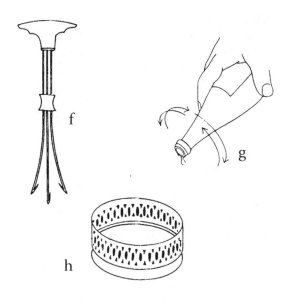

Figure 7.9 (continued)

of the host; the second-best, while it is still in the wine cooler/bucket; the third-best is on the table on a plate coaster or napkin; and lastly, in the hand. If it is a red wine which has sediment, present it to the host in the cradle, then open it still in the cradle on a cart or guéridon, or on the table prior to decanting (see p. 160). If it is without sediment open it on a cart or guéridon, or on the table on a plate/coaster or napkin; as the last choice, in the hand. For banquet service, it is acceptable to open red and white wines in the hand.

The capsule of the bottle must be cut *below* the glass ring on the top of the bottle and the part of the capsule above this point must be removed, otherwise small particles of dirt from under the capsule may get into the wine. Old red wines with lead capsules are likely to have lead oxides under the capsule and these would get into the wine if the capsule is cut too high. The knife of the corkscrew should be angled up against this glass ring so that a clean straight cut is obtained (Figure 7.9b). The top of the neck of the bottle is then wiped clean with the clean service cloth or napkin.

The corkscrew must be inserted into the centre of the cork and screwed down enough for the screw to reach to the base of the cork, but not go through the bottom of it (Figure 7.9c). Brace the lever of the corkscrew on the top edge of the bottle. Lever the cork almost out of the bottle with the right hand (left if left-handed) steadying the lever with the forefinger of the left hand and holding the neck of the bottle with the rest of this hand. The lever should be kept vertical during this part of the process (Figure 7.9d). The cork is finally removed by gripping the cork with the right thumb and forefinger and easing it out (without making a popping noise). The cork should then be removed from the corkscrew and the neck of the bottle wiped clean (Figure 7.9e). The cork should be presented to the host on a side plate or small tray. In some establishments it is house policy to present it in a small glass. Left-handed corkscrews are produced with the worm (screw) twisted in the opposite direction.

If a small piece of cork breaks off and falls into a bottle of wine, the sommelier should remove this by giving the bottle a sharp flick into the cloth without the customer seeing this, or over a sink if in a dispense bar or service area. The piece of cork should come out. If the cork or part of the cork gets pushed right into the wine in the bottle, it should be removed with a cork extractor (Figure 7.9f). This should be done at the side-table, not at the customer's table. If it is impossible to remove the cork in this way, the bottle should be replaced and decanted for sale by the glass. Most establishments' house policies will be to replace the bottle in any case and use the wine for the by-the-glass programme.

Pouring the wine

A small quantity is poured into the glass of the host or hostess, from the right-hand side of the customer, ensuring that the label is in full view. When the host has accepted the wine, the other guests on the table should be served, starting with the guest on the host's right, then serving the other guests in a clockwise direction round the table, and finally topping up the host's glass. If there is a guest of honour, he or she should be served first; then the older women, younger women, older men and younger men. At a function, the chairperson is served first and then the guest on his or her right, who will be the principal guest. When pouring wine, the sommelier should move in a clockwise direction round a table or from right to the left on a long table.

When pouring wine from a bottle, it should be held so that the label is facing and open to the customer's inspection. The wine should be poured firmly into the glass. When sufficient has been poured, the neck should be tilted upwards and a small twist given to the bottle; this should cause any drips to be spread around the glass ring of the bottle instead of dripping onto the tablecloth (Figure 7.9g). The neck should then be wiped with the clean cloth behind the guest before pouring wine for the next customer. Glasses should be half to two-thirds filled but never more than two-thirds full, to enable the bouquet to be fully appreciated. When large glasses are used they should be filled less than half-full.

The bottle may be placed back into the bucket or cooler for white wine, or placed on a plate or coaster on the table. The cork should be placed on the plate with the bottle or on a separate plate. A doily should not be placed on the plate. Condensation on a cold bottle will cause the doily to stick to the bottle when it is picked up. After all, the plate is only a substitute for a coaster, which is usually made from a wooden base with a silver surround; coasters never have a doily put in them (Figure 7.9h). Ensure that the bottle or cooler/ice bucket is in a safe position and not likely to be knocked over.

In some restaurants it is the house policy for the sommelier to pour a very small quantity into a glass and to smell and taste it before offering it to the host, but many customers might object to this, so permission from the customer should be obtained first.

When serving at a function, every fresh bottle of wine is not checked by the customer, and is often used to top up wine which is already in the glasses.

It is therefore sensible for the sommelier to quickly smell the top of the bottle out of sight of the table to ensure that the wine is sound and will not spoil the wine already in the glasses. This is sometimes done in the dispense bar when set wines are being served. A bad or corky bottle of wine served in this way would cause many glasses of wine to be affected.

Further service

The sommelier should keep an eye on the customers' glasses and refill as and when necessary, following the same order as before but without offering a taster to the host. Always serve the host last.

The sommelier should ask the customer if he or she would like a further bottle (of the same wine) before the first one is emptied, if he thinks the customer might require one. He would then have time to prepare a second bottle for service.

The correct form of service for this second bottle would be to place fresh glasses in front of the host and each guest, and to present the bottle to the host. A taster should be served to the host before serving the other guests at the table as for the first bottle. It is common practice to offer just the host a fresh glass to taste it and to check its quality and condition, before topping up the other glasses.

The wine from the second bottle must not be mixed in the glasses with wine from the first bottle before it has been tasted and checked, as it could be 'off', in which case it would ruin all the wine in the glass. In high-class establishments the sommelier might be expected to smell or even sample this second bottle to ensure that its condition and quality are correct; but the customer's permission should be obtained first.

The glasses should be removed from the table when they are finished with. If some of the wine served with an earlier course of the meal is left in the glass when wine offered with a later course has been served, the customer should be asked if he or she has finished with it, and it should only be removed if this is the case.

Decanting

Wine is decanted for two basic reasons:

1 To remove wine from the sediment which has formed in the bottle.
2 To allow the wine to take in oxygen – to 'breathe'.

Wine which has sediment should be treated with great care so that the sediment does not get mixed up in the wine, causing it to become cloudy. If this should happen, the wine should not be decanted but should be left unopened to allow the sediment to settle.

If sufficient notice is given by the customer, for example 48 hours, then the wine may be stood up. This will make the decanting process that much easier. Less than 48 hours' notice may be sufficient for some wines, depending on the type of sediment.

Method of decanting

Before starting to decant, ensure that the following *mise-en-place* is prepared. A cart or guéridon or small table should be prepared with a glass decanter and a decanting funnel if used, both previously rinsed with clean warm water. A piece of clean muslin is often placed into the top of the funnel. A lighted candle is made ready and two side-plates or one side plate and a small tray, are placed on the cart or guéridon. Remove the wine from the rack in the cellar with extreme care and place it in a wine cradle or basket. This should be presented to the customer, then taken to the cart or guéridon where the decanting will take place. In high-class establishments the wine is decanted on a small table cart or guéridon, to the right of the host.

The front of the cradle should be placed on an upside-down side plate, to prevent wine from dripping from the bottle when it has been opened. The capsule should be cut very carefully below the glass ring of the bottle, making sure the bottle is kept perfectly still in the cradle by gripping it with the other hand. The neck should be wiped with a clean service cloth or napkin. The corkscrew should be screwed into the cork, again holding the bottle steady in the cradle with the other hand. The lever is placed on the top of the neck of the bottle and the cork extracted in the usual way, being careful to keep the bottle still. Make sure the cork is eased out of the bottle carefully, so that wine is not sucked out with it. For very old wines, a *screwpull* bottle opener may prove to be more suitable than the traditional 'waiter's friend' type. Where it is the house policy, the sommelier will very gently pour a little wine into a glass on the cart or guéridon in order to taste it.

The decanting funnel, if used, is placed into the decanter and a piece of muslin placed in the funnel if this is required. The bottle should be held firmly with one hand while the cradle is removed with the other, and the wine is then poured steadily into the top of the funnel or decanter with the shoulder of the bottle held over the candle flame. If the bottle is held too close to the flame, soot may form on the underneath of the bottle, which will prevent the person decanting from seeing the sediment moving up the bottle to the neck. The pouring action should be continuous until the sediment reaches the shoulder of the bottle. At this point pouring must stop before *any* of the sediment passes into the decanter. If the cradle is one of the open silver varieties, the bottle need not be removed for decanting as the sommelier will be able to see the light from the candle shining through the wine.

The bottle should be replaced in the basket with the cork for presentation to the host. However, the cork is usually presented to the right of the host on one of the small trays or side plates. Sometimes the cork is fastened to the neck of the decanter with an ornamental clip, or failing this an elastic band. The decanter stopper should be placed in the decanter.

The wine will be offered for service as for a bottle; the host is offered a taste, and then the guests are served. The decanter is then left on a coaster or plate on the table. When part-empty bottles or

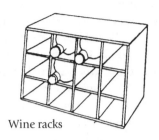

Wine racks

1 Wine basket

2 Cut capsule then wipe neck of bottle

3 Remove cork

4 Wipe neck of bottle again

5 Remove bottle from basket (can be left in if the cradle is of the open silver variety)

Open silver variety

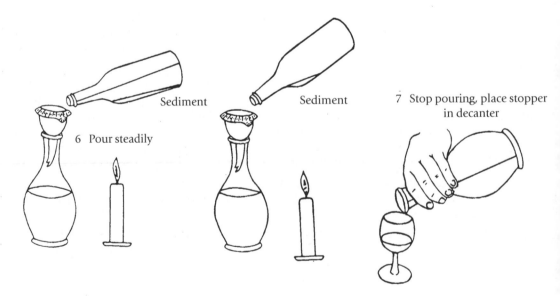

Sediment

6 Pour steadily

Sediment

7 Stop pouring, place stopper in decanter

Figure 7.10 *Decanting*

decanters are placed on the table, they should be placed in front of the host. Remember to present the bottle in the wine cradle when presenting the decanter.

If all bottles of a red wine requested are found to be too cold, it is sensible for the sommelier to apologize to the host and to ask the host if he or she would like the wine decanted. This will help the wine to come to room temperature more quickly. The glass decanter may be rinsed out with warm water, and this will speed up the process. It may also be suggested to the customer that he or she warms the glass of wine in the hands.

Note that the decanting basket was not designed for the service of wine at the table. To serve a red wine containing sediment from a basket will cause a quantity of the wine to be wasted. The wine will wash up and down the inside of the bottle as it is tilted up and down when pouring and lifted after pouring, thus causing the sediment to be disturbed. To serve a red wine which has no sediment in it from a basket just makes the service of the wine more difficult.

Service of sparkling wines

Champagne and sparkling wine should be chilled down to 6–8°C, either by keeping it in a refrigerated cabinet or by placing it in an ice bucket when the wine has been ordered. The wine should be presented to the host, then placed or replaced into an ice bucket or wine cooler with a napkin draped over the top. To open the bottle remove it from the ice or cooler and wipe it dry with another clean napkin or service cloth. Either cut the foil below the wire twist (the foil is usually perforated at the correct point) or pull the maker's tab which will also remove the foil at the correct point, although cutting the foil is safer as the tabs often break. Hold the bottle at an angle of 30° with the cork pointing away from the customer. Lift the wire twist from beneath the foil and untwist it while gripping the cork and neck of the bottle, with the other hand holding an unfolded napkin. Open out the wire cage and grip the cork firmly with one hand and the bottle firmly with the other. Twist the bottle,

not the cork, keeping the cork steady. As the cork loosens, ease it out of the bottle while still holding the bottle at an angle, being sure to keep the hand over the top of the cork. There should be only a slight hiss as the cork is removed. If the wine froths, keep the bottle at an angle, with the cloth held under the neck to absorb the wine.

Stubborn corks may be eased out by inserting champagne tweezers between the cork head and the top of the bottle. Do not twist the tweezers, just lever the cork up. As soon as the cork is eased, remove it as described above.

Offer a small amount to the host to taste and then serve the other guests as for still wine. Care must be taken when pouring the sparkling wine to ensure the wine does not froth up in the glass and overflow. For less experienced sommeliers it may be best to part-fill the glasses first before filling to the correct level, although experienced sommeliers will usually be able to fill the glass with one pour. The glasses should be filled half to two-thirds full.

When the customers have been served, replace the bottle in the wine bucket or cooler and drape the clean napkin over the bucket. A second acceptable method is to open the bottle while it is still in the bucket, then to proceed in the same way as above.

Remember that the pressure in a bottle of Champagne is six atmospheres, so at no time let go of the cork or allow it to point towards anyone, once starting to unwind the wire twist. A released Champagne cork will be a severe safety hazard and can blind a person if it strikes an eye at short range. The cork should be presented in the normal way.

Dealing with faults in the wine

Corky wine
The real meaning of the term corked is that the bottle is sealed with a cork. However, when a customer uses this term to describe a wine, they usually mean that the wine is corky, that is, it has the smell and taste of cork. This condition is caused by a faulty cork (see p. 35).

The sommelier should apologize to the customer, remove the wine, check it himself, and if it is out of condition, replace the bottle with another of the same type. If the wine is in the correct condition, it is prudent to offer a replacement wine of another type rather than have an argument about it. If the sommelier has detected this corkiness before serving the wine he should replace it with another bottle of the same type without offering the faulty one to the customer.

When the sommelier opens a bottle he may smell the wine (not the cork), if out of sight of the customer, as this will indicate to an experienced sommelier whether the wine is in good condition or not.

Broken cork

If a cork breaks and part falls into the bottle of wine, remove this with a cork extractor or decant the bottle. Do this away from the table. Alternatively replace the bottle and use the decanted wine for the wine-by-the-glass programme.

Effervescent wine

If the wine is seen to be 'fizzing' or is slightly effervescent when it is known that it is a still wine variety, this will probably indicate that the wine has undergone a secondary fermentation. It is therefore out of condition and should be replaced. This condition will often make the wine smell yeasty. Always check that the replacement bottle is not in the same condition before serving it to the customer.

Cloudy wine

If the wine is cloudy when it is poured into the glass it is out of condition for service. The sommelier should apologize to the customer, remove the glass and the bottle and replace with another bottle and a fresh glass.

Oxidized wine

When white wine becomes oxidized it usually becomes darker in colour and has a woody, toffee-like smell to it. A bad case of oxidation will cause the white wine to turn brown. It has been caused by the wine being exposed to air (oxygen) either during the production or storage periods. To obtain an example of this, a less than half-full bottle can be left open for a few days. Note: only use a low-priced wine for this experiment!

There are wines that are intentionally oxidized, e.g. Sherry and Madeira.

Maderized wine

Wine which is maderized has very similar characteristics to wine which has become oxidized. It is usually caused by the wine experiencing excessive heat either in the production process, in transportation or in storage. This condition can occur when the wine has been exposed to the sun. It produces much the same effect and has a strong 'sherry' or 'Madeira' smell to it, hence the name. To obtain an example of this, a small bottle of wine can be subjected to heat. Once again only use a low-priced wine for this experiment!

Other conditions

There are many other reasons why the wine may be out of condition. Always replace a bottle if the customer rejects it, and provide a fresh glass. If there is nothing wrong with the wine, suggest another wine to the customer saying that the rest of this wine came from the same delivery/case and that it will probably be in the same condition. The rejected wine can then be sold off by the glass or, in extreme cases, used in cooking.

SERVING SPIRITS, BEERS AND OTHER DRINKS

When serving any drinks at either the table or bar, ensure that the correct glasses are used and that they are scrupulously clean (for the correct glasses, see earlier in this chapter). A careful check must be kept that the full correct measures are served, and that the drinks are served at the right temperatures and with the right garnishes where appropriate. *Never* refill glasses; serve each drink in a fresh clean glass.

Drinks should be carried to a lounge or restaurant table on a salver. The glasses should be placed to the right of the customer, and the barperson or sommelier should stand on the right of each customer when placing his or her drink. At a bar or lounge table the drinks are often placed on beer mats or flat paper 'coasters' which may be used to advertise specific drinks or the establishment. Where tankards or glasses with handles are served, the handle should be placed to the right of the customer. Where a spirit is being served with a mixer, the spirit should be placed in the glass and the *mixer* added in front of the customer, either at the bar or at the table, to enable the guest to have the quantity he or she requires.

Sommeliers and bartenders should pick up glasses by the handle if there is one, or by the stem or the bottom half of the glass if there is not. The fingers of the hand must never be placed in or around the top of a glass, whether it is a clean one, a used one or one containing a drink.

MIXED DRINKS AND COCKTAILS

Preparation methods

Mixing

Mixed drinks are prepared by gently stirring ingredients in the glass to be used for the service of the drink. An example of this type of drink is an Americano.

Shaking

Cocktails may be shaken in either a Boston or a standard shaker (see Figures 2.15, 2.16).

Assemble all the ingredients and make ready any garnishes required before commencing preparation of the cocktail. Once the ice has been placed in the shaker, it will start to melt. If some ingredients are placed in the shaker with the ice, it will melt more quickly; if the bartender then finds that an ingredient is not to hand, the drink will become diluted.

Plenty of ice should be placed into the shaker and any excess water should be strained off. The ingredients are then poured into the shaker onto the ice and the top is put on securely. Holding the top and bottom of the shaker together with both hands for the Boston shaker, and with one or both hands for the standard shaker, shake vigorously so that the ice moves up and down the inside of the shaker quickly, cooling and thoroughly mixing the ingredients. The drink is then strained out of the shaker into the glass or glasses, which have been previously prepared.

Shaken cocktails are always opaque. This method of making a cocktail is used when ingredients of vastly different specific gravities are used together, and when egg white, sugar or cream are among the ingredients.

A Boston shaker is used in conjunction with a Hawthorn strainer (see Figure 2.20) and is the best type when large quantities are being prepared. The standard shaker has a built-in strainer in its top and is more suitable for shaking a single cocktail.

Ingredients containing carbon dioxide, such as soda water, lemonade and cola, must *never* be shaken in a cocktail shaker, otherwise the shaker will burst open. If they are an ingredient of the cocktail they should always be added to the shaken mixture. These ingredients should not be used in a mixing glass or blender either.

Blending

Blended drinks are prepared by mixing the ingredients in a blender (see Figure 2.17). This method is very suitable for drinks which require a purée of fruit in them, for long drinks and for multiple drinks. Crushed ice is usually used in the blender in place of ice cubes. Piña Colada is a drink which is suitable for this method of preparation.

Stirring

The ingredients for stirred cocktails are mixed together with a bar spoon in a mixing glass containing plenty of ice. The cocktail is then strained through a Hawthorn strainer (Figures 2.19, 2.20).

Plenty of ice should be placed in the mixing glass and then any water strained off before adding any ingredients. As for shaken cocktails, the ingredients, garnishes and glasses should be assembled before any ice is added to the glass, to prevent loss of time and excess melting of ice, which will weaken the cocktail.

When the ingredients are all in the glass the bar spoon should be stirred round and round the inside of the glass vigorously, causing the ice to mix and cool the liquors. The spoon is removed and the Hawthorn strainer is placed in the top of the mixing glass, which is then tilted to strain the mixed drink into the cocktail glass. If the drink being prepared is for more than one person, half fill each of the glasses then top up each, so obtaining an equal strength of the drink in each glass. The prepared drink in the mixing glass becomes more dilute towards the end because of the continually melting ice. Stirred cocktails are always clear, for example Dry Martini cocktail (see p. 168).

After a cocktail shaker or mixing glass has been used, the ice left in it must be thrown away and the equipment washed.

Ice

Ice is made in various shapes and sizes in ice machines. It must be clear and clean and plentiful in supply. For shaken and stirred cocktails and mixed drinks, small cubes or double chips are the most suitable. These are also the best shapes for regular bar drinks such as gin and tonic. Crushed or shaved ice is best for use in blenders and can either be produced in a machine that makes shaved ice or by putting ice cubes through an ice-crushing machine. Always ensure that there is a plentiful supply of ice readily available.

When ice is put into an insulated container to stand on the bar, a splash of soda will help to prevent the cubes of ice sticking together. Ice tongs or a spoon should be placed in or by the container.

When serving drinks which normally take ice with them, such as a gin and tonic or a dry vermouth, ask the customer if he or she would like ice; do not put it in without asking.

When preparing a stirred or shaken cocktail, at least half fill the mixing glass or shaker with ice. The mixing glass or shaker will be at the temperature of the bar and will therefore melt some of the ice while it cools down, so strain off any excess water before adding any ingredients of the cocktail.

Ingredients and accompaniments

Presentation of drinks is extremely important. However, although it is acceptable to dress up certain drinks, it should be remembered that drinks are for drinking. Do not over-decorate them with items which add nothing to the taste of the drink.

Lemon and limes

Fresh lemons and limes are essential commodities in any bar. Remove any sticky labels and wipe the fruit thoroughly before putting them into the bar for use.

Lemon and lime zest is used, twisted, over drinks such as Dry Martini cocktails to extract the oils, which will settle on the top of the drink, giving a delicate lemon smell and taste to it. The peel should not be put into the drink after extracting the oils (many barpersons do put it in).
Lemon and lime slices or half-slices are used as ingredients in many drinks such as gin and tonic and Cinzano Bianco. As with ice, always ask the customer before adding the sliced fruit. Don't slice them too thinly and don't put them in automatically.
Fresh lemon juice is used in a large number of cocktails, for example Sours, White Lady and Collins. Bottled fresh lemon juice is available and is easy to use, but does not have quite the same visual impact as fresh lemons. Slightly warm lemons give more juice than cold. Never use lemon squash or cordial for drinks where lemon juice is required.

Cherries

Cherries bottled in a light maraschino syrup are used for cocktails and other mixed drinks and add colour and flavour. There are bottled maraschino cherries available which have their stalks left on, which adds to the presentation of some drinks where the cherry is more of a decoration.

Oranges
Remove any sticky labels from the oranges and wipe them thoroughly before putting them into a bar for use.

Orange zest is used in a few drinks in the same way as lemon zest.
Orange slices, half-slices and wedges are used for drinks such as Champagne cocktails, an Old-Fashioned and Campari.
Fresh orange juice is used in cocktails and mixed drinks such as Buck's Fizz, and on its own, and is prepared as for lemon juice. Slightly warm oranges give more juice than cold ones. Never use orange drinks, squashes or cordials when orange juice is stated in the recipe of a drink.

Mint
Fresh mint leaves are used as an ingredient of juleps, and sprigs of mint are used as a decoration for these and other drinks. As for fresh fruit used in drinks, it is essential that the mint is clean, and it should be washed in cold water before placing it in the bar for use.

Olives
Both black and green olives are used as ingredients in some drinks, as well as for table accompaniments in the bar.

Other ingredients
Other accompaniments or ingredients which should be available in a bar include:

Castor and cube sugars
Coffee beans
Cream
Eggs
Nutmeg and grater
Pearl onions

Salt and pepper
Tabasco sauce
Worcestershire sauce
Cucumber (for Pimms if offered)

Cocktail recipes
Cocktails are combinations of drinks and other ingredients which are mixed together in predetermined quantities according to set recipes. They should taste of a mélange or mixture without any one ingredient predominating.

Cocktails are usually accepted as being short drinks of 2–4 fl oz (5–12cl). The majority are drinks which are suitable to be drunk as apéritifs, stimulating the gastric juices for the meal to come. Others are suitable as after-dinner drinks, such as a Brandy Alexander. The many longer drinks, which are in vogue at present, are usually referred to as mixed drinks.

Cocktails fall into three basic categories:

1   Those prepared by shaking the ingredients together with ice, in a cocktail shaker, then straining the drink into a glass.
2   Those prepared by stirring the ingredients together through ice in a mixing glass, then straining the drink into a glass.
3   Those prepared by *building* (pouring) the ingredients into the glass with no pre-mixing.
4   Those prepared by blending the ingredients in an electric blender, e.g. piña colada.

Although there are cocktails which are made up of just two ingredients, the vast majority comprise three, and there are often more than three. These three parts are usually:

1   A base, usually of spirit
2   A sweetening, which may be a syrup, sugar or liqueur
3   A souring, often fresh fruit juice, bitters or other ingredients.

For example:

	Base	Sweet	Sour
White Lady	gin	Cointreau	lemon juice
Bronx	gin	vermouth	orange juice
Old Nick	Rye whiskey	Drambuie	lemon juice orange juice orange bitters

This is a helpful way to remember the ingredients of recipes.

Both alcoholic and non-alcoholic cocktails may be prepared by shaking or stirring. Other mixed drinks are prepared by combining various ingredients together.

Americano
1 measure Campari
1 measure sweet vermouth
Soda water

An Americano is prepared by building equal quantities of Campari and sweet vermouth into either a highball glass or Old-Fashioned glass half filled with ice, and topping this with soda water. Add a half-slice of orange, a thick wedge of orange or a twist of lemon zest and serve.

Black Velvet
Equal quantities of Champagne and Guinness are built into a beer or highball glass.

Bloody Mary
1 measure vodka
1 baby-size bottle tomato juice
2–3 dashes Worcestershire sauce
1 dash lemon juice

A Bloody Mary may be prepared by shaking, stirring or combining the ingredients together in the glass for service. The most suitable method is to stir it in a mixing glass. Serve in a highball glass or Old-Fashioned glass. Some people like Tabasco sauce, cayenne pepper, mill pepper and celery salt incorporated in this drink. A Virgin Mary is like a Bloody Mary but without the vodka.

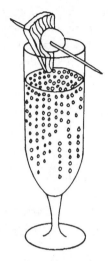

Figure 7.11 *Champagne cocktail*

Buck's Fizz
⅓ orange juice
⅔ Champagne

Champagne Cocktail
1 glass of dry Champagne
1 teaspoon Cognac
1 cube of sugar
Angostura bitters

Place a cube of sugar in a Champagne glass and saturate it with Angostura bitters. Add cold champagne and top with approximately one teaspoon of Cognac. Finish with a half-slice of orange or a thick wedge of orange. This drink may be decorated with a maraschino cherry and a wedge of orange, on a cocktail stick, resting on the top of the glass (Figure 7.11). A slightly less dry version of this drink can be prepared by substituting Grand Marnier for the Cognac. When preparing large numbers of this drink for a reception, the glasses, each containing an Angostura-soaked cube of sugar and a wedge of orange, may be half filled with Champagne a short while in advance and topped up with Champagne and Cognac as the guests arrive.

Cosmopolitan
1 measure of vodka
1 measure of cranberry juice
½ measure of Cointreau/Triple Sec
Juice of half a fresh lime

Build the ingredients into a highball glass half filled with ice, serve with a straw.

Cuba Libre
1 measure white rum
Juice of half a fresh lime
Cola

This drink is classed as a highball. It is made by adding the rum and lime juice to a highball glass half filled with ice and topping up with cola. Stir with a bar spoon and decorate with a thick slice of fresh lime. Serve with straws.

Daiquiri
¾ white rum
¼ fresh lime juice
3 dashes Gomme

Shake and strain.

Fizzes
Fizzes are similar to the Collins except that all the ingredients apart from the soda water are shaken. *Gin Fizz* is made from exactly the same ingredients as a Tom/John Collins. Shake the gin, lemon juice and Gomme together, strain into a highball glass and top up with soda water, stirring with a bar spoon.
Silver Fizz As for a Gin Fizz with white of egg added to the cocktail shaker.
Golden Fizz As for Gin Fizz with yolk of egg added to the cocktail shaker.
Royal Fizz As for Gin Fizz with a whole egg added to the cocktail shaker.

Frappés
Frappés are made by pouring a measure of a liqueur into a 4 oz (12 cl) cocktail glass, a brandy glass or a short-stemmed glass filled with crushed ice, and serve with two half-straws. Three of the most popular *frappés* are:
Crème de menthe frappé (using green Crème de Menthe)
Cointreau frappé
Bailey's *frappé*

Harvey Wallbanger
1 large measure (50 ml/2 oz) vodka
1 baby-size bottle orange juice
½ measure Galliano

This popular mixed drink is prepared by combining a large measure of vodka with a bottle of orange juice in a highball glass half filled with ice. Half a measure of Galliano is poured on the top, and the drink is served with straws.

Highballs
Highballs are long drinks comprising a spirit and an effervescent mixer, and sometimes a third ingredient. They are all served in highball glasses.

Horse's Neck
1 measure brandy
Ginger ale
Peel of one lemon

Peel the skin off a lemon in one long spiral, placing one end in the bottom of a highball glass and the other over the top edge. Place ice into the glass, add the brandy and top up with ginger ale.

Rye Highball
1 measure rye whiskey
Ginger ale or soda water

A measure of rye whiskey is placed in a highball glass half filled with ice, and topped up with ginger ale or soda water, stirring with a bar spoon. A twist of lemon may be added.
 A *rye and dry* in the UK is rye whiskey, ice and ginger ale.

John or Tom Collins
1 measure of London dry gin
Juice of 1 medium-sized lemon
1 teaspoon/bar spoon Gomme syrup
Soda water

Half fill a highball glass with ice. Add the gin, lemon juice and Gomme, then top up with soda water, stirring with a bar spoon. Decorate with a slice of lemon and serve with straws.

Kir
Kir is a mixture of ½ oz (12 ml) of *Crème de Cassis* topped up with dry white wine and served in a wine glass.
   Kir Royal is a mixture of ½ oz (12 ml) of *Crème de Cassis* topped up with Champagne and served in a Champagne glass.

Mai Tai
1 measure white rum
1 measure golden run
½ measure curaçao
¼ measure orgeat
1 dash grenadine
Juice of a lime

Build the ingredients into a highball or Old-Fashioned glass filled with ice. Decorate with a slice of fresh lime, slice of pineapple, a cherry and sprig of mint. Serve with straws.

Manhattan
There are three types of Manhattan: sweet, medium and dry. They are all mixtures of rye whiskey and vermouth.

Sweet Manhattan
1½ measures rye whiskey
¾ measure sweet vermouth
1 dash Angostura bitters

Stir and strain into a small cocktail glass and add a maraschino cherry.

Medium Manhattan
1½ measures rye whiskey
⅜ measure sweet vermouth
⅜ measure dry vermouth

Stir and strain into a small cocktail glass, add a cherry and twist of lemon.

Dry Manhattan
1½ measures rye whiskey
¾ measure dry vermouth

Stir and strain into a small cocktail glass and finish with a twist of lemon.

Martini cocktails
There are three types of Martini cocktail: sweet, medium and dry.

Sweet Martini
1½ measures gin
⅜ measure sweet vermouth

Stir and strain into a small cocktail glass and finish with a maraschino cherry.

Medium Martini
1½ measures gin
⅜ measure sweet vermouth
⅜ measure dry vermouth

Stir and strain into a small cocktail glass and finish with a twist of lemon.

Dry Martini
1½ measures gin
¾ measure dry vermouth (this will vary considerably with taste)

Stir and strain into a small cocktail glass and finish with a twist of lemon. A dryer version of the Dry Martini is sometimes referred to as an American Dry Martini. This is mixed in the ratio of five parts of gin to one part dry vermouth. It has become the fashion to drink Martinis very dry. If this is served with a pearl onion instead of the twist of lemon zest, it is called a *Gibson*.

Negroni
⅓ gin
⅓ sweet vermouth
⅓ Campari
Soda water is optional

Build the gin, vermouth and Campari into a high-ball glass half filled with ice. Add soda water if desired and finish with a half-slice of orange.

Old-Fashioned
1 large measure (25 ml/1 oz) rye whiskey
Angostura bitters
Cube of sugar
Little water

A small cube of sugar is placed into an Old-Fashioned glass and saturated with Angostura bitters. A little water is added to dissolve the sugar, which is broken up with a bar spoon. Half fill the glass with ice, then add the rye whiskey. Decorate the drink with a half-slice or wedge of orange and a maraschino cherry. It is normal to serve a stirrer with this drink.

Pimm's
There are now only two types of Pimms:
Pimm's No. 1, which is gin based. Half fill a 10 oz Highball glass with ice, pour on one measure (1 oz) of Pimm's, top up with lemonade and stir. Decorate with a slice of cucumber peel in the glass, and a cocktail stick with a slice of lemon, slice of orange and a cocktail cherry across the top of the glass.
Vodka Pimm's, which is vodka based.

Pink Gin
1 measure Plymouth gin
Angostura bitters
Iced water
The original Pink Gin was made with Plymouth

gin, and this is still recognized as the correct ingredient. Angostura bitters are shaken into a spirit glass. The glass is twisted around to allow the bitters to coat the inside of the glass; any excess bitters may be emptied out. The gin is added, and the drink is served topped up with iced water.

Pink Lady
1 large measure (2 oz/50 ml) dry gin
½ measure Grenadine
1 egg white

All the ingredients are shaken and strained into a small cocktail glass.

Piña Colada
1 large measure white rum
½ baby-size bottle pineapple juice
1 measure coconut cream or slightly less Malibu

The ingredients are blended with crushed ice and served in a highball glass or 10 oz (28 cl) Paris goblet. The drink is decorated with fresh pineapple and a maraschino cherry and served with short straws.

Pousse-Café
These drinks are made by layering syrups, liqueurs and spirits on top of each other in a narrow glass (Figure 7.12). The order in which the liquors are added depends on the specific gravity of each ingredient. Syrups are the heaviest, liqueurs are the next and spirits are the lightest. The bottles of ingredients should be lined up in order. A small quantity of each is poured down the inside edge of the glass onto the bowl of a small spoon, usually a coffee spoon or teaspoon, which is held against the inside of the glass and the opposite top inside edge (see Figure 7.12). Some people prefer to drink this through a short straw.

Rob Roy
Equal quantities of Scotch whisky and sweet vermouth
1 dash Angostura bitters

Figure 7.12 *Pousse-café*

Build into an Old-Fashioned glass with or without ice. Stir, and serve with a cherry.

Rusty Nail
⅔ Scotch whisky
⅓ Drambuie
Build into an Old-Fashioned glass, half filled with ice, serve with a twist of lemon.

Screwdriver
1 measure vodka
1 baby-size bottle of orange juice

The vodka and orange juice are built into a highball glass half filled with ice, and the drink is stirred with a bar spoon.

Sidecar
1 measure Brandy
½ measure Cointreau
½ measure fresh lemon juice

Shake and strain into a small cocktail glass.

Sours
Sours are shaken cocktails of fresh fruit juice, a

spirit and a sweetening (either a syrup or a liqueur). The drink is usually enhanced by incorporating a little white of egg.

Whisky Sour
1½ measures Scotch whisky
1 measure lemon juice
½ measure Gomme
½ white of egg

Shake and strain into a large cocktail glass and decorate with a half-slice of lemon.

Tequila Sunrise
1 measure tequila
1 baby-size bottle orange juice
Little Grenadine

The tequila is combined with the orange juice in a highball glass half filled with ice. A little Grenadine is poured down the inside of the glass. Decorate with a half-slice of orange and a maraschino cherry, and serve with straws.

White Lady
1 measure gin
½ measure Cointreau
½ measure fresh lemon juice

Shake and strain into a small cocktail glass.

NON-ALCOHOLIC

There are many non-alcoholic drinks and cocktails. They can be made by using combinations of fruit juices, syrups, non-alcoholic cordials, milk, cream and eggs. These may be topped up with soda water, lemonade or other non-alcoholic mixers.

A very popular drink with sportsmen and women is a mixture of fresh orange juice and lemonade.

The best-known non-alcoholic cocktail is the Pussyfoot cocktail. This is a mixture of equal quantities of orange, lemon and lime juice, a dash of grenadine, and an egg yolk, shaken and strained into a large cocktail glass or highball glass.

TABLE AND COCKTAIL BAR ACCOMPANIMENTS

It is the practice in many establishments to put a few small snack items of food in dishes on the bar for the customers to consume while they are drinking.

Many of these items are intended to make the customer thirsty and thus buy extra drinks. An example of this was the introduction of potato crisps. They were not very popular until the manufacturer inserted a small bag of salt into the packet of crisps. They then became very popular with publicans because their customers did in fact drink more when eating them. They were of course generally sold to the customer, which also increased profits. Nowadays many crisps are ready-salted or flavoured, the flavourings having a salty or spicy taste to them.

Other items which are put out as cocktail-bar table accompaniments or are sold in packets to the customers are:

Cheese cubes
Salted biscuits
Chipples, chipsticks
Cocktail gherkins
Dry roasted nuts
Plain nuts
Nuts and raisins
Salted nuts
Olives – black, green, stuffed
Pearl onions
Pickled onions
Pork scratchings
Pretzels
Other proprietary cocktail snacks

CIGARS AND CIGARETTES

Cigars

Cigars should be kept at a temperature of 60–65°F (15–18°C) and a relative humidity of 65–70 per cent. However, this is not the normal environment of a restaurant or bar, so establishments do not usually keep great numbers of quality cigars in stock. Dry heat, drastic variations of temperature, damp and smells are detrimental to cigars. Cigars which have become dry may be restored by putting them in their box for a few days in a damp cellar or atmosphere. Cigars should not normally be stored in these conditions, as if they get very damp they may go mouldy. If a white powder is seen on them this should be removed with a soft brush or handkerchief, it is a 'heat mould' and is not detrimental to the cigar. If boxes of cigars are to be kept for some time, store them upside down; this allows the cigars to breathe through the uncovered bottom of the cedar wood box.

Cigars are often kept and presented in humidor boxes. A humidor is a cabinet or box that has a flush fitting lid with a moisture pad in it. This will regulate the humidity by moisturizing the air if it is too dry. If the atmosphere is too damp then the pad must be used dry and it will then absorb any excess moisture.

Many cigars are individually packed in metal tubes. These are very good for establishments which are situated close to the sea, as salt air has a detrimental effect on a cigar. Inside the tube there is a thin piece of cedar wood around the cigar.

As smoking is offensive to many customers it is common practice in many restaurants to provide a separate room or Cigar Terrace for smoking. In a number of North American states there is a total ban on smoking in restaurants, hotels and public areas. Cigars are usually offered at the end of a meal with the Port or Brandy and coffee. If there is a liqueur trolley, the cigars may be presented from this, from a guéridon or in the box on a salver. The sommelier should ensure that on the trolley there are side-plates, matches, cedar strips if used and a

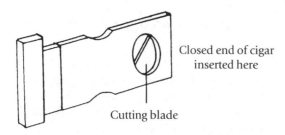

Figure 7.13 *Guillotine cigar cutter*

Closed end of cigar inserted here

Cutting blade

cigar cutter before offering cigars or cigarettes. If there is no trolley then these items must be readily available. There must be sufficient ashtrays on the table, preferably one for each smoker. Cigars which are kept in a cedarwood box or humidor should be shown to the customer from the left. When the customer has selected the cigar, the sommelier should then carefully remove it, taking care not to catch the wrapper of any of the cigars in the box with a fingernail and thus break the outer wrapper. It is a good idea to place a cigar in the box in such a way that the customer can pick it up easily without catching another cigar, and possibly ruining it.

The sommelier should then offer to prepare the cigar for smoking and carry it back to the guéridon. If the cigar is encased in cellophane, tear the tab and carefully ease the cigar out by gentle pressure at the end of the cellophane tube. Do not touch the head of the cigar. Place the cellophane in a pocket or place it on a side plate on the guéridon. The closed end of the cigar has to be opened, and the best way to do this is to use a cigar cutter – either a flat guillotine cutter (Figure 7.13) or a V-shaped cutter. Enquire whether the customer prefers a light, medium or full draw and then cut to suit, but don't cut above the cap, as this seals the wrapper. The cigar should not be pierced as this leaves an opening which is too small for the cigar to be enjoyed to its full potential. The cigar must be handled with great care to ensure that the outer wrapper leaf, which is very thin, is not broken. A cigar which is in good condition will be firm but yielding to light pressure from the fin-

gers, so that it can be held firmly while cutting it. When cut, the cigar should be tapped over a side plate to remove any small particles left from the cutting operation. The cigar should be returned to the customer on another side plate or small tray from the left and offered a light from a cedar wood strip, a wooden match or gas lighter – never from sulphur or wax matches or a petrol lighter, as these will spoil the flavour of the cigar. The end of the cigar should be held in the flame and charred evenly. To assist combustion, the cigar may be waved so that air passes through it. The smoke of the cigar should now be drawn by the customer, with the light held a half-inch away from the tip of the flame. The practice of warming the cigar along its whole length with a lighted match is unnecessary. This practice came about years ago to burn off an unpleasant-tasting glue which was used to secure the wrapper of the cigar. This glue is now no longer used, so it is a redundant practice. Whether to remove the band prior to smoking or not is really up to the smoker's preference. The best time for the customer to remove it would be after the cigar has been smoked for a while and the cigar has warmed up a little and shrunk. The band can then be removed easily without damage to the wrapper.

Although the taste and strength of a cigar cannot be judged from its colour, the following colour markings are often to be found on cigar boxes:

CCC   *Claro*, a light brown colour
CC   *Colorado claro*, a little darker brown
C   *Colorado*, a darker brown still
          Maduro darker still

Maduro or *Colorado-Maduro* is another less-used colour grading, and means very dark brown. 'Green' cigars are not green in colour; the word is used to indicate that the cigar is very fresh and has been neither dried nor conditioned. These are usually sold in hermetically sealed glass jars. A Candela cigar is the name of a greenish-yellow cigar which is popular with some customers.

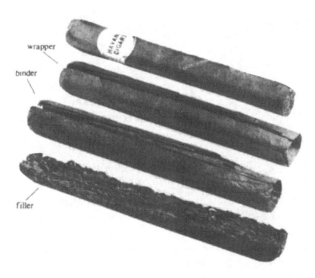

Figure 7.14 *A Havana cigar*

Havana or Habana cigars, which are produced in Cuba, are accepted as being the best, followed by Jamaican cigars. All boxes of Havana cigars have a green and white Cuban government label of guarantee on them. There are five main cigar tobacco-growing districts in Cuba: Vuelta Abajo, Semi-Vuelto, Partidos, Remedios and Oreinte. The Vuelto Abajo is where the wrapper leaf is grown and is considered to be the most important district. The tobacco leaves are harvested in February and March, first dried in barns then in piles in the sun. At this point the tobacco undergoes a fermentation before being tied, five to the bunch, packed into bales and matured for up to two years. A Havana cigar is made in three parts (Figure 7.14):

1 The filler
2 The binder or bunch-binder
3 The wrapper

The wrapper is the most expensive part of the cigar and may be as much as two-thirds of the total cost of the cigar.

Cigars are made in various sizes of length and girth, which are given names. The girth is by a ring gauge. A Corona is sold as having a girth of 42 gauge.

A Corona is 5½ inches or 140 mm in length and has a closed, rounded end. A Petite Corona is 5 inches or 127 mm in length and has the same girth as a Corona. As Cuban cigars are not permitted to be imported into the USA, the cigars from a number of other countries are becoming popular, for example: Dominican, Nicaraguan, Mexican, American from Connecticut and Dutch.

Cigars which are packed in cedarwood boxes of 25 are pressed cigars and appear to be slightly square in cross-section. Cigars tied with a yellow silk ribbon in bundles of 50 and packed in a cedarwood box are called 'cabinet selection'.

Cigarettes

If a customer orders a packet of cigarettes, it should be presented to the customer on a silver or stainless steel salver, or failing this a plate. The cellophane cover should be removed from the packet. The top of the packet should be opened and the small piece of light foil removed from the inside, exposing the cigarettes. This is the correct service of cigarettes at a table in a restaurant or lounge (see Figure 7.15).

Figure 7.15 *Serving cigarettes*

If the restaurant or bar permits smoking, ashtrays which have been used should be changed for clean ones. The procedure to be followed is to approach the table with a salver holding a clean ashtray and something such as a coffee saucer or another ashtray to cover the dirty ashtray. The cover is placed over the used ashtray to prevent the ash from flying, and this is replaced with the clean ashtray; the used one is placed on the salver.

SPECIALITY COFFEES

Speciality coffees are made by placing a measure of the chosen spirit or liqueur into a warmed speciality coffee glass or a Paris goblet, adding brown sugar to taste. Hot black coffee is poured into the glass to within 15 mm of the top, stirring all the time to dissolve the sugar. Double cream is poured gently over a teaspoon to float on the surface of the coffee (Figure 7.16).

The glass is served on a doilied side plate with a teaspoon – in the centre of the cover, not to the right-hand side. These coffees are usually prepared on a trolley or table in front of the customer. Some examples of speciality coffees are:

Name	Liqueur or spirit
Calypso	Tia Maria
Caribbean	Rum
DOM or Monk's	Bénédictine
Gaelic or Highland	Scotch whisky
Irish	Irish whiskey
Prince Charles	Drambuie
Royal	Cognac, flamed
Rüdesheimer	Asbach brandy
Witches	Strega

A Viennese coffee has no liqueur or spirit added, but it is served in the same way with the cream floated on top and grated chocolate sprinkled over it.

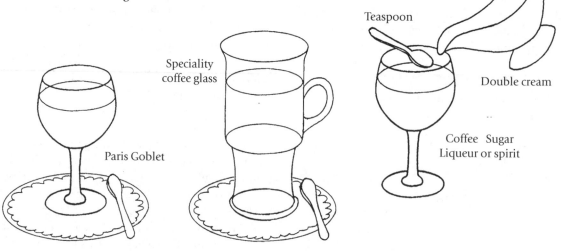

Figure 7.16 *Speciality coffee*

CHAPTER EIGHT

Maintaining and Increasing Sales

OBJECTIVES OF SELLING AND MERCHANDIZING

The objectives of selling and merchandizing are:

1 Gaining customer confidence
2 Achieving customer satisfaction
3 Achieving and maximizing sales

Whenever customers enter a public house or restaurant, they do so to purchase refreshment. It is therefore up to the beverage sales staff to satisfy the customers' requirements and to sell them as much as they will be happy to purchase. In most restaurants more net profit is made on wine and other drinks per unit than on food. It is also very much easier and quicker to serve a drink from the bar or a bottle of wine at the table, than to prepare a course of a meal or a whole meal that sells for the same price as the bottle of wine.

To gain the confidence of the customers, the staff must greet them politely and in a welcoming manner, making them feel comfortable and wanted (see p. 181). The sommelier is required to take drinks orders, advising where necessary, and to serve these drinks in the correct condition and in the correct manner. If a customer has to ask for the wine list, a sale might already have been lost, and the customer's respect most certainly will have been. It is wrong to rush a customer into making a decision on his or her choice; and not being available when the customer is ready to order or requires advice is another negative.

The sommelier needs to be able to judge which customers would welcome advice, but may be too embarrassed or nervous to ask for it. The sommelier can 'test the water' so to speak by asking one or two simple questions such as 'Are you looking for a red or white wine sir/madam?' If the answer is 'White', then to follow with 'If you like a dry wine may I suggest *a* or *b*, or *x*, if you prefer something a little sweeter.' An appropriate conversation could follow if red wine was requested. These suggestions should be at a price which the sommelier thinks will be acceptable to the customer; the *a* or *b* suggestions should be at medium price and medium-plus price levels. The basics of taking beverage orders will be described in Chapter Nine.

METHODS OF MAINTAINING AND INCREASING SALES

The beverage staff should be trained in food and beverage operations and should be encouraged to learn as much as possible about the products which they will be selling. This inevitably means they should be provided with tutored tastings of the listed wines. In this way they will become confident and skilful in the service of drinks.

It is of major importance to the maximizing of sales that the sommelier and barperson have a good knowledge of the range of products on offer. They will then be able to make suggestions and recommendations for drinks to accompany courses and meals and to answer customers' questions. In addition, to maximize sales the beverage service staff need to be able to assess the spending potential of the customer so that they can suggest and recommend drinks which will be appropriate to their requirements.

Good and correct presentation of drinks in the restaurant and bar is of vital importance, as this will help to sell them. Many customers are also attracted to a bar by the showmanship of the barperson and their efficient and attractive service.

Customers also like to be treated as individuals and to feel that their custom is valued.

Cleanliness and tidiness is always important, and should be maintained from opening right through the service time. This means wiping up spillages as soon as they happen, replacing used ashtrays, and ensuring that any tables and service surfaces are kept clean.

Glasses and stemware must always be sound (unchipped) and highly polished. Each time a drink is served in a bar a fresh glass should be used. Wine glasses should be placed in the correct position on the restaurant tables and for functions (see p. 155), and care should be taken to ensure that they are lined up evenly. Good clean, crisp linen shows off glasses well and should be used whenever possible, unless the tables are highly polished wood.

Wine lists must be clean and attractive, well laid out, easy to keep clean and legible, with explanations where necessary to help the customers choose their requirements. Descriptions of the wines, which are printed on the wine list, must be accurate and interesting. These descriptions are very important with the introduction into the market of many lesser-known wines, and the increase in price of the more traditional ones. If whole-page maps of the wine regions are part of the wine list, ensure the wines from the depicted country are shown on the opposite page. Bin numbers should always be used on wine lists to identify the various wines; these enable customers to have confidence when ordering. If they feel embarrassed at not knowing the correct pronunciation of a wine, they will often order a different wine (usually a cheaper one) to hide their ignorance. Bin numbers will also reduce the chance of the wrong bottle of wine being sent up by the cellar or fetched by the sommelier. These points will help to make the customer feel comfortable and

at ease which might encourage them to stay longer on their visit. The longer they remain happily enjoying themselves in your establishment, the more sales you are likely to make. They are also likely to return again in the future and to recommend your establishment to their friends.

Tent cards recommending particular drinks may be placed on the tables in the bar and restaurant. These are proven aids to sales, as are displays of items you wish to promote, but these cards must be changed whenever they become soiled. The display shelves in a bar should be used to *sell*; therefore they should be used for the display of drinks. They should not be used as a holding place for glasses which are to be used for service, as this is a waste of highly effective promotional space. Posters may be displayed recommending particular drinks, and examples of new drinks may be prepared and displayed on the bar, sometimes for customers to sample.

Awareness and anticipation of customers' needs are two qualities which come with training and experience.

POSITIVE SELLING

Customers arriving for a meal should be asked what they would like to drink as an apéritif, for example 'May I take your apéritif order?' or 'What apéritif may I bring you?' This approach does not give the customer the option of saying 'No' quite so easily. Alternatively, the suggestion of a named drink might be made to them, e.g. 'May I suggest a glass of Champagne as an apéritif?' This saves the customer having to make suggestions to his guests, or having to think about what he or she might like to drink. It makes life easy for the customer, relieves any stress that might be there and also ensures an up-market sale. If the apéritif glasses become rather low while the guests are in the bar or lounge areas, the staff should ask them if they require the same order again rather than waiting for them to make a request for more drinks.

The wine list should be presented to the customer with the menu. If the customer makes an order for wine, which is obviously meant to accompany the main course, the sommelier could ask if he would like a wine with the starter course.

If a single bottle of wine is ordered by a party of six persons or more, then it would be sensible to ensure that a second bottle is prepared unopened. This will then be in the correct condition for service and can be offered for service when the first bottle is nearly finished. It is a good idea to mention to the customer that you will have a second bottle available if he or she should want it. Another approach which could be made when the first bottle is ordered would be for the sommelier to ask 'Two bottles, sir/madam?' It is advantageous to good service and sales if a wine order can be taken while the customers are still drinking their apéritifs in the restaurant bar area so that it can be properly prepared and ready for the customers when they arrive at the dining table. This will be seen by the customer as quality service and will encourage them to start drinking the wine immediately, which may well lead to the sale of a further bottle of wine.

The sommelier should offer liqueurs, brandies or port at the end of the meal, just prior to the service of coffee. A liqueur trolley will certainly help sales, as will sweet wine and vintage port offered for sale by the glass and displayed on this trolley. If the restaurant is too small for a trolley, then other techniques can be used to maximize sales. For example, if a customer orders a brandy the sommelier could bring a range of three Cognacs and an Armagnac plus a measure (UK) and glasses to the table on a salver. Very often the best-quality and most expensive brandy is sold in this instance, and the customer will appreciate seeing a full measure (UK) being poured out in front of him/her, even though there is no legal requirement to serve a set measure of brandy. It is better still to free pour the brandy first ensuring the price is sufficient for the projected pour. If a liqueur had been ordered as well, then this would be brought on the same salver with a liqueur glass and would also be poured out in front of the customer at the table. Another positive approach would be to ask the customer if he would like a VSOP, and if he says 'Yes' to bring only VSOP brandies and older on the salver.

A form of positive selling is to use an initial approach which assumes that a sale has been made, and that the only decision to be made by the customer is which item to choose. An example when taking a wine order would be: 'Would you prefer a dry or medium dry wine with the prawn cocktails, sir/madam?' instead of 'Would you like anything to drink with the first course, sir/madam?' or 'Do you require wine with your meal sir/madam?' To help explain this concept fully, the following is an example of negative selling: 'You won't require anything to drink with the first course, will you sir/madam?' The positive approach is directing the customer as to his or her choice, whereas the negative approach is suggesting that no drink will be required. Customers may be encouraged into ordering by a positive approach when they might otherwise not have bothered.

It is vital for sales that any drink ordered is served in good time. The customer must not have to ask for his or her drink to be served once he or she has made the order. It is more obvious in a bar, but equally true in a restaurant, that while a customer is waiting to be served with a drink, sales are being lost. It is therefore essential that sufficient and efficient staff are available, who are alert and always keeping an eye on the customer.

Properly-run bonus schemes can be an incentive to staff to increase sales.

UP-SELLING

Net Profit is a major requirement for any successful commercial undertaking. The average turnover to earn in the:

USA	UK
$1000 net profit	£500 net profit
would be	would be
$5882 ex. Tax	£2941 ex. VAT
$6235 inc. 6% Sales Tax	£3455 inc. 17.5% VAT

When sales increase above the break-even sales point, the gross percentage profit earned in effect becomes net profit for the business.

One obvious example of up-selling is selling mineral water instead of jug water.

The gross profit on a jug of tap water is $0.00 (£0.00), the net profit is a minus amount as there is a cost involved in providing glasses and the water jug, and having them washed. A percentage of the glassware will get broken in time, further raising the losses. The staff to serve the water is an added cost. For the purposes of this example a gross profit of 80 per cent for mineral water and 70 per cent for wine has been applied.

To increase profit by **$1000**		To increase profit by **£500**	

Example 1

USA		*UK*	
Selling price 1 litre mineral water	$5.00	Selling price 1 litre mineral water	£3.00
Less Sales Tax	$4.72	Less VAT	£2.55
Gross profit based on N/C 95c	$3.77	Gross profit based on N/C 51p	£2.04
Up-sell 6 jugs of tap water to		Up-sell 5 jugs of tap water to	
6 litres of mineral water per week		5 litres of mineral water per week	
(just one per night for 6 nights) will		(just one per night for 5 nights) will	
increase the GP by 6 × $3.77 × 52	**$1176.24**	increase the GP by 5 × $2.04 × 52	**£530.40**

Example 2

Selling price of house wine	$18	Selling price of house wine	£10.00
Less Sales Tax	$16.98	Less VAT	£8.51
Gross profit	$11.89	Gross profit	£5.96
Selling price of Chardonnay	$25	Selling price of Chardonnay	£13.00
Less Sales Tax	$23.58	Less VAT	£11.06
Gross profit	$16.50	Gross profit	£7.74
Up-sell 1 house wine to Chardonnay		Up-sell 1 house wine to Chardonnay	
5 days per week and the		5 days per week and the	
increased G.P. will be		increased G.P. will be	
5 × $4.61 × 52	**$1198.60**	5 × £1.78 × 52	**£462.80**
Selling price of Shiraz	$28	Selling price of Shiraz	£15.00
Less Sales Tax	$26.41	Less VAT	£12.76
Gross profit	$18.49	Gross profit	£9.44

Up-sell 1 house wine to Shiraz
   5 days per week and the
   increased G.P. will be
   5 × $6.60 × 52   **$1716.14**

To increase profit by   **$2300**
Each week of the year up-sell just
   2 bottles of house red wine to Shiraz
   3 bottles of house white to Chardonnay
   5 jugs of water to mineral water

  $(13.20 × 52) + (13.83 × 52) + (18.85 × 52)$

  = $686.40 + 719.16 + 980.20   **$2385.76**

Up-sell 1 house wine to Shiraz
   5 days per week and the
   increased G.P. will be
   5 × £3.48 × 52   **£904.80**

To increase profit by   **£1400**
Each week of the year up-sell just
   2 bottles of house red wine to Shiraz
   3 bottles of house white to Chardonnay
   5 jugs of water to mineral water

  £$(6.96 × 52) + (10.44 × 52) + (10.20 × 52)$

  = £361.92 + 542.88 + 530.40   **£1435.20**

CHAPTER NINE

Taking Beverage Orders

TAKING ORDERS AT THE TABLE

Wine list presentation

The host is the person who will give the drinks order to the sommelier. He or she may be identified as a person who has made the booking and, on arrival at the restaurant, the person who confirms his or her booking with the head waiter or restaurant manager. The head waiter or restaurant manager should inform the sommelier as to who is the host when the party has been seated.

If the customers are a chance party then the sommelier can approach the table and say 'Good evening, may I take your apéritif order?' The host normally takes charge and places the order; the sommelier will then know to whom he should offer the (opened) wine list. If the party is two people, a woman and a man, it is normal procedure for the sommelier to say 'Good evening, madam, sir, may I take your apéritif order?' addressing this request to the gentleman, unless you have already identified the host as the lady. The 'madam, sir' may be replaced by 'Good evening, ladies' or 'Good evening gentlemen' if the party is greater than two. It is important to establish a good rapport with the customers at this point and to make them feel at ease with you serving them. To put the customers more at ease the 'Good evenings' might be better followed by: 'My name is —— , I am your sommelier for this evening.' The actual wording of the greeting will vary from country to country and from establishment to establishment, but it should be designed to make the customers feel comfortable.

The sommelier should then stand to the right of the host when taking the order. The beverage list is the 'shop window' for the drinks of the establishment. The sommelier must ensure that all these lists are clean, and that he/she has a working knowledge of all the drinks on the list and the composition of the dishes on the menu, so that recommendations may be made to customers. If any item on the list is temporarily unavailable, the sommelier should point this fact out to the customer when the list is presented.

Writing the check

The sommelier will take the order from the right of the host and then should repeat it back to the host to prevent any error; the sommelier will then prepare a check in duplicate or triplicate. Some small establishments will use a single-sheet check pad, and this will be used by the person who prepares the bill. The following should always be included on the check :

1   Date
2   Table number
3   Number of covers
4   Initials of the sommelier
5   Customer's room number if he or she is a resident of the hotel
6   Customer's signature (usually) if he or she is a resident
7   Name, or bin number if wine, quantity and price of drink required

The order must be clearly written, and, if a wine is ordered, it should be written on the check as the bin number shown on the wine list (see Figure 9.1).

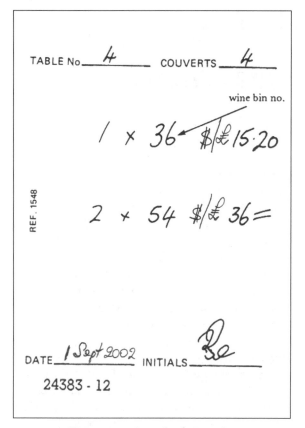

REF. 1548

TABLE No. _4_   COUVERTS _4_

wine bin no.

1 × 36 $/£ 15·20

2 × 54 $/£ 36 =

DATE _1 Sept 2002_   INITIALS _____

24383 - 12

Figure 9.1 *Example of wine order*

The top copy should always be presented to the issuing department, that is the dispense, cellar or bar. The duplicate copy should be used by the person who prepares the bill. This copy will then be sent with a copy of the bill to the control office. It will be married up (matched) with the top copy, which will have come from the issuing department. If the establishment has a fully computerized billing programme the details of the bill will be entered on to the system.

A few establishments use electronic point-of-order pads which are fully computerized, but these are still in the minority.

Recommending wines
The sommelier must have a full knowledge of the preparation and cooking process for every dish on the menu, and a total understanding of the char-

acteristics of every wine in the cellar. When making recommendations the sommelier needs to judge the quality and price range with which the customer will be happy. He or she must also be able to interpret the customer's requirements and recommend accordingly. The sommelier must realize that it is the customer who has to be pleased with the choice, not the sommelier! Consequently the character of the wine must be made clear to the customer, for example whether the wine is red or white, still or sparkling, dry or sweet.

As a starting point for the new sommelier when making recommendations, the following *general* rules may be helpful. It should be stressed that these are only a starting point and are not to be taken with absolute rigidity.

1   Dry wines before sweet wines
2   White wines before red wines
3   White wines with white fish and some white meats
4   Light red wines with red and white meats
5   Off dry or demi-sec wines with spicy foods
6   Strongly flavoured red wines with strongly flavoured meat dishes, red meats and game
7   Sweet still and sparkling wines with sweets

However, there is much more to recommending than this, as within each category of wine there is a wide range of products. For example, the ubiquitous Chardonnay comes in a wide variety of forms, from some thin light citrousy Vin de Pays and Italian examples, to strong pineapple/melon and toasted butterscotch flavours of some high alcohol and oaky Californian and Australian Chardonnays, but it is a base to build on.

Matching wine with food
Much has been written about matching wine with food, and people's ideas and preferences do vary as to which wines complement which dishes. No one sat down and made the rules up: the classic marriages of wine and food came about by common usage.

Some writers have suggested that drinking the 'right' wine with the 'right' food is just snobbishness and not really necessary. However, consider the following:

1   Chablis served with curry.
2   Rioja Gran Reserva Tinto served with a poached fillet of sole with a white wine sauce.

In the first example, an excellent wine will be completely overpowered by the strong spicy flavours of the curry, and thus wasted. In the second, the reverse is the case, with the strong oaky flavour of the wine overpowering the delicate flavours of the fish dish and leaving an unpleasant fishy taste in the mouth. Difficulties will also emerge when the garnishes and accompanying vegetables are of a different strength and flavour from the main meat or fish item in a main course. It is apparent from these examples that care should be taken when recommending wines with foods, in order to achieve the best combinations and enable the maximum enjoyment and value to be obtained from both the wine and food.

A perfect marriage of wine and food is when the wine tastes better when drunk with a certain dish, and the dish is enhanced when served with this wine. Ideally the enjoyment value of the wine and the dish together should exceed the sum of the enjoyment of the two individual components on their own.

When recommending or selecting a wine or wines, thought must also be given to what is to follow, so that an earlier wine does not spoil one which is drunk later. The following guidelines, some of which have already been mentioned, will help: dry wine before sweet; light wine before heavy; young wine before old; white wine before red; except for the heavy sweet white wines which are served with the sweet or at the end of a meal; and some light red or rosé wines which may marry well with some of the stronger starter courses.

There are other factors, besides the menu, which will affect the customer's choice and satisfaction.

The occasion, whether on holiday and or in a foreign country, the weather, the time of the day, the time of year and the price structure of the wine list, all will have an effect on the selection.

Regional dishes are often best accompanied by a wine from the same region, as historically wines were produced for the local people and the local cuisine.

Suggesting apéritifs
The purpose of the apéritif before a meal is threefold: to stimulate the palate for the meal to come, to satisfy a thirst, and to help the person feel relaxed. Some suggestions for apéritifs are:

Champagne and other dry or off-dry sparkling wines.
Dry crisp white wines such as white Burgundies, Muscadet, white and rosé Sancerre, white Graves, Alsace Riesling and Silvaner, Albariño, Mosel trocken and halb-trocken, Californian Sauvignon Blanc or Fumé Blanc.
Dry sherries (Manzanillas and Finos), medium sherries (Amontillados).
Vermouths.
Cocktails.
Mixed drinks such as gin and tonic.

Recommendations for specific dishes
When recommending wines to accompany individual courses, remember that it is unusual for people to have a separate wine with each course of a long meal, and that customers invariably choose different dishes for different courses. It is often necessary therefore to recommend a 'compromise' wine or (wines) which will satisfy all parties. Alternatively if you have a good wine-by-the-glass programme, the individual customers in a party would be able to have a suitable wine with each course.

The following suggestions for wines with foods is intended to be an introductory guide, and is not a full list of all the suitable wines. It is essential that the sommelier knows the wines on the list thoroughly as the producers and vintages of wines can cause them to be vastly different from each other, even when they originate from the same district. It must also be accepted that the composition of sauces, the method of cooking the dish, and any vegetables which might be accompanying a fish or meat course, must be taken into consideration when making the recommendation. Further reading and research in this area will be required to develop an expertise in food and wine combinations.

Hors-d'oeuvres   Hors-d'oeuvres will vary in their content. Those containing a lot of vinegar should be served without wine, as vinegar will kill most wines. However, a Sercial Madeira or Fino Sherry may well stand up to a light vinegary dressing. For most non-fruit starters the following will usually be suitable: Chablis, Alsace Riesling, Sylvaner and Tokay-Pinot Gris, Soave, Muscadet de Sèvre et Main sur lie, Sancerre, Pouilly-Fumé, Mâcon Blanc, Pinot Grigio, Albariño and other dry white wines. With dishes such as fresh asparagus, a New Zealand, Chilean, French or Californian Sauvignon Blanc would be ideal. With spicy oily or fatty dishes, a demi-sec Chenin, Rhine and Mosel Kabinet, New World off-dry Semillon, or Alsace Pinot Gris, would probably suit.

Shellfish and other fish dishes   Recommend dry white wines similar to those for the starters, plus the fuller-bodied white Burgundies, Mosel wines, some medium dry wines such as Vouvray, and Chenin Blanc wines from South Africa, California and Australia. Chablis is an outstanding match for most shellfish. The stronger the flavour of the fish or the sauce, the stronger and more full-bodied the wine should be. Although it was suggested that white wines should accompany fish dishes, a number of rosé wines and some young light red wines will be suitable for fish dishes such as grilled or baked salmon/tuna seasoned with herbs, and other dishes cooked with garlic, mushrooms and strong sauces.

Chinese meals and quiches   Try white Dão, white Graves, Vinho Verde, Arneis, Californian Sauvignon Blanc, Rhine and Mosel wines, medium dry Loire white wines, white Zinfandel (blush) and Beaujolais. Oriental foods have been found to marry well with off-dry wines and wines with a little more residual sugar.

Strong-flavoured pasta dishes   With spaghetti bolognese and other pasta dishes, suggest Chianti, Valpolicella, Spanna and other red Italian wines, Navarra, Valdepeñas, Bairrada, Fitou, Corbières and Côtes du Rhône reds.

Light-flavoured pasta dishes   White Burgundies, white Graves, Grüner Veltliner, Californian and New Zealand Chardonnays and Vernaccia and Vermentino based wines.

White meat dishes and chicken   Recommend light red wines such as Beaujolais; red and white Touraine; Valpolicella; rosé wines; Grüner Veltliner, New World Chardonnays, German Rieslings. Roast turkey will work with red Burgundies, Californian, Oregon or Australian Pinot Noirs, mature Merlot-based Clarets, Italian Sangiovese or Spanish Tempranilla-based wines.

Grilled meats, roast meats, game, stews, casseroles, offals   Suggest *crus* Beaujolais, clarets (particularly with roast lamb), Chinon, red Burgundy, red Dão, Northern Côtes du Rhône reds, Barolo, Barbaresco, Chianti and other red Italian wines, Pinotage, red Rioja, Californian, Chilean and Australian Cabernets, Merlots and Shiraz.

Cheese   The wine served with the red meat course will accompany most hard and semi-hard cheeses. The French take the cheese course directly after the main course, continuing with the same wine; however, many of the soft cheeses of France such as Brie do not marry well with strong red wines. Strong cheeses require strong wines, mild cheeses less strong wines. If a separate wine is to be served, then try a tawny, LBV or vintage port, with the stronger hard cheeses, and a Chianti Classico or red Burgundy with lighter flavoured hard/semi-hard cheeses. In rare cases suggest heavy sweet wines, e.g. Monbazillac or Château d'Yquem with Roquefort cheese, as offered at Château d'Yquem.

Sweets   Wines with sweets, often referred to a little irreverently as pudding wines, are making a comeback in popularity. The wine should be sweet and luscious, or medium to sweet and sparkling. Suggest Champagne, Asti, light red or rosé sparkling Italian wines such as Malvasia; or still wines such as *Spätlese* and *Auslese* Rhine and Mosels, Sauternes, Barsac, Coteaux-du-Layon, Muscat-de-Beaumes-de-Venise, Muscat de Rivesaltes, Californian Orange Muscat, Australian Muscatel or New World Late Harvest Riesling or Sémillon.

Coffee   Serve with Cognac, Armagnac, liqueurs or port.

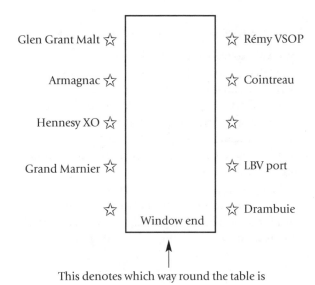

Figure 9.2   *Sketch of table for taking liqueur and brandy order*

Functions

Advance orders for functions should be entered on the banqueting memorandum, and a confirmation of this order should be sent in writing to the organizer.

Credit drinks sold during the course of a function should be authorized by the organizer and signed for at the end of the function. Where there is a request for a credit bar for before or after a meal, it is normal practice to agree a maximum cost. If this is to be exceeded, authorization should be obtained from the organizer before it is allowed to occur.

When taking liqueur and brandy orders at the table, it is sensible to make a sketch of the table and to write in the orders showing the position of the people who have ordered them (see Figure 9.2). If the sommelier cannot distinguish the drinks by appearance, he can place them on the tray in the same order as shown on the sketch.

Cash drinks at functions

Shortened wine lists are usually provided for functions. These will reduce the chance of a wine running out. In addition the wines can be pre-

pared with more confidence for service in advance, that is chilling white and sparkling wines, and ensuring that red wines are at the correct temperature. If set wine is being served from a dispense bar for a function, as a general rule the bottles should have had their corks removed in advance.

Normally the majority of the cash wine orders are taken from the guests at a desk in the reception area close to the table plan. The staff taking the orders write down the customer's name, table number and the order before passing this on to the sommelier who is serving the table. In some establishments this is the top one or two copies of the check; in others, the sommelier will write out the check for the order. The sommelier is therefore able to obtain and prepare the wine in advance. He/she will pass on one copy to the dispense bar or other issuing department, keeping the other copy or copies to present one to the customer when the liqueurs and brandies have been served. If the triplicate system is used, one of the copies is available to be given to the customer as a receipt.

TAKING ORDERS AT THE BAR

Suitable drinks for receptions

Most dry and off-dry white wines and sparkling wines are suitable for apéritifs and reception drinks. Cocktails are also suitable for apéritifs, but not for a large number at a reception as they take time to prepare. An exception to this is a Champagne Cocktail, as this is easily prepared for large numbers.

Sherries, spirits and mixers, vermouths and many other drinks are excellent for these occasions. Soft drinks should always be offered, juices and mineral waters being universally popular.

Recording orders and sales

Orders should be made out on check pads for table orders. One copy should be presented to the dispense bar as described earlier.

In an open bar, sales should be recorded on an electronic or mechanical till and the correct cash value placed in the till drawer. The till drawer must always be kept closed when not being used for a sale. The till roll will record all sales as entered on the keys of the till. It is a sensible control to enter different categories of drinks under different keys so that an analysis can be produced at the end of the service, for example:

Key 1: enter all cash drinks.
Key 2: enter all booked bar drinks.
Key 3: enter all booked wines.
Key 4: enter all bar snacks money.

If the drinks are to be booked to a room number, the room number must be written clearly on the check and the customer's signature obtained. These checks are entered on a summary sheet and sent with this sheet to the cashier.

When a bill or note is offered for payment for drinks, state the value of the note and place it outside the till drawer (some tills have clips for this purpose) until the correct change has been taken from the till and checked. The bill or note should then be placed in the till drawer and the drawer closed.

If an electronic credit card scanner and validation swipe machine is not part of the system, credit cards should be checked against any list of stolen cards which is available. Check the date of validity and the name of the holder. The signature of the customer, which must be written on the voucher in front of the cashier, must be compared with the signature on the card. If the value required is high, a check on whether this amount of credit is available to the customer may be made by telephoning the credit card company.

Customer accounts should be prepared before the customer leaves the establishment, and they should be agreed and signed by the customer. A headed bill should be prepared and sent to the customer as soon as possible.

If cheques are to be accepted for payment, these must be accompanied by a cheque card and the following confirmed:

1   The dates of validity must be checked.
2   The name on the card must coincide with the name on the cheque.
3   The cheque must come from the same bank as the one stated on the card.
4   The value of the cheque must not exceed the limit stated on the card.
5   The signature on the card must match the one written on the cheque in front of the receiver. If there is any doubt as to the authenticity of the signature, the customer should be requested to sign his name on the back of the cheque.
6   The cheque card number must be recorded by the receiver on the back of the cheque.

CHAPTER TEN

Staff Practice and Customer Relations

PERSONAL PRESENTATION AND HYGIENE

Exemplary standards of hygiene, personal presentation and politeness are probably the most important attributes of any staff employed in a service industry. Everyone involved in serving customers, and in particular those concerned with the service of food and drink, must be totally acceptable to the customer. Good health is an essential requirement for a barperson or sommelier; these two jobs entail many hours of walking and standing.

Appearance and personal hygiene must be of a very high standard. Body odour and bad breath are both unacceptable. It can be most unpleasant for a customer to be served by someone suffering from one of these problems. Staff should wash frequently with soap and water, shower or bathe at least once a day, and clean their teeth regularly. An anti-perspirant should be used by all service staff.

The following rules should also be adhered to:

1 Hands and nails must be clean, there must be no nicotine stains on the fingers, and nails must be well manicured and short. Nail varnish should not be worn.
2 Hair must be kept clean, neat and well groomed. If it is long it should be tied back.
3 Staff must wash their hands after visiting the toilet, by law (see Chapter Eleven). They should also wash their hands after doing any dirty jobs such as bottling-up shelves.
4 Staff should not touch their hair, nose or mouth, and then handle glasses or food.
5 Staff must not serve food or drink when suffering from diarrhoea, food poisoning or infectious diseases.
6 Staff must not cough, spit or sneeze over food or drink.
7 Staff must not smoke or take snuff in a food or drink area.
   NB It is also an offence for a barman to smoke behind the bar.
8 Staff suffering from cuts, burns or abrasions must cover these with a waterproof dressing to reduce the chances of infection.
9 Heavy perfume should not be worn as it will detract from the food and wine and may offend the customer.
10 Service cloths must be changed when soiled and must *never* be put under the arm.

In general, staff should practise good hygienic standards and habits. They must comply with the Hygiene Regulations (see Chapter Eleven).

Clothing which is worn outside the working area should be either changed or covered with a uniform. This must be clean, well pressed and well fitting. Shoes must be comfortable, well fitting and highly polished.

Earrings, bracelets, rings other than wedding and signet rings, and hanging jewellery are all unacceptable in the working environment.

ATTITUDES AND BEHAVIOUR

Staff must remember that the customer is the most important person in any restaurant and must always be treated as such. Without

187

customers there will be no business and therefore no work for the staff.

Staff should be positive in their movements. They should stand without leaning on a table, bar or sideboard, and should appear smart and alert at all times.

It is important that service staff enunciate clearly so that the customer is able to understand them, bearing in mind that a restaurant or bar is a noisy place at most times. Staff should speak at a medium pace. If the words are garbled, the customer may have difficulty in understanding and will become impatient. It is important that staff never use bad language, even away from the customer, as the spoken word has a habit of carrying much further than is anticipated.

Staff should greet customers with a smile and welcome them to the establishment and they should show a readiness to oblige the customer. Customers are not paying the staff to be discourteous to them. The customer should be treated pleasantly and politely; in this way he or she will become relaxed more quickly and feel at ease. *Civility* means being pleasant and courteous, and must be practised by the service staff. This must not be confused with *servility*, which means to cringe, to 'bow and scrape'. This behaviour must not be practised.

To be tactful is to be diplomatic and to be able to say the right things when the customer has a complaint or problem. If a customer complains about the wine or the service, listen attentively and take the criticism seriously. Apologize for any actual or perceived problem and make amends as a matter of urgency. It is also important to be tactful and patient when conversing with other members of staff. Cheerfulness and good humour produce a happy atmosphere and can help when dealing with difficult situations. These are essential attributes of all good food and beverage staff.

The customer is entitled to be served by a person with a pleasant and cheerful manner. The meal experience should be a pleasurable occasion for the customer, and the attitude and demeanour of the service staff are major factors in achieving this.

Employees in this service industry should be fully aware of the importance of punctuality and reliability. When a member of staff is late or absent from work, the restaurant or bar will still open. The same number of customers will walk into the premises to be served and this will mean that the remaining staff will have to work harder. The late arrival for work of a hotel manager will not usually cause a great problem, but the late arrival of a barperson could cause a drop in the quality of service and a loss of revenue. Unlike many office jobs, 'the show must go on'.

Self-confidence comes with knowledge, training, practice and experience, and is a requirement of any salesperson. Sommeliers must believe in their own ability and recommendations to the customer, and must project this belief to the customer. A lack of confidence on the part of a barperson or sommelier may lead to a loss in sales and may be the cause of accidents.

On occasions a customer can be very difficult to serve. He or she may complain unnecessarily and may appear to be objectionable to a member of staff. The staff member must always keep an even temper and be polite. Usually the customer will then calm down. If a situation is arrived at where the member of staff is unable to cope with the problem, he or she should ask a superior to deal with it.

Social skills are also about getting on with people. To do this fully it is necessary to understand how other people think and react to certain situations. It is necessary on occasions to think before speaking to ensure that unintentional offence is not given. In particular, people who live in a multiracial society as we do must give consideration to the cultures of people from countries and backgrounds other than their own.

TEAMWORK AND COMMUNICATION

When information is received, ensure that it is passed on in the correct form to the necessary people. A customer may arrive and give you some detail about their party which is booked for dinner, for example that there will be two fewer for the dinner, or that somebody's birthday is being celebrated. This information must be passed on immediately to the restaurant manager.

If a telephone message is taken, the date and time that it was received must be recorded on the message slip. The person to whom it is intended should be clearly stated, plus the name of the person who received it.

To create a pleasant and efficient working atmosphere, staff should work together and help each other. A simple example is when a member of staff fetches a piece of equipment which he requires and at the same time fetches a similar piece for another member of staff, which will save the other person either forgetting it or having to fetch it. This is achieved without doing anything extra at all, but is an example of teamwork or working together to get something done.

A pleasant and efficient working atmosphere will only be achieved by people thinking of others rather than just themselves, and by staff looking around (when they are not busy) for things which need doing or for ways in which others can be assisted.

Staff should be polite and respectful to supervisors and should follow their instructions. If the section is running as a team with the objective of creating a pleasant and efficient environment for the service of customers, any criticism given is probably meant for the good of the operation, and is really meant to help rather than to criticize. Staff who can accept criticism and act upon it will become more accomplished at their job and will get more job satisfaction.

If staff are to do a good job, they must be motivated. To be friendly but firm with subordinates is a very important contribution to their motivation. When pointing out faults or errors to a subordinate, ensure the comments are constructive and not destructive. They need to feel that you are really interested in them and that you are trying to help them. It is important to offer praise when things are done well. Give credit where credit is due, rather than take credit oneself when others

have earned it. Offer advice and encouragement should a member of staff find difficulty with a task. This can be done with a smile and a joke so that the person feels at ease.

When giving directions or instructions to subordinates, make sure that they are clear and unambiguous, and that the person to whom they are given understands them.

The whole establishment as well as the food and beverage service section must work as a team, so it is essential to co-operate with other departments and to give them information which may be useful to them. Often an occasion will arise when you receive information which will be useful for another department to know about. For example, the barman may notice that a party of 22 persons has arrived when he knows the restaurant is expecting 19. He should pass this information on immediately. The restaurant manager would then pass this same information on to the head chef.

RECOGNIZED PROCEDURES

Telephone practice

Telephone enquiries should be received in the following manner:

1 The telephone should be answered as promptly as possible; a good standard is to ensure the call is answered after no more than three rings.
2 Lift the receiver, say 'Good morning/afternoon/evening', announce the name of the bar or restaurant, then say 'How may I help you?' Speak steadily and clearly and speak directly into the mouthpiece of the handset. If you are unable to deal with the call immediately, apologize and either ask if the caller can hold for a short while or take the caller's number and phone them back.
3 Never lift the receiver off and put it down on the side without speaking to the caller; this is extremely rude and frustrating for the caller.
4 Never lift and replace the receiver, thus cutting the caller off.

5 When receiving enquiries for bookings, note the date and time the customer wishes to book for, the name of the caller, their telephone number, and the number of persons they wish to book for.

6 Note any other details, for example ruby wedding celebration, with the names of the two principal people.

7 If you have to leave the phone to obtain some information, tell the caller and keep the time away from the phone as short as possible.

8 When putting the phone down while the person is still connected, avoid banging it as this may be uncomfortable for the person on the other end of the call.

9 Never leave the receiver dangling on the end of the wire while you go to fetch some information.

10 Remember that all noise and spoken words will be picked up by the receiver and transmitted to the caller.

11 At the end of the call, thank the person for calling and place the receiver back in position.

12 Always remember that it is a potential customer on the phone, not a machine. Carry on the conversation as if you were speaking to the person face to face, using your normal voice inflections, facial expressions and changes of tone.

Personal enquiries

Enquiries received from customers in person should be dealt with as efficiently as possible in much the same way as telephone enquiries. Any queries received from customers should be dealt with as quickly as possible and in a polite manner.

Compliments

Compliments offered by customers should be received with courtesy and the customer should be thanked politely. The compliment should then be passed on to the persons or section concerned if it is for someone other than or in addition to yourself. For example, a customer may compli-

ment you on the quality of the wine which you have served. This information should be passed on to the person responsible for preparing the wine list and ordering the wine.

Elderly, children and disabled

Due consideration must be given to elderly customers, children and handicapped persons. Elderly people may require a little more time and patience.

Very young children may require immediate attention. They are usually less of a problem to the parents and the establishment when they have been served with a drink of fruit juice, lemonade, cola, etc.

Disabled customers like to be treated in as normal a way as possible. They generally make light of their disability.

Complaints

Minor complaints should be dealt with by the service personnel themselves. If the problem is more serious it must be reported to the management who should speak directly to the customer concerned. Complaints received from customers are very important and must be recorded. Many establishments keep a complaints book where these are noted down. Action should then be taken to ensure that the same thing does not occur again. In particular, when next this customer comes into the bar or restaurant, special care must be taken to ensure that everything goes smoothly.

Drunken customers

Customers sometimes arrive on the premises under the influence of alcohol, or become inebriated while on the premises. UK law clearly states that such customers should not be served with any more alcohol. The same will almost certainly apply in other countries.

If either of these situations should occur, the management should be called to deal with the problem. It is often at this point that the customer will become unpleasant and abusive. This can be very disruptive to other guests, and a good manager will usually speak to the customer concerned in a quiet but firm manner. Sometimes the manager will be able to conduct the conversation away from the main public area.

If a customer does become drunk while on the premises it is advisable to have as little contact as possible with him or her.

Fire and bomb warnings

In the case of a fire or bomb warning, the procedures laid down for the establishment must be immediately followed (see Chapter Eleven). Reassure customers and help them to evacuate the premises in an orderly manner. If you discover the fire or suspected bomb yourself, you should raise the alarm immediately.

In the event of a fire, after alarm and evacuation close all windows and doors and attack the fire with fire-fighting equipment. It is important to use the correct type of extinguisher for the fire. There is a colour code for British-made fire extinguishers indicating for which type of fire each is suitable (see Chapter Eleven).

Customer illness or accident

Every effort should be made to prevent accidents taking place. Accidents occur unexpectedly and can result in injury to a customer, damage to a customer's belongings, and/or damage to the property of the establishment. If an accident causes damage to the customer's belongings the matter must be reported to the restaurant manager or general manager, who will note all the particulars and take any action which is thought to be necessary. If a customer is injured or taken ill, it will depend on the extent of the injury or the seriousness of the illness as to the procedure to be followed. In any case the restaurant manager or bar manager must be informed.

Very often a customer who feels unwell is helped by being moved to a cooler and quieter place, for example from the bar or restaurant to a private room or a vacated reception bar area, and given a glass of water. If there is a severe problem, a doctor or ambulance should be called. If the customer is very ill or injured badly and cannot be moved from a public room or area, screens should be placed round the table and a member of staff should remain with the customer until the doctor arrives. Whichever of these situations occurs, the details must be carefully recorded.

Theft or loss of customers' property

It is necessary to display a printed notice declaring that the management of the bar or restaurant will take no responsibility for the loss of any property belonging to a customer. If accommodation has not been booked in the establishment there is no liability on behalf of the proprietor unless negligence can be proved. In this case the establishment is held to be liable.

If coats are taken by the establishment and hung up in a cloakroom then liability does exist. Under the law of bailment, if property is handed to and received by another person, he or she is duty bound to return it in the same condition as he or she received it.

If a theft or loss is reported by a customer the manager must be notified. He or she will take down all particulars and will probably notify the police.

Apologies to customers

If it is necessary to apologize to a customer, this must be done in a respectful, courteous and sincere manner.

ANTICIPATING AND SATISFYING CUSTOMER NEEDS

Welcoming

When a customer arrives in an establishment he or she must be noticed and welcomed, not left standing about. Staff should greet customers in a pleasant and courteous manner on their first contact with them. The attitudes and behaviour of staff have been discussed earlier in this chapter.

Depending on the relationship between the customer and the staff of the establishment, the form of address will vary. The normal form of address for an evening would be 'Good evening, sir; good evening, madam', or 'Good evening, ladies and gentlemen' if there are more than one of each.

Some correct forms of address

The following list of forms of verbal address is not intended to be comprehensive, or indeed a toast-master's 'bible'. It is meant to be an accurate guide as to the correct way to speak to the people mentioned as customers.

The Queen   One should not begin a conversation with the Queen. On answering her, use 'Your Majesty' in the first instance and 'Ma'am' afterwards (pronounced Mam).

Royal princes and princesses   Once again a conversation should not be begun by a member of staff. On answering, use 'Your Royal Highness', and afterwards 'Sir' or 'Ma'am'.

Dukes and duchesses are formally addressed as 'Your Grace'.

Peers and peeresses below duke and duchess are addressed as 'My Lord' and 'My Lady'.

Archbishops are formally addressed as 'Your Grace'.

Bishops should be addressed as 'My Lord' or 'My Lord Bishop'.

Cardinals are addressed as 'Your Eminence'.

Lord Mayors and Lady Mayoresses   Address them as 'My Lord' and 'My Lady'.

Mayors (male and female)   Address them as 'Your Worship' or 'Mr/Madam Mayor'.

Mayoresses   Address them as 'Mayoress'.

For a comprehensive list of the correct modes of address, consult *Debrett's Correct Form*.

Treating customers

The approach of staff to treating customers has already been mentioned earlier in this chapter. Customers should always be spoken to in a polite manner and treated with respect. Staff should converse with customers to discuss their requirements, their choice and often other things such as local information. Be prepared to listen and to talk to customers if they want to, but do not force yourself on to them, or interrupt their conversations. Staff should never repeat conversations which they have overheard.

Ensure that customers do not have to wait for you to serve them because you are holding a long conversation with another customer.

Customers' departure

When customers leave the bar or restaurant, say for example 'Goodnight, sir, madam (ladies and gentlemen), it has been a pleasure having you with us, and we look forward to your next visit', or 'Thank you for coming ', or 'We hope you have enjoyed your evening', or a combination of these or similar phrases. Ensure that they have taken all their personal belongings with them by scanning their tables and chairs and the surrounding areas.

CHAPTER ELEVEN

Health and Safety

This chapter gives an outline of the main conditions of the various laws and acts which affect UK food and beverage sales and service operations, but it should not be taken to be a complete work on these areas. For a fuller understanding the author suggests that a book devoted to the law should be consulted. Although these laws are not enforceable outside the UK, they provide a useful guide to follow.

HEALTH AND SAFETY AT WORK ACT 1974

The Health and Safety at Work Act 1974, as amended by the Fire Precaution Act 1971, in effect makes it obligatory for any premises used for the sale of food and drink to obtain a fire certificate.

The employer (hereafter referred to as 'he') must take reasonable precautions to ensure the employees' health, safety and welfare, as far as is reasonably practical, while they are at work. He must provide a safe place of work and take all reasonable precautions to see that it remains safe. He must also ensure the health and safety of customers and guests as far as is reasonably practical. This includes the safe structure of the building; electrical and gas installations; safe floor and stair coverings (for example no frayed or turned-up carpet edges); and dry and uncluttered floors.

All fire and emergency exits must be kept clear. The employer must provide equipment which is safe when used correctly, and which must be correctly installed and maintained. He must provide adequate training for staff so that they know the correct methods and techniques of using the equipment.

He must provide safe methods of access to all rooms.

In establishments with more than five employees the employer must provide a written health and safety policy which is shown to the employees. A record must be kept of any accident to an employee causing him to be unable to work for three or more days. Serious accidents or occurrences regarding dangerous situations must be reported to the environmental health officer immediately. All accidents to employees which occur at their place of work must by law be recorded. A standard accident book is available from HMSO.

Although the employer is held responsible for any act of negligence causing loss or injury to a customer, an employee must exercise reasonable care and skill in the performance of his duties and could be held liable for any loss or injury to a customer. The employee must safeguard the health and safety of colleagues as well as himself.

No person shall intentionally or recklessly interfere with or misuse anything provided in the interests of health, safety or welfare.

OFFICES, SHOPS AND RAILWAY PREMISES ACT 1963

This Act covers people employed in the sales and service of beverages in hotels and restaurants, but excludes employees of registered clubs and purely residential hotels.

It requires that the work and public areas are kept clean, clear and well lit. Non-public work areas must be kept at a minimum of 16°C.

Drinking water with cups, or a drinking

fountain, must be available for employees. Sufficient toilets and washing facilities must be available which are suitable for the requirements of staff of both sexes. A place must be provided for the employees' outdoor clothing.

Staircases must be well lit and must have handrails. Any equipment which is in any way dangerous must have its dangerous parts guarded. Employees must not be asked to lift loads which are liable to cause them injury.

First-aid boxes must be available, and one member of staff must be in charge of and be competent in first aid. Other employees must not tamper with or interfere with these first-aid materials.

The environmental health officers have right of entry and inspection at their convenience.

FOOD HYGIENE REGULATIONS

Many of the points covered under the Offices, Shops and Railway Premises Act are also dealt with under the Food Hygiene (General) Regulations 1970, and Food Hygiene (Scotland) Regulations 1959, as amended. Beverages are regarded as food under these regulations, so beverage sales and service activities are governed by them.

Food and beverage business premises must be sanitary, and all equipment which is likely to come into contact with food and drink must be able to be kept clean and free from contamination. This equipment must then be kept clean. The work area must be kept clear of accumulated refuse. Food must be kept at least 450 mm (18 inches) from the ground, but this does not include items such as bottles of beer which are in sealed bottles. All food rooms must be kept in a good state of repair and must be properly lit and ventilated.

Spare gas cylinders, whether empty or full, should be stored in the open air with the valves uppermost and closed. Safety caps where provided must be in place. The storage area must be well away from buildings, drains, cellars or basements, and combustible materials.

Clean toilet facilities must be provided away from food areas, and wash basins, water, soap, nailbrushes and hand-drying facilities must also be provided. Notices must be displayed in the toilet areas telling employees to wash their hands after using the toilet.

All beverage sales and service staff must keep themselves and their clothes clean. All cuts and abrasions must be covered with blue plasters. Staff must not smoke, spit or take snuff in a beverage service area with open food. It is an offence under these regulations to smoke behind the bar. Employees suffering from certain diseases and illnesses must not work near food.

ACCIDENTS: CAUSES AND PREVENTION

There are three main categories of accident:

1 Those caused by human error
2 Those caused by unsafe or defective equipment and/or working areas
3 Those caused by the effects of alcohol.

Human error

Many accidents are caused by employees drinking on or off duty. It is a fact that alcohol slows down the human reaction time considerably, and increases errors of judgement. People who have taken drugs may have the same problems. Remember that medicines prescribed for common illnesses are drugs and may have adverse effects, including drowsiness.

Fatigue is a major cause of accidents.

Comfortable, well-made solid shoes which give protection to the top of the foot should be worn, and they should be kept in good repair. Badly worn, open toe and high-heeled shoes are very dangerous and are unsuitable for this type of work.

Other accidents are caused by using the wrong equipment for a task, or by the incorrect use of equipment. These may be due to a lack of instruction or supervision; over-familiarity; laziness, which is a form of carelessness; untidiness, which may be caused by pressure of work, poor storage and worktop facilities; and carelessness, for example carrying too many glasses on a tray.

Broken glass in a sink and broken bottles in beer crates or skips can cause serious cuts. Dirty glasses should be washed in glass-washing machines. Chipped or cracked glasses should be thrown away, and care should be taken when emptying bottle skips and full beer crates. Always wrap broken glass in plenty of paper.

Many accidents end with a person falling, and falling is in fact the most common cause of injury on licensed premises. There are two very common types of fall. They are those caused by tripping over items such as flexes, wires, boxes, frayed carpets and other obstructions; and those caused by people falling off items such as chairs or tables on to which they have climbed instead of a ladder. The next most common fall is off a ladder or stairs, so always use a proper set of steps rather than a chair, table, box or other items. It is therefore imperative to keep all corridors, passageways, staircases and work areas clear of boxes, crates, bottles, litter and other obstructions; they must also be kept well lit.

Most people now recognize that drinking alcohol will slow down a person's co-ordination and reaction times. This is the cause of a large number of accidents in the work place. They also recognize that alcoholic intake can be measured by units of alcohol. There is only guidance available for what is a safe limit, as each person has a different tolerance level. It is a fact that the tolerance level of females is lower than that of males. Unfortunately there is a misconception that one glass of wine is equal to one unit of alcohol. If the amount of wine in the glass is 125 cl and the wine is only 8% abv then this is correct, but few wines are this low in alcoholic content. To calculate the number of units consumed, the number of milligrams of the drink is multiplied by the percentage of alcohol by volume (abv) in the drink and 0.001. For example, one 175 ml glass of a wine of 12% of alcohol will equal $175 \times 12 \times 0.001 = 2.1$ units.

Equipment and working areas

Poor lighting, heating and ventilation all cause accidents. Uneven, slippery and cluttered floor areas, badly maintained or broken equipment and furniture, unguarded dangerous equipment, unclean equipment and work area, and unsafe and untidy storage of commodities and equipment are other causes of accidents.

All crates and empties must be stored neatly and tidily.

Remember that under the UK Health and Safety at Work Act the employer is responsible for the safety of the public as well as the staff, so that if a delivery of liquor entails the use of a hatchway, trapdoor, lift or hoist, inside or outside the premises, a person must be designated to guard these areas to protect staff and public from accidents.

Many accidents can be prevented by employers and employees taking a reasonable amount of care.

The employer must ensure that employees are aware of possible dangers. They must be encouraged to report faulty equipment, problem areas or any potential hazard which becomes apparent. They must be trained to keep all areas clean and to clear up spillages as they occur.

Posters and notices should be displayed reminding employees of potential hazards and how to deal with them. The correct use of machinery and equipment instructions should be posted up by the respective items.

As the Health and Safety at Work Act states, employees as well as employers must take every precaution to safeguard the health and safety not only of themselves but also of their colleagues.

All employers and employees must know what action to take in the event of fire (see later in this chapter).

ELECTRIC SHOCK

Accidents involving electricity usually cause electric shocks to people and may also result in a fire.

All electrical equipment must be installed by a

qualified electrician: many accidents are caused by faulty installations.

It is important that the correct fuse is used for each piece of equipment and that the plug is wired up correctly. Many accidents are caused in the hotel and catering industry by faulty or damaged plugs, wires and flexes.

Any electrically operated piece of equipment is usually quite safe when used correctly and well maintained, but it can be a potential hazard to health and safety and must be checked frequently. Electrical heaters are sometimes used to dry bar cloths by draping them over the outlet of the hot air. This practice is extremely dangerous and will quite likely lead to a fire.

Water and other liquids are good conductors of electricity and will make any electric shock worse if associated with any electrical fault. Therefore electrical equipment must never be touched with wet hands. Electrical wires and flexes should be kept away from water and from areas which often get splashed with water.

Flexes and wires should be kept out of the way so that staff and customers cannot trip over them. Counter mountings and display material in bars must have a low voltage supply, *never* mains voltage (consult a qualified electrician if in doubt). Lights should be switched off before attempting to clean them. It is dangerous to use multi-plug adapters in bar areas.

Electrical equipment should be switched off at the mains before dealing with any fault.

Procedure in the event of electric shock

The electricity supply must be switched off immediately. If this is not possible, pull the person clear without touching the person's skin, and do not stand in water.

Call for medical help, and attempt resuscitation if the person has stopped breathing.

A card clearly explaining the correct treatment for electric shock should be displayed in any area where electrical equipment is used.

FIRES

Fires are very dangerous and cause loss of life. However, it must be recognized that smoke and fumes account for more deaths, so it is important to consider this when furnishing or decorating a room. The smoke produced when modern furniture burns is highly poisonous and often fatal.

Fire procedures

To cause a fire there needs to be a combination of a combustible material or substance, oxygen (usually air) and heat. Once the fire has started it will provide its own heat. Open windows and doors will supply air and a draught to fan the flames.

If a small fire has started, the fire alarm should be sounded, any fuel supply switched off and the fire attacked with the correct type of fire extinguisher. Any combustible material nearby should be moved away from the fire, thus isolating it from further fuel.

All members of staff should be instructed in what they should do on the outbreak of a fire. The employer must prepare a fire routine for the establishment. Notices detailing this procedure should be displayed in staff quarters, public rooms and (for hotels) in the guests' bedrooms as well (Figure 11.1). Proficiency in operating this procedure should be maintained by carrying out regular fire drills and instruction.

The employer must ensure that the fire alarm system, emergency lighting and fire-fighting equipment provided in the premises are checked at regular intervals by a competent person. A suitable record must be kept of the dates of the routine inspections, together with the signature of the person carrying out the inspection (Figure 11.2).

Fire extinguishers still have coded colours but the whole of the fire extinguishers no longer has to be of this colour. They will have the following colour clearly identified on the outside.

FIRE ROUTINE

notice for
display at
fire alarm
callpoints

1 If you discover a fire, immediately raise the alarm by operating the nearest fire alarm callpoint.

2 On hearing the fire alarm (continuously ringing bell) leave the building via the nearest available escape route and assemble at
   * ....

3 Do not use the lift/s.

4 Do not stop to collect personal belongings.

5 Do not re-enter the building until told it is safe to do so.

NB Make yourself familiar with the escape routes from the building NOW.

FIRE ROUTINE

notice for
guest
bedrooms

1 If you discover a fire immediately raise the alarm. The nearest alarm callpoint to your room is * ....
   ....

2 On hearing the fire alarm (a continuously ringing bell) leave the building via the nearest available escape route and assemble at
   * ....

3 Do not use the lift/s.

4 Do not stop to collect personal belongings.

5 Do not re-enter the building until told it is safe to do so.

NB Make yourself familiar with the escape routes from the building NOW.

FIRE ROUTINE

notice for
display in
staff areas

IF YOU DISCOVER A FIRE

1 Immediately operate the nearest fire alarm callpoint.

2 Attack the fire, if possible, with the appliances provided but without taking personal risks.

ON HEARING THE FIRE ALARM

3 .... * will call the fire brigade immediately (Dial 999 — ask for FIRE BRIGADE).

4 Leave the building via the nearest available escape route and report to the person in charge of the assembly point at
   .... *

5 .... * will take charge of any evacuation and ensure so far as it is possible, that no one has been left in the building.

6 Do not use lift/s.

7 Do not stop to collect personal belongings.

8 Do not re-enter the building until told it is safe to do so.

* (Note: Complete as appropriate)

Figure 11.1 *Fire safety notices*

Extinguisher type	Colour	Main uses
Water	Red	Wood, paper, fabrics
Foam	White or cream	Petrol, oil, fat and paint equipment
Carbon dioxide	Black	Liquids, gases, electrical and electronic apparatus
Powder	Blue	Liquids but not chip-pan fires

Fire prevention

Many outbreaks of fire are caused by smoking, by un-extinguished cigarette ends being put into waste bins, and by accidents while using a naked flame such as a lighted match. Self-extinguishing bins should be used in bars, and care should be taken when emptying ashtrays, particularly at the end of a service, to ensure that all cigarette ends are extinguished. Paper and combustible materials must not be allowed to accumulate.

Lights and shades must be well maintained; faulty electrical equipment and wiring, and

FIRE EXTINGUISHERS – RECORD OF TESTS AND INSPECTIONS

Date	Location or Number	Inspected or tested?	Satisfactory Yes/No	Remedial action taken	Signature

FIRE INSTRUCTIONS AND DRILLS – RECORD OF WHEN GIVEN

Date	Instruction Duration	Fire Drill Evacuation Time	Person/Department Receiving Instruction/Drill	Nature of Instruction/Drill	Observations of Instructor etc	Signature of Instructor etc

Figure 11.2 *Fire prevention log book headings*

electric lights in contact with lampshades, cause fires. All gas appliances should be well maintained and faults promptly rectified. Care should be taken when changing bottled gas cylinders. Spare and empty cylinders should be stored outside the main building.

Fire prevention is the responsibility of both the management and the staff. Before leaving a public room or premises at night or at the end of a service, a routine should be followed. Empty all ashtrays, check carpets and furniture for dropped cigarettes, switch off all electrical equipment and remove power plugs. Check that gas taps are turned off, and close all doors to all rooms and staircases. This procedure is absolutely essential.

PEST INFESTATION

Insect and/or rodent infestation is likely to occur in even the most hygienically run operation, although a high standard of hygiene will reduce the likelihood of this happening. Although many infestations such as cockroaches and rodents, should be treated by a professional pest-control company, successful individual spot treatments can be carried out on some of the most common pests. Only those materials which have been cleared by the Pesticide Safety Precaution Scheme should be used.

The following pests are the most common to be found in a beverage sales and service area.

Why you should practise correct handling and lifting

Because you then use those muscles best fitted for the job.
Because it takes the strain out of handling and helps you to carry out handling movements more easily.
Because it protects you from sudden injury by strain and rupture, or ill health arising out of unconsciously using bad handling methods. Such bad methods are often responsible for what we call 'rheumatism', 'fibrositis', or 'slipped disc'.
Because it enables you to finish the day fresh to enjoy your leisure.
Because every job can be made easier by correct handling.

These points are essential for smooth and easy handling of all kinds

1 CORRECT GRIP
Use the palms and roots of the fingers and thumb.

2 STRAIGHT BACK
Lift with the legs and relax the knees.

3 CHIN IN
Raise the top of the head and tuck the chin in.

4 CORRECT FEET POSITIONS
Stand with feet apart, but no wider than the hips, with one foot forward in the direction you intend to follow.

5 ARMS CLOSE TO THE BODY
This enables you to use the body muscles correctly.

6 BODY WEIGHT
Use your body as a counterbalance. Its weight can reduce the muscular effort necessary.

Figure 11.3 *Handling and lifting loads*

199

Ants Ants will infest food and drink areas, particularly in the summer. Ensure that all bottles are securely sealed. If the nest can be identified it should be treated with a proprietary ant-control product. If it cannot then the point of entry of the ants should be traced back and this point plus the ant run within the establishment should be treated.

Silverfish Treat the infected areas such as cracks and crevices and the inside of cupboards with a proprietary crawling insect killer.

Flies Pyrethrum or pyrethroid fly sprays are particularly effective for use in bars and service areas, but all items of open food must be covered when they are used and for a short time afterwards. In areas other than public rooms, an ultraviolet fly-control unit may be most suitable.

Cockroaches Apply an insecticidal lacquer aerosol or a proprietary crawling insect killer to cracks, crevices and other affected areas. It is advisable to seek the services of a professional pest control company.

Rodents Seek the services of a professional pest-control company. The most satisfactory method of pest control in hotels and catering establishments is to employ a professional pest-control company on a contractual basis.

LIFTING AND CARRYING LOADS

Do not attempt to lift a load which is too heavy. As a general rule these are loads over 20 kg, but this weight depends on the shape and size of the load and the strength of the lifter. Where possible use a sack barrow to move beer crates. This can also be used to move beer kegs if a keg trolley is not available.

When lifting an item from the ground, squat down with the knees apart (Figure 11.3). Take a firm hold on the load using a full palm grip. Keep the back straight and upright. Bend the knees and let the legs do the work. Keep the arms straight and close to the body. Do not twist the body whilst lifting; avoid sudden movements and twisting of the spine. Take account of the centre of gravity of the load when lifting.

If a load is too heavy, call for assistance. Do not rush into lifting a heavy load; try the weight cautiously first. Plan the move to avoid unnecessary lifting. Move a load by the simplest method. Clear all obstacles from the area and from the place you intend to deposit the load.

Be careful not to cause injury to other people. Avoid wearing rings and bracelets. Wear protective gloves to avoid injuries from sharp edges.

Appendices

APPENDIX 1: 1855 CLASSIFICATION OF THE MÉDOC

Where a château has altered its name, the new name is quoted.

Premiers crus

Vineyard	*Commune and AOC*	
Château Lafite	Pauillac	
Château Margaux	Margaux	
Château Latour	Pauillac	
Château Haut-Brion	Pessac;	AOC Pessac-Léognan
Château Mouton-Rothschild(upgraded to first growth 1973)	Pauillac	

Deuxièmes crus

Château Rausan-Ségla	Margaux	
Château Rauzan-Gassies	Margaux	
Château Léoville-Las-Cases	St Julien	
Château Léoville-Poyferré	St Julien	
Château Léoville-Barton	St Julien	
Château Durfort-Vivens	Margaux	
Château Gruaud-Larose	St Julien	
Château Lascombes	Margaux	
Château Brane-Cantenac	Cantenac;	AOC Margaux
Château Pichon-Longueville Baron	Pauillac;	
Château Pichon-Longueville Comtesse de Lalande	Pauillac	
Château Ducru-Beaucaillou	St Julien	
Château Cos d'Estournel	St Estèphe	
Château Montrose	St Estèphe	

Troisièmes crus

Château Kirwan	Cantenac;	AOC Margaux
Château d'Issan	Cantenac;	AOC Margaux
Château Lagrange	St Julien	
Château Langoa-Barton	St Julien	
Château Giscours	Labarde;	AOC Margaux
Château Malescot-St-Exupéry	Margaux	
Château Boyd-Cantenac	Cantenac;	AOC Margaux
Château Cantenac-Brown	Cantenac;	AOC Margaux
Château Palmer	Cantenac;	AOC Margaux
Château Lagune	Ludon;	AOC Haut-Médoc
Château Desmirail	Margaux	
Château Calon-Ségur	St Estèphe	
Château Ferrière	Margaux	
Château Marquis d'Alesme Becker	Margaux	

Quatrièmes crus

Château St Pierre	St Julien	
Château Talbot	St Julien	
Château Branaire-Ducru	St Julien	
Château Duhart-Milon-Rothschild	Pauillac	
Château Pouget	Cantenac;	AOC Margaux
Château La Tour-Carnet	St Laurent;	AOC Haut-Médoc
Château Lafon Rochet	St Estèphe	
Château Beychevelle	St Julien	
Château Prieuré-Lichine	Cantenac;	AOC Margaux
Château Marquis de Terme	Margaux	

Cinquièmes crus

Château Pontet-Canet	Pauillac
Château Batailley	Pauillac
Château Haut-Batailley	Pauillac
Château Grand-Puy-Lacoste	Pauillac
Château Grand-Puy-Ducasse	Pauillac
Château Lynch-Bages	Pauillac

Château Lynch-Moussas	Pauillac	
Château Dauzac	Labarde;	AOC Margaux
Château d'Armaihaq (previously Mouton-Baron-Philippe)	Pauillac	
Château du Tertre	Arsac;	AOC Margaux
Château Haut-Bages-Libéral	Pauillac	
Château Pédesclaux	Pauillac	
Château Belgrave	St Laurent;	AOC Haut-Médoc
Château Camensac	St Laurent;	AOC Haut-Médoc
Château Cos-Labory	St Estèphe	
Château Clerc-Milon	Pauillac	
Château Croizet- Bages	Pauillac	
Château Cantemerle	Macau;	AOC Haut-Médoc

APPENDIX 2:
CLASSIFICATION OF GRAVES 1953
MODIFIED IN 1959

Crus classés (rouges)

Château Bouscaut
Domaine de Chevalier
Château Carbonnieux
Château de Fieuzal
Château Haut-Brion (also classified in 1855 Médoc)
Château Haut-Bailly
Château La Tour-Martillac
Château La Mission Haut-Brion
Château Latour Haut-Brion
Château Malartic-Lagravière
Château Olivier
Château Pape-Clément
Château Smith-Haut-Lafitte

Crus classés (blancs)

Château Bouscaut
Château Carbonnieux
Château Domaine de Chevalier
Château Couhins
Château Couhins-Lurton
Château Haut-Brion
Château Laville-Haut-Brion
Château La Tour-Martillac
Château Olivier
Château Malartie-Lagravière

APPENDIX 3: 1855 CLASSIFICATION
OF SAUTERNES AND BARSAC

Premier Grand crus

| *Vineyard* | *Commune* |
| Château d'Yquem | Sauternes |

Premiers crus

Château La Tour-Blanche	Bommes
Château Lafaurie-Peyraguey	Bommes
Château Haut-Peyraguey	Bommes
Château Rayne-Vigneau	Bommes
Château Suduiraut	Preignac
Château Coutet	Barsac
Château Climens	Barsac
Château Guiraud	Sauternes
Château Rieussec	Fargues
Château Rabaud-Promis	Bommes
Château Sigalas-Rabaud	Bommes

Deuxièmes crus

Château Myrat	Barsac
Château Doisy-Daëne	Barsac
Château Doisy-Dubroca	Barsac
Château Doisy-Védrines	Barsac
Château d'Arche	Sauternes
Château Filhot	Sauternes
Château Broustet	Barsac
Château Nairac	Barsac
Château Caillou	Barsac
Château Suau	Barsac
Château de Malle	Preignac
Château Romer	Fargues
Château Romer-du-Hayot	Fargues
Château Lamothe	Sauternes

This Châteaux was split into two in 1961, now Château Lamothe-Despujols and Château Lamothe-Guignard.

APPENDIX 4: 1996 CLASSIFICATION
OF ST-EMILION

Premiers Grand Crus Classé

Category A
Château Ausone
Château Cheval Blanc
These two wines are agreed by all to be superior to other St-Emilion wines.

Category B
Château L'Angélus (promoted in 1996 classification)
Château Beau- Séjour-Bécot (promoted in 1996 classification)
Château Beauséjour-Duffau-Lagarrosse
Château Belair
Château Canon
Château Clos Fourtet
Château Figeac
Château La Gaffelière
Château Magdelaine
Château Pavie
Château Trottevieille

Grands Crus Classés
There are 55 vineyards entitled to use this classification.

APPENDIX 5:
GRAND CRUS OF BURGUNDY

Côtes de Nuits

Grand Cru	*Commune*
Chambertin	Gevrey-Chambertin
Chambertin Clos-de-Bèze	
Chapelle-Chambertin	
Charmes-Chambertin	
Latricières-Chambertin	
Mazis-Chambertin	
Ruchottes-Chambertin	
Bonnes Mares (part)	Morey-St-Denis
Clos de la Roche	
Clos de Tart	
Clos St-Denis	
Clos des Lambrays	
Bonnes Mares (majority)	Chambolle-Musigny
Le Musigny (also little white)	
Clos de Vougeot	Vougeot
Richebourg	Vosne-Romanée
La Romanée	
Romanée-Conti	
Romanée-St-Vivant	
La Tâche	
La Grande Rue	
Echézeau,	Flagey-Echézeau
Grands Echézeau	

Côtes de Beaune

	Commune
Le Corton (red, some white)	Aloxe-Corton
Corton-Charlemagne (white)	Ladoix-Serrigny
Le Montrachet (white)	Puligny-Montrachet
Chevalier-Montrachet (white)	
Bienvenues-Bâtard-Montrachet (white)	
Bâtard-Montrachet (white)	Chassagne-Montrachet
Criots-Bâtard-Montrachet (white)	

APPENDIX 6:
GRAND CRU VILLAGES OF CHAMPAGNE

Ambonnay	Mesnil-sur-Oger
Avize	Oger
Aÿ-Champagne	Oiry
Beaumont-sur-Vesle	Puisieulx
Bouzy	Sillery
Chouilly (white grapes)	Tours-sur-Marne (red grapes)
Cramant	
Louvois	Verzenay
Mailly-Champagne	Verzy

PREMIER CRUS VILLAGES OF CHAMPAGNE

Avenay	Mareuil-sur-Aÿ
Bergères-les-Vertus	Montbré
Bezannes	Mutigny
Billy-le-Grand	Pargny-les-Reims
Bisseuil	Pierry
Chamery	Rilly-la-Montagne
Champillon	Sacy
Chigny-les-Roses	Taissy
Chouilly (red grapes)	Tauxières
Coligny (red grapes)	Tours-sur-Marne (white grapes)
Cormontreuil	Trépail
Cuis	Trois-Puits
Cumières	Vaudemangers
Dizy	Vertus
Ecueil	Villedommage
Etrèchy (red grapes)	Villeneuve-Renneville
Grauves	Villers-Allerand
Hautvillers	Villers-aux-Noeuds
Jouy-les-Reims	Villers-Marmery
Ludes	Voipreux

APPENDIX 7:
AUSTRALIAN WINE ZONES

Western Australia
Central Western Australia
Eastern Plains, Inland and North of Western Australia
Great Perth
South West Australia
West Australia South East Coastal

South Australia
Adelaide
Far North
Fleurion
Lower Murray
Limestone Coast
Mount Lofty Ranges
The Peninsulars

Victoria
Central Victoria
Gippsland
North East Victoria
North West Victoria
Port Phillip
Western Victoria

New South Wales
Big Rivers
Central Ranges
Hunter Valley
Northern Rivers
Northern Slopes
South Coast
Southern New South Wales
Western Plains

APPENDIX 8

South African Wards (43)

Western Cape

Koekenaap	Walker Bay (Overberg)
Vredendal	Elim (Overberg)
Spruitdrift	Aan-de-Doorns (Worcester)
Bamboes Bay	Nuy (Worcester)
Piekenierskloof	Scherpenheuvel (Worcester)
Cederberg	Eilandia (Worcester))
Groenekloof (Swartland)	Vinkrivier (Worcester)
Malmsbury (Swartland)	Le Chasseur (Worcester)
Riebeekberg (Swartland)	Agterkliphoogte (Worcester)
Ceres (Tulbagh)	McGregor (Robertson)
Constantia	Boesmansrivier (Robertson)
Durbanville (Tygerberg)	Bonnievale (Robertson)
Wellington (Paarl)	Stormsvlei (Robertson)
Slanghoek (Worcester)	Hoopsrivier (Klein Karoo Region)
Goudini (Worcester)	Klaasvoogds (Klein Karoo Region)
Bottelary (Stellenbosch)	Montagu (Klein Karoo Region)
Devon Valley (Stellenbosch)	Tradouw (Klein Karoo Region)
Papegaaiberg (Stellenbosch)	Buffeljags (Swellendam)
Simonsberg-Stellenbosch	Herbertsdale (Klein Karoo Region)
Jonjkerhoek Valley (Stellenbosch)	Ruiterbosch (Klein Karoo)
Franschhoek Valley (Overberg)	Swartberg (Klein Karoo)
Elgin (Overberg)	

South African Wards (3)

Northern Cape
Lower Orange
Hartswater
Riet River Free State

APPENDIX 9:
THE VDP ACCORD OF 2002
CLASSIFICATION CRITERIA FOR GREAT GROWTHS – DRY AND LUSCIOUSLY SWEET – AND WINES FROM A CLASSIFIED SITE (PRIVATE LAW REGULATION)

Reproduced with the permission of the VDP

Production criteria for the top level

*Grosses Gewächs (great growth) designates top-quality dry wines from the Rheinhessen, Nahe, Mittelrhein, Württemberg, Baden, Franken and Pfalz regions
** Erstes Gewächs (first growth) designates top-quality dry wines from the Rheingau

- Maximum yield: 50 hl/ha
- Origin is restricted to classified sites
- Choice of grape variety is restricted
- Viticultural measures are subject to control
- Minimum must weight: equivalent to Spätlese
- Selective harvesting, by hand
- Wines are subject to a VDP sensorial exam
- Wines are aged prior to first release

Production criteria for the second level

- Origin is restricted to vineyards that impart discernible, site-specific traits
- Choice of grape variety is determined by the regional associations
- Maximum yield: 65 hl/ha
- Selective harvesting
- Fully ripened crop

Grosses Gewächs*
'great growth'
Erstes Gewächs**
'first growth'
(Rheingau)
dry in style

Auslese
Beerenauslese
Trockenbeerenauslese

Eiswein

lusciously sweet in style

Klassifizierter Lagenwein ('wine from a classified site')
Classification of a region's vineyards – or portions thereof – is the responsibility of regional associations, respectively, in close cooperation with members whose vineyards have already been classified. In the future, vineyard designations on VDP members' labels will be restricted to classified sites only. Only VDP members' finest vineyard appellations will appear on labels; no other site names will be used.

Guts- and Ortswein
('house wine' labeled with a proprietary name and/or the name of a village or region)

General standards of the VDP

- 80% of an estate's holdings are planted with traditional grape varieties typical of their region, as recommended by the VDP
- Maximum yield: 75 hl/ha
- Minimum must weight (higher than prescribed by law) is determined by the regional associations
- Hand harvesting for grapes of Auslese, and riper, quality levels
- Vineyard procedures adhere to measures prescribed for integrated viticulture
- Wines are subject to examination during a VDP estate inspection
- Estates must meet and maintain VDP inspection criteria (30 points)

In general, the VDP national association provides a uniform framework of quality-oriented measures. The regional associations can stipulate stricter conditions.

Self-assessment Questions

CHAPTER 1

1 The HTF is an organization
   (a) which protects the wages of workers in the hotel and catering industry
   (b) which promotes training within the hotel and catering industry
   (c) of hotel and catering teachers
   (d) of hoteliers and caterers.

CHAPTER 2

1 The Hawthorn strainer is used
   (a) to decant old wines containing sediment
   (b) to strain fresh fruit juices
   (c) in conjunction with a standard cocktail shaker
   (d) in conjunction with a mixing glass.
2 Nitrogen and carbon dioxide may be fed into casks of traditional cask-conditioned beer to
   (a) increase the speed of service
   (b) improve the quality of the 'head'
   (c) prevent spoiling bacteria contacting the beer
   (d) speed up the conditioning of the beer.
3 Which of the following is a legal method of dispensing whisky in a public house in the UK?
   (a) straight from the bottle into the glass
   (b) through an unsealed and unstamped optical dispenser
   (c) using a government-stamped thimble measure
   (d) using a lined glass.
4 Coasters are used to
   (a) place wine bottles in on the table
   (b) strain cocktails
   (c) decorate drinks
   (d) put round the neck of a bottle to prevent wine dripping.
5 Muddlers are used to
   (a) take the gas out of sparkling wines
   (b) stir drinks
   (c) make crushed ice
   (d) relieve hangovers.
6 A shive is correctly described as the
   (a) round piece of hard wood or plastic used as a bung in the top of a cask
   (b) round piece of hard wood or plastic used as a bung in the tap hole
   (c) connector which is attached to the top of a keg of beer
   (d) tapered piece of wood used to vent new casks of beer.
7 Detergents should not be mixed together because
   (a) they may give off poisonous fumes
   (b) the strength will be too high
   (c) they might counteract each other's cleaning qualities
   (d) it will be very expensive.
8 The correct way of removing a smear on a glass while polishing it for the table is to
   (a) breathe on it, then polish it with a dry cloth
   (b) hold it over steaming hot water, then polish it with a dry cloth
   (c) polish it with a damp cloth
   (d) rub the smear with a finger then polish it with a dry cloth.
9 Glasses are frosted by
   (a) placing them in a trough of ice cubes
   (b) placing them in a refrigerator
   (c) placing them in a deep freeze
   (d) dipping the rim in egg white and sugar.
10 The most suitable temperature for a beer cellar to be kept at is
   (a) $45°F (7.2°C)$
   (b) $50°F (10°C)$
   (c) $55°F (12.7°C)$
   (d) $60°F (15.6°C)$.
11 Which of the following is correctly described as ullage?
   (a) the stand in the cellar on which casks of beer are placed

(b) the charge made by a hotel on bottles brought in by the customer

(c) any out-of-condition wine which has to be returned to the supplier

(d) non-alcoholic beer.

12 A bursting disc is found on

(a) kegs of beer

(b) gas cylinders

(c) cask-conditioned beers

(d) the top of spirit bottles.

13 A kilderkin of beer will contain

(a) 4½ gallons

(b) 9 gallons

(c) 10 gallons

(d) 18 gallons.

14 What is the main use of a wine cradle?

(a) to improve the appearance of a wine

(b) to carry a bottle of wine containing sediment to the point for decanting

(c) for the service of young red wines

(d) for the storage of wine in a cellar.

15 In a public house selling on average 70 pints of beer per line per day, the beer pipes should be cleaned at least

(a) once a day

(b) twice a week

(c) once a week

(d) each time a keg or cask runs out.

CHAPTER 3

1 Vines are grafted in order to

(a) improve the quality of the wine

(b) help attract *Botrytis cinerea*

(c) increase the yield

(d) counteract *Phylloxera*.

2 Which of the following grapes will produce a wine with a spicy bouquet and flavour?

(a) Chardonnay

(b) Chasselas

(c) Gewürztraminer

(d) Müller-Thurgau.

3 Which of the following grape varieties is important to the production of Hermitage?

(a) Cabernet Sauvignon

(b) Gamay

(c) Grenache

(d) Syrah.

4 The tannin found in wine comes from the

(a) grape pips

(b) grape skins

(c) malolactic fermentation

(d) juice of the grape.

5 The liquor obtained from fermenting the skins and pips left after pressing grapes is called

(a) marc brandy

(b) *vin de goutte*

(c) *vin de presse*

(d) *ratafia*.

6 Which of the following alcohols is found in wine?

(a) butanol

(b) ethanol

(c) methanol

(d) pethanol.

7 *Pelure d'oignon* is a term used to describe

(a) Spanish sparkling wine

(b) German sparkling wine

(c) rosé wine

(d) old Sauternes.

8 Bitterness in wine is tasted

(a) in the centre of the tongue

(b) at the sides of the tongue

(c) at the front of the tongue

(d) at the back of the tongue.

9 Which of the following ACs is considered to be the best?

(a) Bordeaux Supérieur

(b) Haut-Médoc

(c) Médoc

(d) Pauillac.

10 An *Anbaugebiet* is

(a) a wine-growing area for *Qualitätswein*

(b) a quality wine

(c) an official control number

(d) a wine-growing region for *Tafelwein*.

11 *Spätlese* wine is made from

(a) late-gathered grapes

(b) specially selected bunches of grapes

(c) individually selected grapes

(d) frozen grapes.

12 Many sweet liqueur white wines are produced from the

(a) Chardonnay

(b) Sylvaner

(c) Muscadet

(d) Muscat.

13 If the grape pips are crushed in the vinification process the wine will have a

(a) grassy flavour

(b) bitter taste

(c) fuller flavour

(d) darker colour.

14 Wine made from the pressings of red grape skins after they have been removed from the fermenting must is called
(a) *vin de goutte*
(b) *cuvaison*
(c) *marc*
(d) *vin de presse.*

15 During the vinification process, at what percentage of alcohol will all the wild yeasts be killed?
(a) 2%
(b) 4%
(c) 6%
(d) 8%.

16 What is the term for the process of stirring up the lees of the wine?
(a) *batonnage*
(b) *macération pelliculaire*
(c) *soutirage*
(d) *sur lie.*

17 The top quality white Burgundies are produced from the
(a) Chardonnay
(b) Gamay
(c) Sémillon
(d) Sauvignon.

18 Dry white Italian wine will be indicated by the term
(a) *abboccato*
(b) *dolce*
(c) *chiaretto*
(d) *secco.*

19 Which of the following is an EU guarantee of quality and origin?
(a) VdM
(b) VDT
(c) VSOP
(d) VQPRD.

20 Why should the best vines have deep roots?

21 What are the requirements necessary for the production of alcohol?

22 What does fermentation produce besides alcohol?

23 Where does red wine obtain its colour from?

24 Wines produced in the cooler climates usually have a higher . . . . content than those produced in warmer climates.

25 Why is sulphur dioxide gas often used at an early stage in the fermentation process?

CHAPTER 4

1 The most favourable latitudes in the southern hemisphere for wine production are between
(a) 10–30°S
(b) 20–40°S
(c) 30–50°S
(d) 40–60°S.

2 Which of the following would indicate a sweet wine from Alsace?
(a) *sélection de grains nobles*
(b) *passe-tout-grain*
(c) *edelzwicker*
(d) *réserve spéciale.*

3 Sancerre is produced in
(a) Anjou
(b) Central Vineyards
(c) Nantais
(d) Touraine.

4 Which of the following is a sweet wine?
(a) Muscadet de Sèvre-et-Maine
(b) Coteaux de la Loire
(c) Bourgeuil
(d) Bonnezeau.

5 Pauillac is a
(a) commune of Sauternes
(b) good-quality wine from Côte de Beaune
(c) high-quality wine from Pomerol
(d) commune of the Médoc.

6 St Estèphe is a commune of
(a) Médoc
(b) Graves
(c) St-Emilion
(d) Pomerol.

7 The most suitable of the following wines for service with an apple flan would be
(a) Mersault
(b) Château Pétrus
(c) Loupiac
(d) Soave.

8 Pinot noir is the classic grape used in the production of
(a) Beaujolais
(b) Meritage
(c) Nuits St Georges
(d) Pomerol.

9 Mercurey, Rully and Givry are all wine-producing communes in
(a) Touraine
(b) Côte Chalonnais
(c) Beaujolais
(d) Médoc.

10 The main grape used for the production of Orvietto
is the
(a) Alvarinho
(b) Garganega
(c) Verdicchio
(d) Trebbiano.

11 Blanquette de Limoux is famous for its
(a) sparkling wines
(b) 'black' wines
(c) sweet Muscat wines
(d) rosé wines.

12 The *bocksbeutel* is the bottle used for wines from
(a) Alsace
(b) Sekt
(c) Provence
(d) Franconia.

13 The majority of the *Cava DO* is situated in the
Spanish demarcated region called
(a) La Mancha
(b) Rioja
(c) Penedès
(d) Valdepeñas.

14 Which of the following is a DOCG wine?
(a) Asti
(b) Bardolino
(c) Sassicaia
(d) Orvieto.

15 Portugal is the producer of
(a) Navarra
(b) Vougeot
(c) Vinho Verde
(d) Madiran.

16 The Hunter Valley is situated in
(a) North Island
(b) New South Wales
(c) South Australia
(d) Tasmania.

17 Marlborough is a wine-producing district in
(a) Australia
(b) America
(c) South Africa
(d) New Zealand.

18 Commandarie is produced in
(a) Austria
(b) Cyprus
(c) Greece
(d) South Africa.

19 Which of the following groups are all producers of
sweet wines?
(a) Muscat de Beaumes-de-Venise, Rivesaltes,
Cérons

(b) Sauternes, Barsac, Fronsac
(c) Bourg, Graves, Loupiac
(d) St Croix-du-Mont, Fitou, Murrumbidgee.

20 Which of the following villages is renowned for
QbA red wines?
(a) Würzburg
(b) Eitelsbach
(c) Assmanshausen
(d) Kreuznach.

21 In which district of the Loire would you find
Quarts de Chaume?
(a) Saumur
(b) Touraine
(c) Coteaux du Layon
(d) Loire Valley.

22 Which of the following groups are all Grand Cru
Burgundies?
(a) Clos de Vougeot, Mersault, Clos de Tart
(b) Clos de la Roche, Vosne-Romanée, Fixin
(c) Charmes-Chambertin, Clos des Lambrays,
Bonnes-Mares
(d) Richebourg, Le Montrachet, Aloxe-Corton.

23 What is the name of the most important town in
Cava DO?

24 Where is Vega Sicilia produced?

CHAPTER 5

1 Which of the following produces the carbon dioxide in a bottle of Champagne?
(a) *dégorgement*
(b) *dosage*
(c) *liqueur de tirage*
(d) *remuage*.

2 Coteaux Champenois is correctly described as
(a) champagne with half the usual gas pressure
(b) the range of hills south of Reims
(c) still white wine from Champagne
(d) a premium brand of champagne.

3 Sherry fermentation is carried out in
(a) *bodegas*
(b) *criaderas*
(c) *estufados*
(d) *soleras*.

4 *Venencia* refers to the
(a) new wine of a single year
(b) sherry tasting glass
(c) town where *fino* sherries mature and take on a
salty taste
(d) long-handled cup used to extract samples
from a sherry cask.

5 *Vin doux naturel* is a
   (a) sweet unfortified wine
   (b) the sweetening used to sweeten sherry
   (c) sweet fortified wine
   (d) wine produced without the use of chemicals.

6 Manzanilla sherry is correctly described as a
   (a) light-coloured dry sherry
   (b) golden-coloured dry sherry
   (c) light-coloured sweet sherry
   (d) dark-coloured sweet sherry.

7 Dom Pérignon was cellar master at an abbey in
   (a) Cramant
   (b) Verzenay
   (c) Hautvillers
   (d) Aÿ.

8 The German wine term meaning slightly sparkling is
   (a) steinwein
   (b) spritzig
   (c) spätlese
   (d) mozzer.

9 The number of years late bottled vintage port remains in cask before being bottled is between
   (a) 2–4
   (b) 4–6
   (c) 6–8
   (d) 8–10.

CHAPTER 6

1 Irish whiskey is made from
   (a) barley and other grain, and distilled twice in a pot still
   (b) maize only, and distilled twice in a continuous still
   (c) barley and other grain, and distilled three times in a pot still
   (d) maize only, and distilled once in a continuous still.

2 The part of the distillate from which Cognac is finally produced is called
   (a) *bois ordinaires*
   (b) *bonne chauffe*
   (c) *brouillis*
   (d) *bons bois.*

3 Fine Champagne is made entirely from grapes which have been grown in the
   (a) Grande Champagne
   (b) Montagne de Reims
   (c) Grande Champagne and Fins Bois
   (d) Petite Champagne and Grande Champagne.

4 Which of the following spirits would *not* be correctly referred to as *alcool blanc*?
   (a) Calvados
   (b) Framboise
   (c) Mirabelle
   (d) Poire William.

5 Angostura bitters is produced in
   (a) Antigua
   (b) Cuba
   (c) Puerto Rico
   (d) Trinidad.

6 Which of the following has a flavour of caraway?
   (a) Amaretto
   (b) Galliano
   (c) Kümmel
   (d) Sambuca.

7 The mash tun is used in the production of beer to
   (a) steep barley to encourage growth
   (b) boil the hops, wort and sugar together
   (c) extract the flavour from the malt
   (d) grind or crack the grains of malt.

8 Apollinaris is produced in
   (a) Belgium
   (b) France
   (c) Germany
   (d) Italy.

9 Which of the following mineral waters is produced in France?
   (a) Vichy Catalán
   (b) Henniez
   (c) Spar Reine
   (d) Vittel.

10 Quinine is one of the ingredients of
   (a) Bitter lemon
   (b) Ginger ale
   (c) Ruschian
   (d) Soda water.

CHAPTER 7

1 Which style of glass would be the most suitable to serve a lager beer in?
   (a) Thistle
   (b) Titan
   (c) Sleever
   (d) Pilsner.

2 Which one of the following cocktail ingredients must never be shaken in a cocktail shaker?
   (a) Angostura bitters
   (b) Cream
   (c) Egg white

(d) Soda water.

3 Which of the following drinks contains Campari?
   (a) Americano
   (b) Bloody Mary
   (c) Sidecar
   (d) Pink Lady.

4 A White Lady cocktail contains
   (a) fresh orange juice
   (b) fresh lemon juice
   (c) a cube of sugar
   (d) vodka

5 Havana cigars should be kept at a temperature of
   (a) 10–12.8°C
   (b) 12.8–15.6°C
   (c) 15.6–18.3°C
   (d) 18.3–21.1°C.

6 A Corona cigar is best prepared for smoking by
   (a) warming it over its whole length with a lighted match
   (b) cutting the sealed end with a guillotine cutter
   (c) piercing the sealed end with a cigar piercer
   (d) crackling it between the fingers.

7 The wood associated with cigars is
   (a) apple
   (b) cedar
   (c) chestnut
   (d) oak.

8 Prince Charles coffee is prepared with
   (a) Cognac
   (b) Drambuie
   (c) Glayva
   (d) Scotch whisky.

9 When a second bottle of the same wine is ordered by a party of four, the sommelier should present the bottle to the host then
   (a) provide clean glasses to all the customers and pour the wine
   (b) provide clean glasses to all the customers, offer the host a taste, then pour the wine
   (c) pour the wine into the existing glasses
   (d) supply the host with a clean glass, offer him a taste, then pour the wine.

10 If the customer complains that the wine is corked, the sommelier should apologize, check it himself, then
   (a) decant the wine
   (b) pass the wine through muslin
   (c) change the wine for another bottle
   (d) remove the cork.

11 What causes oxidation of wine?

12 What causes wine to become 'maderizé'?

CHAPTER 8

1 Which of the following would be the best approach to a customer who orders a wine which is suitable for the main course?
   (a) 'Would you like a wine before this one, sir?'
   (b) 'Would you like a wine to accompany your first course, sir?'
   (c) 'Anything else to drink sir?'
   (d) 'You don't require a drink with your first course then, sir?'

2 Suggest ways in which the sale of sweet wine may be increased.

3 Why are bin numbers used on wine lists?

CHAPTER 9

1 Which one of the following combinations should prove to be the most satisfactory?
   (a) Barolo with grilled Dover sole
   (b) Fitou with spaghetti bolognese
   (c) Californian Chenin Blanc with roast rib of beef
   (d) Châteauneuf-du-Pape with a selection of hors-d'oeuvres.

2 Which one of the following drinks is most suitable to serve as an apéritif?
   (a) Red Dão
   (b) Schloss Johannisberg Riesling Auslese
   (c) Alsace Riesling
   (d) Amaroni.

3 Suggest three wines which would be suitable to accompany grilled king prawns.

4 Suggest three wines which would be suitable to be recommended with a cheese board.

5 What drinks should be offered with the service of coffee?

CHAPTER 10

1 If a member of staff is having difficulty performing a task, his superior should
   (a) take over the task
   (b) offer advice and encouragement
   (c) upbraid the person for not being efficient
   (d) make a written report and give the member of staff a warning.

2 The correct form of address for a duke is
   (a) 'My Lord'
   (b) 'My Lord Duke'

(c) 'Sir'

(d) 'Your Grace'.

3 The correct form of address for a bishop is

(a) 'My Lord'

(b) 'Your Worship'

(c) 'Your Eminence'

(d) 'Your Grace'.

CHAPTER 11

1 The minimum number of people that an employer may employ in the UK without having to provide a written health and safety policy which is shown to the employees is

(a) 2

(b) 5

(c) 10

(d) 20.

2 The minimum temperature permitted in a non-public work area in the UK is

(a) 50°F (10°C)

(b) 55°F (12.8°C)

(c) 60°F (15.6°C)

(d) 65°F (18.3°C).

3 Which colour on a fire extinguisher indicates the correct one to use on a computer which is on fire?

(a) Green

(b) White

(c) Red

(d) Black.

Answers to Self-assessment Questions

CHAPTER 1

1 b

CHAPTER 2

1 d
2 c
3 c
4 a
5 b
6 a
7 a
8 b
9 d
10 c
11 c
12 b
13 d
14 b
15 c

CHAPTER 3

1 d
2 c
3 d
4 b
5 a
6 b
7 c
8 d
9 d
10 a
11 a

12 d
13 b
14 d
15 b
16 a
17 a
18 d
19 d
20 a) to enable them to withstand extreme weather conditions (drought and severe frosts).
   b) to enable them to extract more trace elements and minerals from the ground.
21 Sugar, yeast, warmth.
22 Carbon dioxide gas and sediment.
23 From the grape skins.
24 Acid.
25 To prevent the growth of wild yeasts.

CHAPTER 4

1 c
2 a
3 b
4 d
5 d
6 a
7 c
8 c
9 b
10 d
11 a
12 d
13 c
14 a
15 c

16 b
17 d
18 b
19 a
20 c
21 c
22 c
23 San Sadurní d'Anoia
24 Ribera del Duero in Spain.

CHAPTER 5

1 c
2 c
3 a
4 d
5 c
6 a
7 c
8 b
9 b

CHAPTER 6

1 c
2 b
3 d
4 a
5 d
6 c
7 c
8 c
9 d
10 a

CHAPTER 7

1 d
2 d
3 a
4 b
5 c
6 b
7 b
8 b

9 b (Note: d is acceptable and is often trade practice).
10 c
11 Contact with air.
12 Usually caused by keeping wine at too high a temperature.

CHAPTER 8

1 b
2 By recommending a sweet wine when the sweet order is placed; by offering sweet wine by the glass; by putting a sweet wine on the sweet trolley; by offering half bottles on the wine list.
3 To help the customer with ordering, and reduce the chance of the incorrect bottle being served.

CHAPTER 9

1 b
2 c
3 Light dry or off-dry white wines.
4 Red port wines, full-bodied red wines and in some cases heavy sweet wines.
5 Liqueurs, brandies, ports.

CHAPTER 10

1 b
2 d
3 a

CHAPTER 11

1 b
2 c
3 d

Index